REMEMBERING THE CULTURAL
OF A CHILDHOOD

To Millie

May you cherish your childhood memories forever

Remembering the Cultural Geographies of a Childhood Home

PETER HUGHES JACHIMIAK
University of South Wales, UK

Routledge
Taylor & Francis Group

LONDON AND NEW YORK

First published 2014 by Ashgate Publishing

2 Park Square, Milton Park, Abingdon, Oxon OX14 4RN
711 Third Avenue, New York, NY 10017, USA

Routledge is an imprint of the Taylor & Francis Group, an informa business

First issued in paperback 2016

British Library Cataloguing in Publication Data
A catalogue record for this book is available from the British Library

The Library of Congress has cataloged the printed edition as follows:
Jachimiak, Peter Hughes.
  Remembering the cultural geographies of a childhood home / by Peter Hughes Jachimiak.
     pages cm
  Includes bibliographical references and index.
  ISBN 978-1-4094-4812-9 (hbk)
  1. Geographical perception in children. 2. Home--Psychological aspects.
  3. Cultural geography. 4. Place attachment. 5. Recollection (Psychology) I. Title.
  HQ784.G45J33 2014
  304.2'3--dc23

                                                                    2014000197

ISBN 978-1-4094-4812-9 (hbk)
ISBN 978-1-138-25783-2 (pbk)

Contents

List of Figures

Acknowledgements

To my darling Katja. Thank you so much for the Berlin trip. As, without which, this would not have been finished.

Danke, also, to Adrian Holder and the boys and girls of The Moment – especially for the nudge that was needed ('Get the book finished fella, it'll be great to be published'). This book is for my family – past, present, and future – and all of the Mamas and the Papas and the Millies everywhere, all through time.

Finally, this book is dedicated to both the memory and legacy of the children's author Roy Brown (R.I.P.). Childhood memories have been enriched by your work for evermore.

Chapter 1

House, Rooms, Cobwebs – An Introduction

A well behaved boy in class who works quietly (Peter's school report, Mynachlog Nedd Junior Mixed, class 2L, summer, 1975).

Young men sent to prison for holding knife to Mr French of Alfred Street. The girl that was most responsible for the attack had Borstal (Millie's diary, Thursday, 5 November 1981).[1]

Rose Tints and Collective Emotions

Remembering the Cultural Geographies of a Childhood Home is about childhood places and a child's perspectives: that is, places to be found within the home, and a child's perspective of a house, its gardens, and its neighbourhood. Indeed, that is its geographical framework. However, its cultural framework – that is, its emotional framework – is one to do with notions of the uncanny, the spiritual, and the otherness of childhood. For, what this book is not about – and not part of – is the rather rose-tinted nostalgia of and for that time. Whilst it does locate all amid the cultural geographies of home within both a Wales- and 1970s-specific context, it is not part of the literary continuum that I term the 'Spacehoppers 'n' Spangles' literature. Just to highlight two particular pertinent examples: it is not akin to either Andrew Lovell's *Tiswas and Tanktops – The Pocket Diary of a 1970s Boy* (2008) or Derek Tait's *A 1970s Childhood – From Glam Rock to Happy Days* (2011). With the former little more than a page-after-page celebration of banal references to 'Skool' and 'Shopz', the latter suggests that, during the 1970s, all children entered into an unquestionable shared experience of that decade. As, throughout, there is this assertion that '[a]ll kids collected stamps back then' (Tait, 2011: 83), that '[w]e always seemed to be out and about doing something' (Tait, 2011: 84), that '[e]veryone had platforms' (Tait, 2011: 99), and that '[w]e all ate Bazooka Joe bubblegum' (Tait, 2011: 109), and so on. Whilst Tait's recollections are grounded in a reasonably thorough overview of all manner of cultural artefacts from the 1970s, Lovell's 'yob prose' is merely that. Furthermore, both of these examples (and many others) contribute, arguably, to what Dave Haslam (2005) terms the 'Abbafication' of the 1970s. In *Not Abba – The Real Story of the 1970s* (2005), Haslam is committed to the eradication of popular collective memory of such 'Abbafication': That is, the distortion of the lived experiences of the 1970s by media-derived clichés – for 'Abbafication has been so successful that some of

---

1 'Millie', or Mildred Rosalind Hughes (née Evans, b.1904, d.1992), was Peter's grandmother on his mother's side.

us who grew up in the 1970s are likely to have begun to doubt the validity of our own memories' (Haslam, 2005: 6).

Even though this book does make specific reference to both children's and adult's cultural texts of the time – the 1970s – it also serves to instil in the reader the notion that the childhood home, of any time, and of any place, is imbued with (often) emotionally derived cultural geographies that transcend time and place. For example, whilst this book is primarily to do with my memories of the experience of living in my own childhood home during the 1970s – Ivy Cottage, Skewen, South Wales – it is as much about living, as a child, centuries before and centuries thereafter. Thus, the following chapters, concerned with the 'Home' (Chapter 2), the 'Garden' (Chapter 3), the 'Street' (Chapter 4), and 'Suburbia' (Chapter 5) are, I hope, of their time and yet timeless. They are about both childhood and the environment within which childhood is immersed. *Remembering the Cultural Geographies of a Childhood Home* is about how cultural geographies are, in essence, collective, emotional experiences.

Home as Awe and Wonder

In *The Spiritual Dimension of Childhood* (2008), Kate Adams et al., in highlighting the pressures many adults feel as a result of being subjected to modern life, ask the question, 'When was the last time you felt awe and wonder?' (Adams et al., 2008: 60). In the assumption that these are experiences that many of us have not felt since childhood, they sympathise, and explain that, unlike adults, '[y]oung children are constantly expressing wonder, asking questions, and are curious to see, touch, taste and smell everything around them', to the extent that, '[f]or some, such moments can be incredibly spiritual' (Adams et al., 2008: 60).

In *Berlin Childhood Around 1900* (2006), Walter Benjamin – reflecting upon his own *fin de siècle* childhood – provides great insights into the delights of a child's innocent experience of the world; an experience that is heightened by an acute awareness of 'colors'. For example, when he watched soap bubbles float lazily through the air, Benjamin confessed that, 'I traveled in them throughout the room and mingled in the play of colors of the cupola, until it burst' (Benjamin, 2006: 110). Thus, it was when, as a young boy, Benjamin looked up at the sky, gazed at stained-glass windows, read a book, used water-based paints, handled a piece of jewellery colours, that, he admits, 'I would lose myself in colors' (Benjamin, 2006: 111). Even when consuming chocolate bars, it was the pattern and hues of the wrapper which appealed first and foremost: 'For before I could succumb to the enticements of the treat, the higher sense in me had all at once outflanked the lower and carried me away' (Benjamin, 2006: 111). Benjamin's notion of being 'carried away' by 'colors', is in keeping, as we will appreciate, with Peter's near-hypnotic gazing up at the living room window through a marble in Chapter 2 and, in Chapter 3, being magnetically drawn to the flames of a garden bonfire.

Brian Dillon's *In The Dark Room – A Journey in Memory* (2005) is a memoir which immerses the reader in a sensual, yet often troubled, remembering of a childhood home that is, throughout, tinged with loss. As the book opens with the author's approach to, and entering of, his parents' house – which, following their deaths, was to be lived in, and eventually, sold by himself and his two brothers – Dillon not only begins to muse philosophically the notion of memory, but recalls, across its opening pages, the very feeling of movement experienced within his childhood family home's physicality and history. One section is so impassioned and so insightful, that it is worth quoting at length:

> What do I remember when I think of a house in which I've lived? More than anything, a sense of what it felt like to move about in that medium. I remember the quality of light in a bedroom at dawn; the sudden acoustic shift that occurred when I opened a bathroom door; the curve near the head of a staircase that was a little too steep to run down and a little too wearying on the way up; the warmth of a kitchen in a house without central heating; a door that nobody, not even your parents, who warned you time and again not to do it, could resist slamming; the knowledge that the house had an attic that you had never actually seen (the tiny hatch was too perilously placed above the staircase) but that, despite all evidence to the contrary, you like to imagine stocked with the fascinating detritus of past generations which an attic ought to contain; the odd sensation, as you wheeled your bicycle along the narrow passageway at the side of the house, that the building was rooted in concrete, in brick foundations, in earth and rock to which you otherwise gave no thought at all (Dillon, 2005: 10).

Thus, *Remembering the Cultural Geographies of a Childhood Home* is – above and beyond everything – written in the wake of having read both Benjamin's and Dillon's remembering of their childhood homes. Through contemplations of such simple childhood pleasures as a near-spiritual appreciation of colour and an acute awareness of moving within, and being attuned to, the medium that is a house, the notion that home is aligned absolutely with the humanness of both our senses and our emotions are achieved. If anything, this book is an attempt to engage with a continuum of cultural geography that is home, senses, emotions. Moreover, it aims to bring about, once again, those intense childhood moments of awe and wonder.

A Cultural Geography of Home

William Norton, in *Cultural Geography – Environments, Landscapes, Identities, Inequalities* (2006), notes that – as per the emerging humanist approach from the early 1970s onwards – 'a new phenomenological understanding of the geographic concept of place' took hold, whereby place was now 'where space and time come together' (Norton, 2006: 334). Instead of merely referring to place as a distinct topography of landscape, a geographical location, or an area of the social where cultural artefacts or people are to be found, 'humanist geographers used place to refer to a territory of meaning and to where we live' (Norton, 2006: 334). For Norton, a particularly insightful humanist application of the term place involves the notion of home, which – as a physical space deeply imbued with symbolism – should be better understood 'as a familiar and usually welcoming setting within some larger, more uncertain world' (Norton, 2006: 334). And it is, perhaps as a result of the world becoming more 'uncertain' as we head into the twenty-first century, that more and more people are expressing some desire to return – to their childhood home especially – whether that return is an actuality or as a result of some creative act.

In *Returning Home – Reconnecting with our Childhoods* (2011), Jerry M. Burger insists that the main reason why people wish to return to the homes of their childhood, 'is to establish a psychological link with their past and the person they once were' (Burger, 2011: 13). Burger explains that such a desire to return is a result of a growing sense of loss or crisis in their lives, as many of his respondents verbally expressed anxieties over 'their childhoods slipping away from them', resulting in a desire, 'to renew memories about who they were and where they had come from', whilst others 'seemed to be going through a type of identity crisis' (Burger, 2011: 13). Meanwhile, Deborah E. Reed-Danahay, in her introduction to *Auto/Ethnography – Rewriting the Self and the Social* (1997), highlights that one of the most distinct aspects of the methodological approach to self-enquiry that is autoethnography – perhaps its very driving force – is an exploration of 'cultural displacement or situation of exile' (Reed-Danahay, 1997: 4). This is when the autoethnographer who, as a researcher – in finding themselves to be 'studying his or her own kind, the native telling his or her life story, or the native anthropologist' – realises that they, engaging in any form of return, are 'not completely "at home"' (Reed-Danahay, 1997: 4). Kevin Mills, in *The Prodigal Sign – A Parable of Criticisms* (2009), considers creativity in relation to prodigality as any artistic endeavour involves, simultaneously, the act of following and a desire not to follow, a striving to be creative, but to be, in turn, critical of that creativity. Thus, '[t]he creative gesture, even as part of the critical process by which we seek out the new in the old, is one of escape, of wanting not to repeat, of espousing, craving, or imagining discontinuity' (Mills, 2009: 5). Quite crucially, creativity 'is also a matter of return, of continuation and repetition' (Mills, 2009: 5). Thus, the writing of this book is to engage in creative prodigality: it not only borrows from existing literature, but, through the act of writing, it is an emotional return to a childhood home that, during our years of growing independence, Peter felt he had escaped from.

Cultural Geography as Structures of Feeling

In a way, *Remembering the Cultural Geographies of a Childhood Home* is an exercise in 'doing' cultural geography, whereby a reading of place-specific texts produces social meaning. Pamela Shurmer-Smith, in *Doing Cultural Geography*

(2002: 123–36), insists that not only can a book be 'read', but also media-generated texts such as paintings, films, aspects of television (that is, advertisements, documentaries, soap operas, news items, etc.), and also more culturally derived events, performances, and rituals. But, perhaps more importantly – certainly as far as the cultural geographer is concerned – aspects of the topographical and geographical can be 'read', such as a map, a landscape, an urban environment, a piece of architecture, and so on, often in conjunction with any of the former (i.e. a television programme to do with a particular landscape painter). However, no matter what text is being 'read', '[i]mplicit in the idea of reading is the assumption that one is making sense out of something experienced' (Shurmer-Smith, 2002: 123). And, indeed, such a 'reading' is not something that is merely conducting in a passive manner, but it is rather an active practice: in conducting such multi-text, place-specific readings founded upon experience, we are 'generating a geography' (Shurmer-Smith, 2002: 133–5), whereby it should be acknowledged 'that every text is generated in the light of grounded experience, subjective view and exposure to other texts' (2002: 134). Thus, in Chapter 3: The Childhood Spaces of the Garden, there is a section – wherein Peter'a memory of entering the garden of Ivy Cottage for the first time is set alongside an excerpt from Laurie Lee's *Cider With Rosie* (1959) – in which two related texts (a memory of a childhood experience, and a novel that revolves around the remembering of a childhood experience) merge to 'generate a geography': specifically that of Ivy Cottage during the early 1970s amid the continuum of children's texts. Thus, in reading the place that is home – in light of other, previous texts – the cultural geography that is generated is that of a 1970s childhood home.

Meanwhile, whilst the term geography would suggest purely some form of mapping of the physical environment, its pairing with culture brings about an interpretive element to 'doing' cultural geography that prioritises internal significance over external aesthetics. Thus, Peter Jackson in *Maps of Meaning* (1989), in putting forward an early agenda for cultural geography, explains that this emphasis upon internal significance not only involves the shift of appreciation 'from a world of exterior surfaces and appearances to an inner world of meaning and experience' (Jackson, 1989: 177), but is an insistence upon 'the idea of landscape as a social construction or a 'way of seeing' rather than as reducible to a series of physical traits' (Jackson, 1989: 181). Furthermore, Nigel Thrift (1994) – in an effort to conceptualise humans coming to terms with the increasingly mechanical inhuman geographies encountered since the Industrial Revolution – highlights the emergence of an empirical structure of feeling that is committed to the highlighting of the physicality of experience in relation to interpretation of environment. That is, the experience of environment as something which is irreducible, where the 'structure of feeling necessarily involves calling on emotion, bodily practices, the physical character of places, all those differentiated and differentiating elements of comportment which are crucial to a culture' (Thrift, 1994: 193). Additionally, this notion of a structure of feeling, should be interpreted as more than a methodology, 'but as actually reflecting a specific historical period in which almost/not quite effects become more palpable', whereby a structure of feeling 'describes a kind of shadow world which is now coming out into the light' (Thrift, 1994: 193–4). Indeed, any cultural geography-derived structure of feeling is imbued with even more meaningful emotions when combined with an autoethnographic approach, as, in their introduction to *Auto-Ethnographies – The Anthropology of Academic Practices* (2005), Anne Meneley and Donna J. Young insist that '[t]his volume is animated by complex structures of feeling', whereby 'feelings of humanity linked to an ironic awareness of our selves as social actors and feelings of quiet resolve', is 'born out of a conviction that what we have to say about the world we live in is important' (Meneley and Young, 2005: 15). Furthermore, Mike Hayler, in *Autoethnography, Self-Narrative and Teacher Education* (2011), underlines that autoethnography, with its 'focus upon the memories of events, feelings, thoughts and emotions', manages to 'contribute through varying methods of recall, collection and analysis towards different types of systematic introspection in order to illuminate and to facilitate understanding' (Hayler, 2011: 19).

Thus, such a systematic structure of feeling – borne out of resolve, conviction, and introspection – is occasionally the result of (often private) shadow worlds emerging into (public) light, and, to stress, it is often an emotional process. Owain Jones (2005), in offering an interpretive ecology of the landscapes of his own childhood home – where memory, emotion, and self collide – alludes to the complexities that are a result of such geographies being grounded in our own emotions and experiences of being our younger selves. For, '[g]eographies of memories and memories of geographies are complex and emotional, not least because some, perhaps the most powerful, will be the geographies of our childhood' (Jones, 2005: 215). Indeed, Jones's childhood home – a farm – no longer exists, with the farm land now housing estates and the farmhouse itself converted into an apartment. Thus, Jones's childhood home only exists as an emotional geography of the mind that, in Jones's own memory, is gradually being eroded with the passing of time and his increasing inability to remember. Thus, it now only exists as an emotional geography of the mind that, when only partially remembered, brings about an overwhelming sense of loss: 'So it has all gone, doubly – as time and as space. I get a feeling of panic, that my whole existence is thinned as the spaces of the past have been eradicated' (Jones, 2005: 217). However, on a less personal – and more collectively empowering note that encapsulates the power of autoethnography – such an emotional loss of childhood geographies 'is a story of losses of kinds which many have faced, and in a way, which we all face, the loss of past geographical selves' (Jones, 2005: 217).

Autobiographies and Autoethnography

Peter H. Mann, in *Methods of Social Investigation* (1985), explains (in a rather gendered way, that is indicative of its time) that any form of autobiography – that is, in its way, a form of memoir – is an attempt to provide 'a systematic and chronological record of the author's life, with himself at the centre of the story' (Mann, 1985: 79). Thus, for Mann, a seminal piece of critical autobiographical writing is Robert Roberts' memoir of his days as a child in Salford, *The Classic Slum* (1971). Providing an evocative picture of a 'lost' way of life that existed either side of World War One, it is not only an engaging social history, but a sociological text that provides great insights into a period of immense cultural change. Significantly, though, *The Classic Slum* was written by Roberts when he was in late middle-age, and both a fully fledged sociologist and a self-declared socialist. As such, throughout the book, the author has 'a tendency to see things rather more 'socially' than one might expect from a child of the local corner shop' (Mann, 1985: 81). Thus, *Remembering the Cultural Geographies of a Childhood Home*, is, like Robert Roberts' *The Classic Slum*, not some innocent remembering of childhood. Instead, it is an academically tinged account – through the inclusion of memories of childhood written in adulthood, followed by cultural criticism of those memories – of a time now past, but reflected upon from the contemporary perspective of the author as cultural geographer.

In order to reiterate what is meant by autobiographies – and turning to Patrick McNeill's *Research Methods* (1990) – they are not only 'first-person descriptions of social events, written by an individual who was involved in or witnessed those happenings', but they fundamentally 'include the writer's attitudes towards those events' (McNeill, 1990: 109). Sociologists and cultural historians who use such documents have to ask themselves whether the evidence therein is authentic, whether it is complete, how representative it is of the experiences described, whether it is distorted by the personal bias of the writer, and why is it written' (McNeill, 1990: 109). Furthermore, according to Martyn Hammersley and Paul Atkinson, in *Ethnography – Principles in Practice* (1992), any form of autobiographical document will often display forms of bias and prejudice that attempt to present the author in a highly favourable manner (and, in doing so, make excuses for, or attempt to justify, questionable behaviour), and are, in the worst instances, merely platforms for spiteful revenge. At the very least, Hammersley and Atkinson warn us that, as '[t]hey are often writing with the benefit of hindsight', such autobiographical-based forms of writing 'are thus subject to the usual problems of long-term recall' (Hammersley and Atkinson, 1992: 130). However, whilst we should indeed be very much aware of such pitfalls in the writing of any kind of autobiographies, the author's biased mode of writing and analysis should not always be interpreted as a negative, for 'sources of 'bias' are, looked at from another perspective, data in themselves' (Hammersley and Atkinson, 1992: 130). Thus, the tendency for ethnographers to engage increasingly with 'narratives of the self' – and, in doing so, their striving to incorporate more poetic forms of creative writing into their analytical prose – is, according to Norman K. Denzin, in *Interpretive Ethnography – Ethnographic Practices for the 21st Century* (1997), a central element of autoethnography. That is, this is where there is 'a turning of the ethnographic gaze inward on the self (auto), while maintaining the outward gaze of ethnography', in order to, ultimately, consider 'the larger context wherein self experiences occur' (Denzin, 1997: 227).

Awkward Snapshots and Autoethnography

Mike Bender and Doug Chernack's *Awkward Family Photographs* (2010) – whilst being essentially an opportunity to collate mirth-inducing posed photographs of various families – does include a brief introduction which discusses the sometimes problematic relationship between human beings and the camera. For Bender and Chernack, it is as a result of individual family members coming together within the proximity of the camera that a certain photogenic awkwardness is inevitable. Indeed, they insist that any such awkward photographs are a direct consequence of the awkwardness of the family itself:

> So, let's just put it out there – *family is awkward*. That's right. When a group of people with the same name and different personalities are forced to spend most of their lives together, plenty of uncomfortable moments are sure to follow. And when a camera is there to capture one of those moments, an awkward family photo is born (Bender and Chirnack, 2010: 8).

I would also insist that even photographs of family individuals – as they are often taken by another member of the family within the confines of the family home and garden – result in awkwardness. Thus, whether of the family unit, or of individual family members, 'as long as the viewer feels some level of discomfort, there is awkwardness' (Bender and Chirnack, 2010: 9). And many of the photographs in this book are no different. For, *Remembering the Cultural Geographies of a Childhood Home* contains a number of photographs in which Peter (perhaps as a result of being a rather shy, self-conscious boy and, then, teenager) stands stiffly straight with a forced, fixed grin, staring inanely into the camera. Yet, such family snapshots are – to Tessa Muncey in *Creating Autoethnographies* (2010) – crucial to the study of the self, whereby '[i]n a sixtieth of a second the camera can capture an image that will serve to add a visual dimension to a memory' (2010: 58). Moreover, for Muncey, the snapshot is one of countless artefacts that, when analysed, 'conjure up feelings and thoughts' (2010: 55) which, as a result 'connect to deep personal experiences' (2010: 59). Thus, Peter's childhood snapshots – taken, of course, in a pre-digital photography age – are awkward photographs, which, taken now, would be deleted, and certainly not printed off in any shape or form. However, they are included here, as – from an era when taking a photograph was still a rare, special moment – they are amongst the few such photographs that exist that capture a young Peter, at home, in the 1970s. As such, they have a significance all of their own, and are, as a result, insightful snapshots with regards the relationship between us and visually orientated cultural artefacts.

Joanne Garde-Hansen, in *Media and Memory* (2011), notes, '[w]hat at first glance appear to be simple childhood photos become media texts that can be analysed socially, culturally, technologically and historically' (2011: 35). In turn, it is through such analysis – and from an autoethnographic methodological standpoint in particular – that childhood photographs facilitate the act of remembering oneself. Thus, 'personal memory through photography becomes a reflective practice, in that family photographs are used for reminiscence, therapy, trauma, reconciliation and autoethnographic critique' (Garde-Hansen, 2011: 35).

Fundamentally though, Marianne Hirsch, in *Family Frames – Photography, Narrative and Postmemory* (1997), argues that photography and photographs are more than mere memory joggers for individuals and families, they are – by definition – reminders of both death and loss. Thus, to Hirsch, photography and photographs do not simply connect the individual with the memories of others, but they 'bring the past back in the form of a ghostly revenant, emphasizing, at the same time, its immutable and irreversible pastness and irretrievability' (Hirsch, 1997: 20). Such an acute awareness of irreversible pastness and irretrievability, when looking at childhood photographs, was experienced by Owain Jones (2005), as here is his closing paragraph of his chapter in Davidson et al.'s *Emotional Geographies*:

> When searching through the photos I have of the farm and family life there, I found myself leaning right forward, staring at details of the pictures as they came up on the PC screen as if half hoping it was all going to come alive again. I feel overwhelmed by each photograph. Why am I so moved? Why am I so concerned? Inevitably this is lived and personal, the divisions between the public and professional and the private are breeched. This is the point and the challenge of emotional geographies (Jones, 2005: 217).

Ghost Topologies

According to John G. Sabol Jr., in *Ghost Culture – Theories, Context, and Scientific Practice* (2007), everyone has the potential – as we all engage in our day-to-day existence – to contribute to the hauntings of the future. These, what Sabol terms future 'residuals' of ours, might be thought of as ghostly, yet all-the-while normal, by yet-to-be-born researchers of such spectral sightings. Thus, '[t]he memories and experiences we have at locations we inhabit, visit, or investigate will be the basis for own 'personalized' hauntscapes', where '[w]e are both that participant in, and observer of, our own ghostly actions' (Sabol, 2007: 130). For, in short, '[w]e are the subject observing, and the object of some future investigation' (Sabol, 2007: 130). Moreover, Sabol, in *Bodies of Substance, Fragments of Memories – An Archaeological Sensitivity to Ghostly Presence* (2009), insist that ghostly presence – rather than being a paranormal phenomenon – is a reality. A reality that is often played out, again and again, at the same location, '[i]t is the story of individuals and their passions, or their obsessions', and, as such, '[i]t is the experience of how one lived and, perhaps, how one wants to be remembered' (Sabol, 2009: 199). Such hauntings then are often evident in places that are, quite literally, close to home. As, in *What Lurks Beyond – The Paranormal In Your Backyard* (2010), Jason Offutt asks us to contemplate what is just the other side of our back door – for, what is to be found beyond his back door is both mundane and uncanny: 'Pushing it open, I find a broken lawn mower, scattered toys, a dew-covered spider web, and tales of the paranormal', where '[a]ll are strange, close to home, and true' (Offutt, 2010: xi). In relation to the following structure – and themes contained herein – of *Remembering the Cultural Geographies of a Childhood Home*, the flow of Offutt's words are beguiling: moving from space to space – inside to outside, spectacle to spectacle – and the suggestion that the paranormal is both everyday and everywhere. Fundamentally, though, Offutt's words transform the paranormal – that is, what is beyond normal – to that which is normal.

Sabol, in *Ghost Culture Too – Expanding the Contemporary Reality of Past Interactive Interactions* (2012), connects ghostly residuals with aspects of cultural geography by terming the location of a haunting a border – that is, 'a zone of cultural differences', that 'contains particular spaces where many identities and memory practices articulate with one another in the *same* space as *surface* assemblages' (Sabol, 2012: 105). As something which is discussed at length in Chapter 2 (with specific reference to the hallway of Ivy Cottage), these haunted borders are contested spaces, where any form of communication is as a result of respectful negotiation, following an acceptance of ghosts, and an acknowledgement that our engagement with them is deemed a worthy one. Similarly, Julian Wolfreys' chapter, 'Ghosts: Of Ourselves or, Drifting with Hardy, Heidegger, James, and Woolf' (2010), also insists that all hauntings always take place at borders: 'between all those 'ones' and 'others' – alive and dead, present and absent, there and not there, visible and invisible – the pairings of which serve to map out, in a kind of spectro-tropo-topology, the spaces in-between' (Wolfrey, 2010: 16). Yet, despite this spectro-tropo-topology – this semi-solidity – ghosts are, of course, capable of non-physical actions that defy the restrictions of human geographies. Thus, Christopher M. Moreman, in *Beyond the Threshold – Afterlife Beliefs and Experiences in World Religions* (2010), notes that, with regards the anomalous experience that is our encounters with ghosts, all can be reduced to two paradoxical considerations: 'On the one hand, apparitions appear very solid and lifelike. They move about in physical space and behave as though they exist within the confines of their environment'. Yet, vitally, '[o]n the other hand, the apparitions perform feats that would be impossible for a physical being to perform, such as passing through doors, vanishing into thin air, walking without leaving footprints, or making any noise whatsoever' (Moreman, 2010: 204).

Whilst such anomalous experiences occur at contested borders amid this spectro-tropo-topology, it seems that – conversely – they are an essential aspect of normal life. As G. Maxwell-Stuart, in *Ghosts – A History of Phantoms, Ghouls & Other Spirits of the Dead* (2006), states:

> [p]erhaps, then, in spite of everything, the dead are still conceived as integral to the complete sweep of human existence, guarantors both of connection with the past and of continuance in the future, and hence mediators between realms which are otherwise considered distinct (2006: 229–30).

More fundamentally, according to Owen Davies, in *The Haunted – A Social History of Ghosts* (2007), we are fearful that – should we ever stop believing in ghosts – we will rid ourselves of a vital element of our human nature. Thus, '[s]ome of us evidently need ghosts to live as much as they require us to die' (Davies, 2007: 249). No surprise, then, that Avery F. Gordon, in *Ghostly Matters – Haunting and the Sociological Imagination* (2008), highlights the emancipatory, and collective, nature of an experience – that is, seeing a ghost – which is often perceived of as being a purely personal one. As, 'ultimately haunting is about how to transform a shadow of a life into an undiminished life whose shadows touch softly in the spirit of a peaceful reconciliation' (Gordon, 2008: 208). Thus, '[i]n this necessarily collective undertaking, the end, which is not an ending at all, belongs to everyone' (Gordon, 2008: 208). But, perhaps more than anything, ghosts mirror our times. The concluding comment within R.C. Finucane's *Ghosts – Appearances of the Dead & Cultural Transformation* (1996) insists that each and every era manifests its respective spirits according to cultural expectations of the time. As times change, so does the look of ghosts themselves. In short, '[f]rom this point of view it is clear that the suffering souls of purgatory in the days of Aquinas, the shade of a murdered mistress in Charles II's era, and the silent grey ladies of Victoria's reign represent not beings of that other world, but of this' (Finucane, 1996: 223).

The 1970s – The Decade's Self-perceptions

Come the late 1970s, the United Kingdom was in dire-straights, and it knew it. Richard Clutterbuck's *Britain in Agony – The Growth of Political Violence* (1978), outlines the decade's tendency (thus far) to be tainted by inflation, unemployment, poor industrial relations, strikes and picketing, demonstrations, street violence, extremists on both the Left and the Right, an oil crisis, bombing campaigns, and so on. He makes explicit – with the opening line of its Introduction – that '[t]he seven years from 1971 to 1977 must surely be amongst the most agonizing in British history' (Clutterbuck, 1978: 19). Acknowledging that the decade was witness to a rise in violence more generally, Clutterbuck is at pains to differentiate hierarchically between two distinct forms of violence: political violence (often perpetrated by the educated and the affluent, and which was seemingly being tolerated, excused even, by the system), being, for some, more worrying than the other, and crimes of violence:

> Crimes of violence have increased alarmingly and, for robbery with violence and rape, the courts will send a man to prison for several years. But some magistrates seem to regard political violence as morally more forgivable than violence for personal gain. They are wrong, because apart from the few big-time professionals, most criminals have suffered some deprivation, whereas

those organizing political violence are more often people who have many other opportunities open to them (Clutterbuck, 1978: 279).

The same year as Clutterbuck's analysis, violence of a more personal nature – namely, that decade's moral panic that was mugging – was being critically explored as an ideologically imbued, and racially specific, societal phenomenon. Stuart Hall et al.'s *Policing the Crisis – Mugging, the State, and Law and Order* (1978), noted, with resignation, that whilst statistics showed that mugging was carried out by youths irrespective of their ethnic backgrounds, 'few people would deny that, for all practical purposes, the terms 'mugging' and 'black crime' are now virtually synonymous' (Hall et al., 1978: 327). This equation of synonynimity, according to the study's Marxist authors, was as a consequence of a division being created within the working class that was as a result of the irreversible rise of black empowerment:

> For the moment black organisations and the black community defend black youth against the harassment to which they are subject, they appear on the political stage as the 'defenders of street criminals'. Yet not to defend that sector of the class which is being systematically driven into crime is to abandon it to the ranks of those who have been permanently criminalised (Hall et al., 1978: 396).

In 1976, Patrick Hutber's *The Decline and Fall of The Middle Class – And How It Can Fight Back* insisted that, come the middle of the decade, the United Kingdom was characterised by two inter-related crises: that of the nation more generally, and that of the middle classes more specifically, with the latter being 'subjected to unprecedented pressures and, at the same time, to unprecedented denigration' (1976: 9). Significantly, the militancy alluded to in the book's title was a barely shrouded warning that, if the middle class did not 'fight back' – that is, to 'assert and re-assume its wealth-creating role' (1976: 170) – then it would lead to its eventual abdication, whereby 'Britain is not likely to turn, as the more sanguine sort of socialist theorist hopes, into a superior kind of Sweden', but, instead, '[i]t is much more likely to finish up, as far as economic standards are concerned, a less efficient sort of Yugoslavia, or an even less dynamic version of Hungary' (170). Indeed, Hutber, a year or two later, was to edit another Socialist-bashing publication which – focusing upon these growing crises, now dubbed 'the English sickness' – attempted to answer, across its 15 chapters (that offered '15 answers'), the question, *What's Wrong With Britain?* (1978). Hutber's own contribution, the concluding chapter, insisted that the UK's population has 'been bewitched by the false compassion of socialism', itself the consequence of the 'historical accident of a monolithic trade union movement tied to a monolithic Labour Party', whereby 'the fanatics, the extremists and the wreckers in both the unions and the Labour Party are given a false legitimacy' (1978: 111). The 'cure', then, was a stark realisation:

> For perhaps a decade, the task of the Conservatives is not to conserve things but to change them, to make the choices that have so far been evaded, to move

forward towards a more market-orientated economy, and to alter the economic, social and political climate in a revolutionary way (1978: 112).

Furthermore, the 1970s was not only a decade in which there seemed to be social, economic and political turmoil, it was also a time in which the arts themselves were not only a barometer of cultural change, but a means by which the cultural chaos of the time was actually brought about – quite often as the result of some complex and accumulative (and, thus, problematic) intellectuality. For, Edward Lucie-Smith, in *Art in the Seventies* (1980), admits that '[t]he art of the 1970s has been difficult for the public to absorb, because it often seemed that one must hold the whole history of modern art in one's head in order to comprehend it' (Lucie-Smith, 1980: 7–8). Furthermore, such hyper-comprehension had to be engaged with as a revolutionary artistic epoch was being entered into: 'One can go further still, and say that artists of the 1970s, sometimes without fully meaning to do so, have overturned a whole system of categories' (Lucie-Smith, 1980: 8).

The 1970s – Perceptions Since

Yet, in retrospect, all this talk of an overturning of artistic practices and a bringing about of a postmodern condition in which it was necessary to behold all simultaneously, the 1970s – at least in some quarters – have come to be viewed as the decade in which cultural conservatism ruled, as a result of a concerted, and systematic, reduction of the funding of the arts. Bart Moore-Gilbert, with *The Arts in the 1970s – Cultural Closure?* (1994), argues that this was not only due to shrinking fiscal investment during a time of economic hardship, but both the end of Modernism (that is, with the death, during the decade, of such Modernist practitioners as Auden, Picasso, Stravinsky, etc.) and the post-counter-culture collapse of the avant-garde. Fundamentally, though, such cultural conservatism was ushered in by the fanfare that was the 'cult of nostalgia' that typified the 1970s – a nostalgia that was 'exemplified above all in the 1977 Queen's Jubilee' (Moore-Gilbert, 1994: 12). Indeed, such Jubilee-inspired celebrations – exemplified in the undertaking of the street party – often bordered upon the absurd. According to Philip Whitehead in *The Writing on the Wall – Britain in the Seventies* (1985), '[t]he most bizarre street party was held in Queen Street, Rugeley', where '[t]he street no longer existed' as '[i]t had been demolished and built over by planners' (Whitehead, 1985: 305). So, '[f]or the Jubilee, however, its former residents came together on the site', as, '[f]or them, the past really had been better than the present' (Whitehead, 1985: 305). Furthermore, and during a time of uncertainty, when there was perceived to be a decline of both community and the family, it was the way in which the Queen's popularity was bolstered through fervently supportive newspaper and television coverage that was the greatest significance. As, '[t]hrough the mediators the British saw the Queen as they would have liked to see themselves: she had her family troubles, was still respected in the neighbourhood, had managed to hang on to the family property – above all, she was a survivor' (Whitehead, 1985: 308).

Yet, despite the decade's increasingly conservative nostalgic trends, more recent accounts of the 1970s touch upon its extremes. Francis Wheen's *Strange Days Indeed – The Golden Age of Paranoia* (2009) insists that the true flavour of the decade bore 'a pungent *mélange* of apocalyptic dread and conspiratorial fever' (Wheen, 2009: 9). With omnipresent establishment-derived surveillance, underlined by both infamous reality (Watergate) and classic examples of corporeality (Francis Ford Coppola's *The Conversation*, 1974), the 1970s – politically and culturally – are now perceived of as a bad case of paranoid claustrophobia. Indeed, despite the positive-sounding title of *Seventies – The Sights, Sounds and Ideas of a Brilliant Decade* (2006), for its author, Howard Sounes, it was the pivotal year of 1976 – with its drought-inducing summer heatwave that scorched the brown earth and torched the flora black – that brought about a revolution of youth, Punk, that fanned the flames of the public's expectations that the 'apocalypse' would happen 'now'. Punk, a genre of music that was played by thrash-and-bash bands as The Damned and The Clash, and a mode of fashion that was, fundamentally, 'in yer face', the 'look' was everything: 'Punks dyed their hair in strange colours and wore it in weird styles; they pierced their tender skin with safety pins; cut and slashed their clothes, and donned the fetishist apparel of sex shops' (Sounes, 2006: 282). At a time of high-profile hostage-taking and subsequent posted ransom notes, Punk possessed a style of graphics that embraced such lawlessness. This was an inflammatory means of communication that 'used collage and lithographic printing to create stickers, posters and record sleeves, often with lettering cut from newspapers and arranged in the style of a kidnap demand' (Sounes, 2006: 292).

Andy Beckett, the author of *When the Lights Went Out – Britain in the Seventies* (2009), was born in 1969, and he admits that he is able to recall very little with regards the concerns that preoccupied the adults of the 1970s: 'The politics of the seventies, even in their broadest sense, are in the blurriest margins of my childhood memories' (Beckett, 2009: 2). However, as someone who would then grow up through the 1980s and 1990s, he – like many other 'children of Thatcher' – had accepted the post-1979 orthodox perception of that troubled decade: 'After all, it was not just Thatcherites who told it: left-wing people would scorn or regret the Callaghan years; liberals would condemn the brutality towards Irish republicans under Edward Heath; almost no one had a good word for the Harold Wilson administration of 1974–6' (Beckett, 2009: 3). Drawing links with the woes of Germany during the dark days of the 1930s, Beckett's generation often thought of the United Kingdom of the 1970s 'as a kind of Weimar Republic, a spooky parallel often invoked under Wilson and Callaghan' (Beckett, 2009: 3). Yet, in his attempt to rewrite the history of that tarnished decade, Beckett is at pains to – quite literally (as per his book's title) – re-illuminate the more optimistic aspects of life during that time. As, 'British politics in the seventies, for all the gothic prose it usually prompts, was about moments of possibility as well as periods of entropy; about stretches of calm as well as sudden calamity' (Beckett, 2009: 5).

Likewise, a similar rewriting is offered by Alwyn W. Turner in *Crisis? What Crisis? – Britain in the 1970s* (2008). Whilst his work opens with the stark recalling of the 1970s as a dark, bleak time. when '[t]he lights were going out all over Britain, and no one was quite sure if we'd see them lit again in our lifetime' (2008: ix), Turner is also able to pinpoint a significant moment in the new millennium when a major reappraisal of that decade began to take place. In 2004, the New Economics Foundation compiled a report on national performance founded on, not just gross domestic product (a common system of economic measurement), 'but on what it called the measure of domestic progress, incorporating such factors as crime, family stability, pollution and inequality of income', and, as a result, 'concluded that Britain was a happier country in 1976 than it had been in the 30 years since' (Turner, 2008: ix). Come the making public of the NEF's findings, the 1970s were now being re-evaluated as a (albeit, ever-so-slightly rusty) decade that – socially and culturally – shone: 'No longer 'the decade that taste forgot', it was now seen as a golden age of British television, of popular fiction, of low-tech toys and of club football' (Turner, 2008: x). However, and perhaps of greater insight, such a trend to reappraise the 1970s (that is, post-NEF 2004) has resulted in a consequential critique of those '30 years since'. As, Mark Garnett, in *From Anger to Apathy – The British Experience since 1975* (2007), claims that 'it would be more realistic to see the study as a doleful verdict on subsequent developments, rather than a celebration of the real living conditions of 1976' (2007: 2). Offering a more balanced – and sobering – comparison between the mid-decade 1970s and the year of the NEF's report, Garnett draws attention to the Violent Crime Reduction Act (2006). Whilst this piece of legislation, which 'gave teachers the right to search their tender charges for concealed weaponry' (Garnett, 2007: 377) – suggesting a level-headed approach to making the school environment safe – it simultaneously made explicit how different the United Kingdom of 2006 was compared to that of 30 years before, as '[a]lthough many British schools were unsavoury places in 1975, such a legislative measure would have been quite unthinkable at that time' (Garnett, 2007: 377).

Probably the most extensive – that is, especially with regards the amount of words devoted to that purpose – revisiting of the 1970s is that undertaken by Dominic Sandbrook, in his twin tomes *State of Emergency – The Way We Were: Britain, 1970–1974* (2010) and *Seasons in the Sun – The Battle for Britain, 1974–1979* (2012). In the former, Sandbrook – opening the preface with a detailed account of the wedding of Princess Anne and Captain Mark Phillip, 14 November 1973 – makes it clear that, whilst the politics and the significant political figures of the time are all important, it is the personal accounts of the many that are just as vital (if not more so). Thus, *State of Emergency*, attempts to encapsulate the countless number who were, during the first years of the 1970s:

> [D]rinking Watney's Red Barrel and Blue Nun, listening to Elton John and Emerson, Lake and Palmer, laughing at *Morecambe and Wise* and *Bless This House*, and cheering on Kevin Keegan, Jackie Stewart and Red Rum; the kind of people who spent their evening glued to *Crossroads* and *Upstairs, Downstairs*,

their weekends in the supermarket and the garden centre, and their holidays in
Malta and Majorca; the kind of people, indeed, who lined the street with their
flags and banners at the wedding of Princess Anne (Sandbrook, 2010: 14).

Meanwhile, in *Seasons in the Sun* (2012), Sandbrook attempts to encapsulate
the collective mood of the population of the United Kingdom towards the end of
the 1970s, with an overview of the making, and eventual release, of *Star Wars* (a
film that premiered in London on Boxing Day, 1977). Whilst admitting that the
film is a seemingly strange means by which the mood of the nation of the time
can be gauged, Sandbrook is quick to point out that, as it was produced at the (by
then run-down) Elstree Studios across 1976 and into 1977, and often blighted by
Union-led British working practices, 'it was largely a British endeavour' (2012:
xiv). With a significant number of the film's recognisable 'big name' stars, co-stars
and supporting actors, and almost all of its production team being British, this
was truly a futuristic science fiction epic that emerged out of the Home Counties
of the 1970s. More so, it captured the moment at which the optimism for future
space exploration was tarnished by the rot of the present condition that was
Britain in the 1970s. Instead of exhorting the post-1960s 'white heat' of science –
as Kubrick's *2001* has done, with its whiter-than-white interstellar veneer – *Star
Wars* was coated with the faecal dross that was the 1970s. As, for Sandbrook, all
the way through the film there was a perceptible 'healthy distrust of technological
modernity' that, in turn, was 'a message that would have resonated with millions of
British filmgoers in an age of resurgent environmentalism, economic decline and
cultural nostalgia' (2012: xvii). Quite significantly, for Sandbrook, 'beneath the
breathless kinetic spectacle, as so often in the mid-1970s, there was a thick layer
of New Age spirituality', where 'the hero turns off his battle computer, preferring
to rely on his own instincts, informed by the vaguely spiritual Force' (2012: xvii).

The 1970s – Cultural Recollections

Peter Knobler and Greg Mitchell's *Very Seventies – A Cultural History of
the 1970s From the Pages of Crawdaddy* (1995) deliberately places little emphasis
on politics, as, instead, popular culture is, to them, all important. As former
editors of the monthly magazine *Crawdaddy*, the most prominent social actors
in 1970's America 'were not its political leaders but its cultural ones' (Knobler
and Mitchell, 1995: 15). Thus, in America – at the level of the macro – culture was
everything. Likewise, at a micro level, in the United Kingdom, cultural change
occurred amid the cosy confines of the living room. As, in *Nice to See It, To
See It, Nice – The 1970s in Front of the Telly* (2009), Brian Viner (newspaper
television critic and columnist) not only provides an overview of small-screen
fare, for both children and adults, across that decade, but pinpoints the moment
at which the viewing habits of both crossed uncomfortably. A moment that he
describes as 'The Look' – that is, covert eye contact, from parent to parent, when

'adult TV' had just (often accidentally) been viewed by a minor – it not only 'was a signal that something had gone awry in the parental universe', but '[i]n a televisual context it usually concerned robust language or some kind of spectacle deemed inappropriate for my keen young eyes' (Viner, 2009: 9).

However, it was out in the street, and amid the playgrounds, and the like, that immense cultural transformations were taking place. The fleetingly brief youth subcultures and high-street fashions that were witnessed throughout the 1970s (of which Punk was the least subtle), have been well-documented in recent years. Trevor Coote's tenth novel, *Lemon Socks* (2011), attempts to capture on the page a youth subculture/street fashion – Suedehead – at the moment that it comes to both prominence and simultaneous decline. As here, in the Foreword, he describes the novel's protagonist's predicament come 1971, as he strives to climb the hierarchy of a local football hooligan firm:

> Glenn Turley is a 19 year old self-styled suedehead, a brief youth fashion that emerged out of the decline of the original skinheads around 1969, and which retained the fundamental musical and sartorial aspects of that culture … However, he is in a race against time to reach the top rung before he becomes a dinosaur as suedehead fashion disappears before his eyes, along with his youth (Coote, 2011: 9).

Andrew Collins (journalist, presenter, and scriptwriter), in 2003, published his childhood memoir, *Where Did It All Go Right? – Growing Up Normal in the 70s*. Humorous, and drawing heavily from his diaries, Collins insists that '[m]y story is essentially the story of Northampton's 1970s, or if you prefer, any provincial English town's 1970s' (2003: 14). To the other extreme, Paolo Hewitt (music journalist and author), blending autobiography and fiction, offers, in *The Looked After Kid – Memoirs From A Children's Home* (2002), a bleak account of being in care during the 1970s. For here is an extract from Chapter 2, 'Hurt is where the home is. April 1971':

> The shirt I button is thin and nylon, my tie grey and red. I hate my clothes. My friend's clothes at school are brand new, sharp-smelling and colourful. They wear tasselled loafers, Ben Sherman shirts and Levi sta-prest. They are all the latest fashion. Mine aren't. Mine are cheap and shapeless and dull and next to them I feel like a pauper (Hewitt, 2002: 16).

Similarly, Gary Robertson's *Skeem Life – Growing Up in the Seventies* (2010), an autobiographical account of childhood life amid the intimidating social housing estates of 1970s Dundee, is rich in period detail that is all the more enhanced through the author's writing style that draws heavily upon local dialect. Chapter 2, 'A Hoose In The Clouds', recalls (admittedly, with some humour) the squalid conditions endured by a young Robertson and his family, nine floors up, in Whitfield Court tower block, Whitfield:

> Some landings you passed would have anything from dog or human excrement
> or pish or a mix of all them. This delightful spectacle was usually complimented
> with artwork from the local creative literati whose work adorned walls, ceilings
> and floors alike with spray-painted classics such as 'YOUNG SHAMS RULE
> YA BASS' sitting proudly in the centre of the gallery. Vandalism and open toilets
> were accepted and we as bairns never batted an eyelid (Robertson, 2010: 8).

Pish in a tower block in Dundee. Thin, nylon shirts worn in a care home. Provincial
towns. Suedeheads. 'The Look'. The cultural geographies of a 1970's childhood
were – absolutely – place-specific, home-centric, and fleeting.

Conclusion

Fundamentally, *Remembering the Cultural Geographies of a Childhood Home* is
concerned with childhood, family life and the home – and, quite specifically, a time
when childhood found itself wrenched out of a fantasy existence and ditched amid
the harshness of reality. According to Estella Tincknell, in *Mediating the Family –
Gender, Culture and Representation* (2005), this epochal shift – which, admittedly,
originated in the decade before, the 1960s – meant that children's literature 'began
to be dominated by a new social realism in the 1970s' (2005: 86). Thus, embracing
such 'non-childish' issues such as youth culture, sexuality, existential crises, and
so on, such fictional texts highlighted 'a significant cultural move and a series of
complications around the relationship between the way in which the child was
imagined and family structures and emotions' (2005: 86). In the chapters that
follow, Peter's experience of childhood and his resultant memories of his family
home are of their time; whilst there is some element of imagination and fantasy
to be found, much is rooted in the realism and the harshness of the time, whereby
non-childish feelings and emotions are at the core of the everyday experiencing of
a 1970s childhood.

   That stated, it is the childhood home – that is, the house itself – which is the
prime focus of this book. For, Tessa Muncey, in *Creating Autoethnographies*
(2010), encourages 'the use of metaphor to enable deeply personal experiences to
be layered and disguised without losing meaning' (2010: 55). Thus, Muncey makes
much of the use of metaphors, asserting that – not only are they a highly significant
tool of memory research – but those Freudian ones, that draw upon the rooms
of a house are, for Muncey, particularly pertinent metaphors. This is because,
'[h]ouses are full of memories and ghosts that fit well with autobiographical
writing' (2010: 103). Drawing upon the metaphor of memories as ghostly rooms in
a house, we will – across the coming chapters – encounter, room-by-room, Peter's
childhood home of the 1970s: Ivy Cottage, Skewen, South Wales. As Peter's
memories are often both fleeting and fragile, perhaps they are better thought of
as cobwebs within the rooms of Ivy Cottage. Built in the late 1800s, Ivy Cottage
was – by the 1970s, and to Peter especially, as a young boy – an old house. And

it had many a spider's web within it. For *Remembering the Cultural Geographies of a Childhood Home* – combining Peter's memories and cultural artefacts amid – brings together many strands of the spiders' webs.

Chapter 2

The Childhood Spaces of the House

Two years today, Kath and I moved to Skewen to live with Marge, Frank, and boys (Millie's diary, Friday, 21 April 1978).

Lovely day ... Spent a nice quiet day at home with my family ... Peter and Frankie playing dominoes and cards (Millie's diary, Thursday, 1 January 1981).

Introduction

With Chapter 1 having introduced us to the literatures to do with cultural geographies, autoethnography, ghost topologies, and the 1970s, let us now knock on the door of Peter's childhood home: 19 St John's Terrace, Skewen, South Wales – Ivy Cottage.

The Front Door

Akiko Busch, in *Geography of Home – Writings On Where We Live* (1999), considers the demise of the front door during the twentieth century, for – in an era where the entering of a detached, or semi-detached, suburban home is quite often via a side door or entrance at the rear – the front door has become superfluous; or, at best, a decorative element of the front façade of the house. To Peter and his family, living in Ivy Cottage during the 1970s, this was certainly not the case: the front door – as an extension of the garden gate and the flagstone path that led off from the street – was the means by which the house was entered. Indeed, this is akin to Busch's assertion that, to some, 'the front door continues to appeal to our sense of arrival', whereby, in entering a house in such a manner, we are engaging in 'the ceremony of coming home' (Busch, 1999: 33).

Furthermore, the regular use of the front door of Ivy Cottage as a daily ceremony of coming home, is emphasised by the photograph reproduced overleaf (Figure 2.1). With Peter, peering into the rays of a late evening autumnal sun, leaning against the front door of Ivy Cottage, is clearly more than just a way in – it is a proud focal point of residence. The front door of Ivy Cottage – at a time when its usage, more generally, was being increasingly shunned – possessed a familial and social meaning more akin to its original purpose, where '[t]he front door was traditionally designed to present the house to the world at large, to welcome others' (Busch, 1999: 35).

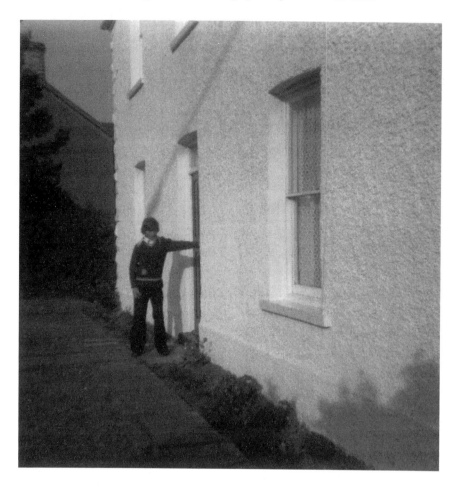

Figure 2.1   Peter at the front door of Ivy Cottage
Source: Author's own collection.

The front door is painted 'caterpillar yellow'; its glowing colour enhanced by the day's last embers of sunlight. It is coated in this colour that has come from tins of paint his father has brought home from his place of work (he was, at the time, a 'paint-sprayer'), where the intended use of the paint – rather than being domestic paint for exterior woodwork – was to provide caterpillar-tracked vehicles with their distinctive 'JCB' colour. To Peter, the front door of Ivy Cottage – in its 'caterpillar yellow' of the 1970s – is forever associated with his father, and his father's workplace of the time. Perhaps even more significantly, this 'caterpillar yellow' front door was a site at which Peter and his mother would often stand of a late afternoon, anxiously awaiting the return of 'Daddy', their husband-come-father, from work.

We're at the door, looking 'up the hill' towards Skewen proper, praying for his bus to appear. Daddy's already over an hour late, and there's still no sign of him. Keeping his dinner warm on the gas cooker, Mammy's standing over me, arms folded, and I can see by her face that she's now getting worried. What if something's happened to him at work? What if he's not coming home!?! I try not to think of what we would do if he didn't come home ... Wait, there's his bus! Coming down the road and indicating, it slows down, and pulls into the stop that is right opposite our front door. A few seconds later, it's off again, heading for Neath. The exhaust fumes clear, and there's Daddy, navy overalls stained in the day's oil and paint, standing, waiting to cross the road home. Me and Mammy breath simultaneously sighs of relief. Now, staggering slightly, grinning coyly, he's across the road, and through the garden gate. With a cheery, and slightly slurred, 'Peter-o!' he's through the front door, and it's obvious he's had a pint or two.

Produced by Hanna-Barbera, and first shown in the United States in 1972, *Wait Till Your Father Gets Home* was a cartoon series (that is, a pilot, and two series of 48 episodes), that portrayed the life of a contemporaneous middle-class, suburban family. With Harry Boyle as the white-collar patriarch who seemed incapable of establishing any form of emotional bond with his children (22-year-old Chet, an unemployed hippy; Jamie, a 9-year-old amoral capitalist; Alice, 16, an overweight 'romantic radical'), *Wait Till Your Father Gets Home* explored an American breadwinner's stressed relationships with his housewife (Irma) and anti-communist neighbour (Ralph). In doing so, the series was 'typical of its time in its promotion of certain social values (i.e. hard work, nuclear family, suburban dwelling, conservatism)' (Lewis, 2001: 320). Yet, as it was genuinely witty, with significant moments of obvious irony, it became one of Hanna-Barbera's most enduring animated legacies. A shame, then, that – when syndicated to the UK shortly after its US airing – it suffered a fate of serious under-exposure. For, '[t]he UK programmers' mistake was to show it during prime kids' TV time, when much of the material was intended to be appreciated by adults, possibly returning from that hard-day-at-the-office' (Lewis, 2006: 320).

Thus, whilst *Wait Till Your Father Gets Home* – specifically the title and the show's theme music – was representative of a mother's threat to a misbehaving child, the series, as a whole, always made Peter think of the moment his blue-collar father would come through the front door from his work (factory- and not office-based workplace). Fundamentally, *Wait Till Your Father Gets Home* was, in fact, about Peter's father's life holistically; both in work, and at home.

For Roger Moore in *The Man Who Haunted Himself* (1970), the front door to the house was very much a contested site of 'coming home'. A psychological thriller, it pits two post-accident doppelgangers against one another – that is, Moore as the two Harold Pelhams (one, a true 'City Gent', the other a more flamboyant 'Kings Road' version) – whose characters swap traits come the end of the movie. Indeed, in the film's closing moments, set during a rain-swept evening, Moore's two characters eventually come face-to-face with each other in the hallway of the Pelham family home. Up until this point the 'good' Pelham, the now 'bad' doppelganger (soaking wet, having 'come home' in an erratic, deranged manner) is challenged by the other – that is, the 'good'-once-'bad' version of Pelham:

Who on earth are you? Who are you?

With his response being a rather unsure and unconvincing 'Pelham!', Luigi (the butler), Alex (business associate and friend), Eve (wife), and Mike and Jamie (the children), all now congregating in the hall, collectively estrange the 'real' Harold Pelham. Indeed, it is his children's reaction which truly contests Pelham's 'coming home': With one stating, 'Mummy, I'm frightened', and the other asking (and, then, demanding), 'Daddy, who's he? Why does he look like you? Make him go away!' Thus, against a backdrop of a thundery, wind-swept night, the confused, challenged Pelham (that is, as opposed to the confident, authoritative version) charges out through the front door, leaving his home and family behind.[1]

It's 1972, it's mid-morning, and it's pouring with rain. Peter and his mother have just returned to the house laden with shopping.

———————————

Walking through the front door, we're relieved. We're back home, but we're sodden. The rain has managed to soak right through my khaki hooded parker, so that even my green polo neck underneath is wet. My arms are aching and stiff from carrying two heavy bags of shopping. Mammy mutters to herself 'Bloody Sam!', as our nostrils catch a whiff of fresh tomcat pee coming up from the patch of carpet just before the entrance to the parlour that he's squatted on continuously since it was fitted all those months ago. Taking off my saturated coat, the hall welcomes us into the house: with doorways on either side, it stretches out endlessly in front of me, on and on, until it reaches the door to the porch. The grey daylight that comes through the porch window, is, in turn, diffused through the glass panels of this door. As a result (and as there's even less grey illumination coming through the fanlight above the front door behind us), the hall itself emerges out of a darkness and into only semi-light. But, on this rainy day, the gloom only places emphasis upon the fact that we're back, and we're home.

———————————

1   The final scene – as with the film's opening moments – is centred upon a car accident. However, on this occasion, the 'real' Pelham (a ghost all along?) re-enters the body of his sinister doppelganger – reversing the physical/personality split which had been initiated by the earlier road accident.

The Hallway

Conducting an anthropological study of the spaces between the front door and the hallway, Céline Rosselin (2006) notes that it is 'in daily rituals of reception, that the threshold of the front door, being the borderline between the private and the public space, is of special importance' (Rosselin, 2006: 53). Thus, for Peter and his mother, such 'daily rituals' as coming through the front door of Ivy Cottage from shopping (the public), and stepping further into the hall (the private), they are overwhelmed with a sense of homecoming at a particular point in the house that can be better understood as a 'threshold'. In a way, this threshold begins with the front door (that is its outward, or public edge) and continues, and eventually ends, with the hall (the inner, or private border of threshold). As such, the threshold of hall itself can be conceptualised as 'a marginal or liminal zone that separates and links two distinct territories' (Rosselin, 2006: 54). Indeed, the hall not only separates the public from the private, it place emphasis upon itself as the final space in the house to do this. For, '[t]he hall is a limit threshold: the last one for the public world and the first one for the private world' (Rosselin, 2006: 56).

Once through the front door, and into the hallway, Ivy Cottage welcomed you in, for '[w]hen you enter a house through the front door, you discover its interiors in a logical progression, passing from public to private realms ... on this journey of progressive congeniality' (Busch, 1999: 37). It is the moving away from the front door, progressing along a hallway – and the notion of doing so as conducting a 'journey of progressive congeniality' – that is of importance here, as whilst the hallway of Ivy Cottage was welcoming, it was also a site of haunting which suggested that this was very much a contested space of the house. As Rosselin (2006) is also at pains to stress 'the marginal, the dangerous, and even the sacred aspect of the hall as a threshold' (Rosselin, 2006: 56).

I'm in the kitchen, and I'm having a drink of pop. Mammy is sitting next to the circular, Formica-topped table, on the chair nearest the door. Having a cigarette, she suddenly looks to her left – out through the door, past the foot of the stairs, to the point in the hall that is just in front of the door opposite to the living room – and she looks startled. A few seconds later, Kathleen, having stepped out from the parlour into the hall, looking just as shocked, and, noticing her expression, asks Mammy in a hurried breath 'Did you just see her as well?' 'Yes!' Mammy said, 'It was her again, in a floral bustle dress! Just a glimpse, like as if she was floating along. And, then – puff! – she went!'

With this memory of Peter's in mind, whereby both his mother and his aunt simultaneously catch a fleeting glimpse of one of Ivy Cottage's resident ghosts, let us further contemplate the space within the house within which this 'Lady in the Floral Bustle' was sighted on a number of occasions: the hallway. Rosselin

(2006), providing the example of inspecting oneself in the mirror (momentarily if there's one in the hall, far more intimately and lasting when in the bathroom or bedroom), makes explicit the fleeting nature of our occupying of this space in the home. That is, '[t]he transitional character of the hall, the area where people are not meant to stay, gives a special temporality to the actions performed there' (Rosselin, 2006: 58). Furthermore, it is 'an in-between of two other worlds' – such as 'interior versus exterior, private versus public, the intimate versus foreign' – where 'the hall does not belong to either of these categories but plays a spatial role in both of them' (Rosselin, 2006: 59). Indeed, '[t]he hall is not a univocal space', as it is the site in the home 'where the reversal between interior and exterior, private and public, and opening and closing are always possible' (Rosselin, 2006: 59).

As such, it is highly significant that the spectral 'Lady in the Floral Bustle' appeared in the hallway of Ivy Cottage: A place where 'people are not meant to stay', here was a space where a spirit seemed to exist forever; the domestic site within which the paths of the living and the dead crossed. To this end, the hallway of Ivy Cottage was very much 'an in-between of two other worlds'. Indeed, if the 'Lady in the Floral Bustle' was a former resident, then a fundamental question has to be asked: Who were to be deemed existing in the 'private' here, and who were to be deemed the 'foreign'? The 'Lady in the Floral Bustle' or Peter and his family? Additionally, the manner in which the 'Lady in the Floral Bustle' occupied and moved along the hall – albeit momentarily – is of interest here, as Alison Lurie, in *The Language of Clothes* (1981), argues that from the mid-nineteenth century onwards the so-called 'ideal woman' was 'at once divine and efficient, the 'angel in the house'' (Lurie, 1981: 69). In an era of crinoline, and shortly thereafter of the bustle, the now raised profile of women within both the domestic and public spheres was heralded 'by their sheer bulk' (Lurie, 1981: 69). Yet, in such bulky clothing, movement was extremely restricted, with walking at a pace hard to do, and running, quite simply, out of the question: 'But then, ladies did not 'walk', since in polite discourse they had no legs – rather they 'glided' or 'swept' across the floor' (Lurie, 1981: 218). A practical explanation, then, as to why the 'Lady in the Floral Bustle' of Ivy Cottage', when fleetingly glimpsed, appeared to 'float', and not walk, along the hallway.

Richard Lewis' *The Encyclopaedia of Cult Children's TV* (2006) places emphasis upon another of Hanna-Barbera's animated outputs – *Scooby Doo, Where Are You?*[2] First broadcast in the USA in 1969, and initially shown on

---

2   Brian Viner, in *Nice to See It, To See It, Nice – The 1970s in Front of the Telly* (2009), adds another dimension to children's watching of *Scooby Doo, Where Are You?*: 'But the best thing I can tell you about *Scooby-Doo* is that my friend Chris Taylor admits to having had "early erotic thoughts" about Scooby's friend Daphne – "the fit one", as Chris still describes her. This admission, I feel, puts into context my own mild feelings for Lady Penelope in *Thunderbirds*, and indeed my reliance on the underwear sections of Littlewoods and Grattan catalogues. It really was an age where you had to find your adolescent thrills in whatever way you could, whether in a mail-order catalogue or a children's cartoon

BBC1 across 1970–1972, the series – based upon the comic exploits of a bunch of teenage ghost-hunters who drove around in a customised VW microbus entitled the 'Mystery Machine' – was fronted by Shaggy (a cowardly, scruffy hippy) and Scooby Doo (an oversized dog, with its trademark husky laugh). In essence, '[t]his lily-livered duo was invariably sent off by the authoritarian Freddy down the darkest passage in the whole Gothic mansion to encounter the 'ghost' and engage in slapstick comedy' (Lewis, 2006: 267). Viner, in slightly exasperated tones, concludes that, with regards each and every episode, and the series as a whole, '[o]f course there were no ghosts' (Lewis, 2006: 268). No, instead, *Scooby Doo* ..., on a weekly basis, revolved around some form of extraordinary construct of a psychic phenomenon, all loosely founded in some local lore in an effort to add authenticity, in order to attempt to put off these 'snooping kids' (and, of course, their canine helper). In doing so, the villains of the series employed 'an enormous network of wires, pulleys, TV cameras, projectors, tape loops, pyrotechnics, electronic voce-altering devices, make up, prosthetic limbs and latex masks' (Lewis, 2006: 268).

Despite the contrived nature of the 'ghosts' in *Scooby Doo* the episodes would often begin with Freddy et al., being genuinely scared, and, as a result, running terrified – as Lewis puts it – 'down the darkest passage in the whole Gothic mansion'. Utilising a repetitive backdrop – that is, the same stretch of animated wall-door-wall-door, again and again – the teenage stars of the show ran away in a blur of on-screen revolving legs, whilst, behind them, the corridors and halls of the supposedly deserted mansion within which they had found themselves took on a never-ending dimension. Indeed, whilst Scooby Doo – as, essentially, an animated farce for children – could hardly be described as 'scary', it was this particular aspect of the animation (however unintentionally – as its 'repetitiveness' was most probably down to budgetary constraints) which lent it a certain uncanny quality.

British children's supernatural television on the other hand, added a certain gay hammyness to the mix, with the *Ghosts of Motley Hall* (ITV, 1976) and *Rentaghost* (BBC, 1975–1984). The latter is 'a masterpiece of low production values', whereby '[r]arely in the course of television history has there been such an ill-advised and embarrassing marriage of poor scripting, poor acting and poor directing' (Lewis, 2006: 258). *Rentaghost*, in essence, in an extremely cringe-inducing manner, portrayed 'the hammily-acted machinations of a group of ghosts who decided to set up in business renting themselves out' (Lewis, 2006: 258). Yet, despite the series' severe shortcomings of production, it is a fondly remembered example of 1970s (and early-1980s) television, and, in many respects, its unique representations of ghosts was particularly embedded in wider popular culture of the time. For example, Fred Mumford (played by Anthony Jackson) had met his end by falling off a cross-channel ferry, and aspects of pantomime and slapstick were very

---

series' (Viner, 2009: 220). Such a sexualised reading of childhood of the 1970s is similar to Peter's experience – detailed in Chapter 3 – of the tabloid newspaper, *The Sun*, and its 'Page 3 girls'.

much the order of the day, whereby '[f]oam pies were thrown, soot dislodged and jets of water issued amid theatrical shrieks and silly voices' (Lewis, 2006: 258). If anything, though, such paranormal activity was delivered – on a weekly basis (and like much of the adult-orientated drama of the period) – as all manner of 'over-acting luvvies appeared' (Lewis, 2006: 258). Likewise, the *Ghosts of Motley Hall* was similar camp, over-acted fare – with this being '[t]he televised blatherings of a whole lot of ghosts ... doomed to haunt their decaying ancestral Home, Motley Hall' (Lewis, 2006: 125). However, what was significant about this example of children's supernatural television was that, here, '[v]arious generations of the hilariously-named Uproar family roamed the dusty carpets and halls as the undead' (Lewis, 2006: 125). With the 'White Lady' as the most otherworldly (that is, 'conventional' – wailing, and so on) of all the on-screen ghosts, it is of interest that such a haunting was set within such domestic surroundings.

The first episode – 'The Last Uproar' (broadcast 25 April 1976) – opens with the spirits of Bodkin (an Elizabethan court jester) and Fanny (an eighteenth century Dandy), bringing up from the cellar a large portrait of General Sir George Uproar (ex-British Army, nineteenth century), which – upon the latter's barked orders – is to be rehung, above the fireplace, in the entrance hall of Motley (that is, placing emphasis upon such everyday domestic activity as putting up a picture). Interestingly, when a hitherto unknown ghost of the estate – a regency era stable boy named Matt – sneezes, Bodkin and Fanny (as they can't see him as yet) are clearly alarmed. Whilst Fanny rather nervously declares 'It's a trespasser!' Bodkin asks, in a scared manner, 'One of us or one of them?' The latter's question, of course, not only makes distinct that life and death co-exist in Motley Hall ('them' being the occasional live visitor to this 'empty' property occupied by 'us', the resident ghosts), but raises the issue of who is actually conducting the haunting in this series – those that are dead, or those that are alive? To the ghosts, who actually 'live' there, it is the trespassing living that, arguably, are doing the 'haunting'. Indeed, still momentarily invisible, Matt vandalises Sir George's oil painting by drawing on it with charcoal from the fireplace, and, upon his return from searching for the source of the sneezing, Fanny looks at the defaced artwork in horror. To which, seeing his shocked expression, Bodkin states 'What's up, you look as if you've seen a person?!?'.

Furthermore, and as if to demonstrate the intertextuality of children's and adults programming during the 1970s, the second episode – 'Old Glory' (shown 2 May 1976) – has the ghosts of Motley Hall being confronted by a Welsh husband-and-wife team of ghosthunters, Jack and Margaret Potter. With Fanny asking in a rather puzzled manner, 'What's the lunatic doing?', Jack Potter – played by Gerald James – enters into a lengthy scene of arranging the varied accoutrements of a ghost hunter carefully around the entrance hall and lower staircase: 48 thermometers, numerous chalk-circled ping-pong balls, strands of cotton that suspend countless bells, layers of shaken out talcum powder, and so on. Playing the role of yet another ghosthunter (or, rather, a 'psychic investigator'), who enters into a similar ritual of placing devices by which ghostly presences can be detected, Gerald James was to appear as George Tully in 'Assignment Two' of the series *Sapphire and Steel*, transmitted just a few years later (31 July– 8 November 1979).[3] If anything, the episode 'Old Glory' – entering into such great detail to do with the 'science' behind ghosthunting – was a classic case of how children's television during the 1970s, especially when tackling 'adult' themes such as the paranormal, did not patronise their young audiences. As if not to ridicule the existence of ghosts (yet, at the same time, undermining the work of her husband), the final scene of this episode of the *Ghosts of Motley Hall* – where, beforehand, she is shown as the uninterested sceptic, constantly knitting away – Margaret Potter, just turning back as they leave the property (and with Jack Potter having been unable to detect any form of psychic activity), smilingly bids farewell to the spirits with the words 'You'll be alright now. I think he's given up ghost hunting!' This, then, is the sceptic as the true 'sensitive' to – and the true respecter of – paranormal activity.

All the while, the series' title is significant as – at a time, the mid-1970s – the hallway had been virtually divorced from its original usage and meaning. As Bill Bryson, in *At Home – A Short History of Private Life* (2010), notes, from the early 1600s onwards, when the private began to relocate itself from single-space, communal housing towards compartmentalised stately homes, 'the hall lost its original purpose and became a mere entrance lobby with a staircase – a room to be received in and pass through on the way to more important spaces' (Bryson, 2010: 70). Yet, whilst the 'hall' as a living space was being made obsolete, its origins were being immortalised – and even expanded upon – through the vogue (certainly by the nineteenth century) of naming extensive, public buildings of note, and even newly-emerging cultural concepts, as 'halls': 'Carnegie Hall, Royal Albert Hall, town hall and hall of fame, among many others' (Bryson, 2010: 70). Thus, the *Ghosts of Motley Hall* – albeit on the level of children's television – was part of this continuum of 'preserving' the hall, as a place of residence, at a time when the hall, to the children of the 1970s (like Peter), was merely somewhere to hang your rain-soaked parker coat. In the final analysis, though, the depictions of ghostly phenomena on children's television of the 1970s – hall-bound or otherwise – was characterised by not only repetition (and, thus, a certain predictability), but by an over-the-top theatricality and campness: No blood and gore, but more the queer *unheimlich* of lashings of Georgian wigs, white face powder, and the faux beauty spots.

According to Graham Kibble-White, in *TV Cream – The Ultimate Guide to 70s and 80s Pop Culture* (2005a), ITV's *Thriller*, broadcast from 1973–1976, 'was a textbook example of straightforward, unpretentious telly drama doing its job beautifully' (2005a: 192). With a title sequence that filtered eerie suburban vistas through a blood-red fish-eye camera lens, to the accompaniment of discordant scales of music, the mood was established 'for each week's dose of macabre

---

3   This episode of *Sapphire and Steel* is concerned with a disused railway station that is haunted by the ghost of a soldier killed in action during the First World War.

happenings in, more often than not, a superficially cosy remote provincial setting' (2005a: 192). Utilising, from a modern-day perspective, 'glacial pacing', deliberately elongated tracking shots of empty rooms – all to a spine-tingling sparse musical score – proved absolutely essential to the mood which the series wished to create: 'Rather than cut rapidly from shot to shot, the direction took its time, almost taunting the viewer with its creeping progress' (192). As a result, the series, each week, created an on-screen 'claustrophobic sense of place and foreboding' (2005a: 192). Yes, limited by studio-bound filming (with very little done on location), *Thriller* – again, by today's standards – possesses a slightly amateurish feel, but even such low production values 'had an atmosphere all their own' (2005a: 192).

One episode of *Thriller*, 'Possession' (transmitted 21 April 1973), places itself – with regards any 'geography of the home' – at the point at which the hallway meets with the cellar (that is, the very point at which we now find ourselves in Ivy Cottage). Set in an old, isolated country house, 'High Pines', the episode begins with the committing of a murder there in 1953. Twenty years later, when newly-weds Ray and Penny Burns move into the property, the repair of a faulty central heating system results in the digging up of the cellar floor, and the discovery of skeletal remains. A police investigation follows, with the body being declared that of a previous owner – Miss Elizabeth Millington, who had 'disappeared' in 1953 (the year, of course, of the opening scene's murder). Just before Elizabeth Millington's body is discovered, the camera (and, thus, the audiences' point-of-view) moves slowly from the floor of the cellar, up its steps to the door into the kitchen, panning across that room, and through the entrance into the hallway. Then, along that space, and up the stairs and into the main bedroom, the camera focuses upon Penny Burns' sleeping face. All the while, this painstakingly slow tracking shot (lasting a total of 1 minute and 22 seconds), is hauntingly accompanied by near silence that is barely punctuated by the ghostly whispering of the melody 'Greensleeves'. As events unfold, the obligatory séance is entered into, with – later in the episode – the medium, Cecily Rafting, being murdered and buried in the cellar. Initially suspecting a 'possession' of some form, it transpires that Ray Burns is the killer of both Millington and Rafting, and has only purchased the house in order to find hidden money that he failed to uncover at the time of his first foul deed (carried out when he was a travelling salesman) in 1953. Indeed, Ray Burns – finally being tackled by arresting police in the kitchen – stumbles backwards through the doorway down into the cellar, and suffers a fatal fall to the floor at the very point at which both bodies had been buried. The episode then ends, to the accompaniment of a whistled 'Greensleeves', with yet another laborious tracking shot, from hallway to cellar, where a feint outline of Ray Burns' body is detectable upon the floor as a suggestion of High Pines' ongoing spiritual possession.

So, with the tune of 'Greensleeves' in our ears, and now at the end of the hallway in Ivy Cottage, just before the back porch, we turn right, and, unlocking the bolt to the cellar door, we go down the steps into its subterranean gloom.

The Cellar

In *Environment and Children – Passive Lessons from the Everyday Environment* (2007), Christopher Day describes – in relation to children and their sense of 'space-mood' – the emotion-derived atmosphere of underground rooms such as basements and cellars: 'Cave-like, they invoke archetypal roots, a magical but disquieting past, and subhuman monsters. They're usually dark, cold and musty – a climate independent of weather' (Day, 2007: 124). Meanwhile, despite its negative resonance, Bryson (2010) places emphasis, quite specifically, on the cellar's 'solidity' – its sheer ability to 'support' the house: 'It isn't a very congenial space, but it does have the compensating virtue of providing some sense of the superstructure of the house – the things that hold it up and keep it together' (Bryson, 2010: 211).

Matthew Manning, the 'child psychic',[4] in his first autobiographical account *The Link* (1974, published when he was just 18), admits that he had felt an 'outsider' since he was 11 years old. For, at that age, Matthew, in the home that he lived in with his parents and younger brother and sister, experienced manifestations of a poltergeist with Matthew as the 'source'. Living in a relatively recently built detached house – where they had already been for seven years – the phenomenon, commencing on the morning of 18 February 1967, lasted a number of weeks, but ended suddenly thereafter. The Manning family then, in November 1968, moved into Queen's House, Linton, near Cambridge. At 15, with Matthew as a boarder at public school, the phenomena returned in a far more potent manner. Thus, it was, in 1971 – three years after the Mannings had moved into Queen's House – that Robert Webbe 'introduces' himself. Webbe, the original builder and owner of this eighteenth-century family home (built in 1731) died in 1733, but remained as a spirit there, attempting to maintain 'ownership' of the property ever since. Seemingly oblivious to the fact that the house has new owners, Webbe enters into 'conversations' with Matthew through bouts of automatic writing in which Webbe describes his everyday eighteenth century existence. This form of communication continues over a six year period, over which time it becomes clear that Webbe not only believes that he still 'exists' (that is, both prior to, and *after* his death), but he fears that his communications with Matthew are actually voices in his own head as insanity sets in. Yet, it was the so-called 'spirit graffiti' that appeared on the walls of Queen's House between the 31 July and 6 August 1971, that Matthew himself describes as amongst 'the most unusual psychic phenomena ever to have manifested themselves' (1974: 87). Webbe, through automatic writing, boasted

---

4   Matthew Manning is the first of this book's 'child psychics' of the 1970s. Welsh-born Stephen O'Brien is the second, discussed later in this chapter. Indeed, as Peter and his family (his mother and aunt in particular) sporadically attended evening services at Neath's Spiritualist Church during the mid-to-late-1970s, such celebrated young psychics and mediums as both Manning and O'Brien (and others, more elderly, such as Doris Stokes) were often the topic of conversation at Ivy Cottage at this time.

that he would provide "half-a-thousand signatures of friends and family" (cited in Manning, 1974: 87). As such, starting with 'Rob. Webbe', and being joined, 20 minutes later, by 'Hannah Webbe' (his daughter's 'signature'), Manning, in *The Strangers – My Conversations With A Ghost* (1978), explains that the walls of his teenage bedroom gradually became adorned with these psychic scrawls – to the extent that '[b]y lunchtime, about two hours after the appearance of the first name, 15 more had appeared; most of them seemed to belong to members of the Webbe family' (1978: 21). Finally, after six full days of intense paranormal activity, an eventual 503 frenzied 'signatures', almost all of them dated, had been scribbled onto the walls of Matthew's bedroom.[5] Indeed, the names extended across an entire panelled wall, its door, and had then over-spilled onto the two walls either side.[6] Covering the cornice, the skirting boards, and even the ceiling, it was the inaccessible points of the walls and ceilings at which much of this 'graffiti' could be found that added to their uncanny quality:

> Many of the names were being written in places where it was quite impossible for any human to have written them. Some were compressed so far into corners that people later inspecting the wall have been unable to get their hands in, let alone write a signature. Others were written in perfect writing on the ceiling, or on the cornices; some were written upside down with apparent ease (Manning, 1978: 24).

Despite Matthew's father demanding that this 'graffiti' come to an immediate end, Webbe not only continued to write on the walls, but he did so whilst vehemently insisting upon his on-going entitlement to do so. For, as one 'automatic' message implored (in contemporaneous 'Olde English'), 'You must relize that it is my wall and I am at liberty to write on my owne walls' (Webbe, cited in Manning, 1978: 21). Here, Webbe's insistence to continue inscribing upon his 'owne walls' is in line with Paul Pennartz's work to do with 'home', and the 'experience of atmosphere', where '[w]alls may function as barriers to communication and therefore give one a feeling of being shut out' (2006: 102). Thus, in this instance, Webbe – feeling, quite possible, 'shut out' from his own home by the Mannings' insistence on their occupation of it – attempts to transform these 'barriers to communication', the walls of *his* own home, into the site of his chosen method of communication with Matthew and his family. Thus, come 3 August, with the list of names

---

5   Eventually, on the walls and doors of Matthew's bedroom, were listed 544 names of Webbe's family, friends, and other contemporaries. Whilst Webbe's own examples – two signatures and six poems – were dated 1733, the remainder ranged from 1355–1870. All names are listed, in alphabetical order, in *The Strangers – My Conversations With A Ghost*, as 'Appendix 2: The Names Inscribed on the Study Walls' (1978: 160–76).

6   *The Strangers – My Conversations With A Ghost* (1978) also includes one photograph, taken in 1971, showing an extensive stretch of the panelled walls and door, all completely covered with writing by Webbe et al.

already exceeding 300, the Manning family had come to the realisation that their ownership of Queen's House was now in dispute: 'By now it was becoming clear that as far as Robert Webbe was concerned, the house belonged to him, and not to us. We were strangers. Furthermore, he seemed to regard himself rather than my father as the master of the house' (Manning, 1978: 28). With Webbe eventually insisting that 'This is myne house. Myne house and myne all' (cited in Manning, 1978: 42), it is now essential that we acknowledge that '[t]he walls of a room are also spatial elements 'to do something with'' (Pennartz, 2006: 105). That is, in the case of Robert Webbe, and his on-going claim of ownership of Queen's House, *his* walls very much offered themselves as a blank canvas of sorts for him 'to do something with' as he saw fit.

Significantly, on 2 April 1972, Webbe communicates that it is 2 April 1727, having written, the year before, that his date (the time in which Webbe, beforehand, seemed to perpetually exist) was 1733. Realising that Webbe was seemingly of the impression that he was now existing in 1727 (again, despite the fact that, the year before, he acknowledged that he had died in 1733), Matthew came to the conclusion that Webbe was 'trapped' in a form of 'postmortal nightmare' from which he could not escape. Indeed, Matthew, at this point, drew an analogy between Webbe's predicament and an aspect of late-1970s culture which is worth quoting at length here:

> Here an image occurred to me. I visualized time as a record being played on a gramophone. The needle moved along the groove and time progressed. If the motor of the gramophone was reversed, one retraced the groove which had already been played and time would be repeated. With Webbe it was as though there was an obstruction in the groove at the point of his death which caused the needle to jump back across the grooves through which it had previously played. Thus Webbe was somehow reliving the final years of his physical life over and over. Sometimes I seemed to communicate with him as the needle reached the obstruction on the surface of the record, and he would be aware that he was now dead, and at other times I would communicate with him after the needle had jumped back again (Manning, 1978: 66).

Furthermore, to Matthew:

> [t]his seemed an attractive image and explained to me why Webbe, when asked what the date was, always gave varying dates between 1727 and 1733 (Manning, 1978: 66).

With final contact between Matthew and Webbe during Christmas 1974, *The Strangers – My Conversations With A Ghost* (1978) concludes with the pondering of whether or not Webbe would return in the manner that he had 'lived again' between the years 1971 and 1974. However, Matthew sensed that Webbe was now a 'spent force': whilst his presence may still remain, Matthew felt it as only 'an empty reservoir'. Commenting upon the quiet nature of Queen's House since 1974, and the associated lack of any form of paranormal activity, Matthew – rather contemplatively – states that it was now 'as if a storm had passed' (Manning, 1978: 118). As such, it is here worth noting that – with Queen's House more generally, and Matthew's teenage bedroom in particular – '[a]gain it is not the spatial enclosure that determines the atmosphere, but the opportunity it provides' (Pennartz, 2006: 105). And it is with a consideration of the 'atmosphere' of the house as 'spatial enclosure' that Matthew signs off with:

> It was another of those halcyon days during the hot summers we have experienced recently: one of those days on which it seemed that nothing strange could happen. After all, strange phenomena are traditionally associated with windswept, creaky houses in the middle of nowhere, and occur on bleak, winter nights. But this was different. The brilliant sunlight swept through the windows, its light falling in broken patterns on the carpeted floor of the bedroom (Manning, 1978: 118).

To Matthew, then, his bedroom now existed 'in a timeless realm', acknowledging that – in essence – Queen's House stood then as it had done for the past 250 years before. With the bright sunlight blazing through the window onto the carpeted floor of his bedroom, Matthew cast his mind back to that morning when the eighteenth-century 'ghost graffiti' had begun to manifest itself, and procrastinated both the passing of time, and the perception of time itself: 'Three years ago seemed to me so very distant. I wondered how long it seemed to Robert Webbe' (Manning, 1978: 119). Furthermore, Matthew sensed that something had fundamentally changed since his communications with Webbe – something that was ushered in at the time of Webbe's death in 1733: it was the realisation that, since that day, two parallel time zones were in existence within the walls of Queen's House – that of the Manning's and that of Webbe's. Yet, upon the 'passing of this storm', time was, once again, reduced to the singular amid this aged family home:

> Now there is only one time scale which is real, and that is our own. The other has been absorbed by history, and has seeped back into the bricks of the house (Manning, 1978: 119).

The Parlour

To Bill Bryson (2010) the room in the house which epitomises comfort is the 'drawing room', noting that its name derives from 'a shortening of the much older 'withdrawing room', meaning a space where the family could withdraw from the rest of the household for greater privacy' (2010: 147). Bryson, though, is at pains to stress that the term 'drawing room' has had difficulty incorporating itself into

**Figure 2.2   Peter, Daddy, Mammy, and 'Taffy Thomas' in the parlour of
                Ivy Cottage**

Source: Author's own collection.

widespread usage within both English language and architecture, as '[f]or a time
in the seventeenth and eighteenth centuries, "drawing room" was challenged in
more refined circles by the French *salon*' (Bryson, 2010: 147). Indeed, in North
America, 'parlour' was preferred the term, and is the one with the most ancient
lineage, as '[i]t is first recorded as a room where monks could go to talk (it is from
the French *parler*, "to speak") in 1225 and was extended to secular contexts by
the last quarter of the following century' (Bryson, 2010: 148). Thus, above is a
photograph (Figure 2.2) of Peter with his mother and father (and his ventriloquist
dummy, 'Taffy Thomas'), in one of their two front parlours at Christmas time,
having 'withdrawn' into that living space in order to mark that year's festivities.

By 'withdrawing' into the parlour for the weeks not only leading up to Christmas but those that took the celebrations (and the lull after) into the new year, both the television (there was no aerial point in the room) and gas-fire heating were shunned. Indeed, it was the early-morning preparing and lighting of that room's coal fire which signalled the arrival of Christmas. Furthermore, to Peter, it was the carpet of the parlour which equated their living through the colder weeks of the year in that space: with a pattern comprising of leaf-like dark browns, greens, and reddy-rusts, just to lie down on it felt like Christmas. Indeed, it was typically 1970s, as, during that decade, 'autumn-coloured 'shag pile' was seen everywhere' (Shepherd and Shepherd, 2012: 33). Meanwhile, the rather spindly tinsel Christmas tree, festooned with home-made crackers made from old toilet rolls and gaudy crepe paper,[7] was typical of those – year-in-year-out – being put up in parlours and living rooms across the land. Gary Robertson, in *Skeem Life – Growing Up in the Seventies* (2010), remembers his family's rather shoddy, artificial perennial Christmas tree being put up in their flat in a multi-storey in early-1970s Dundee:

> Our Christmas tree was more of a sapling than a tree, a sorry-looking wee silver number that seemed very sad and lacked self-esteem. In contrast to the present day's all singing, all dancing, colour changing poser range, our little tree was like a withered dandelion that had been pished on by a cat. Still, we did our best and had it decked out in tinsel and baubles and looking as best as it could (Robertson, 2010: 40–41).

Whilst Peter, his parents, and their Christmas tree are the obvious focal point of this photograph, it is to the nearly-out-of-shot 'Taffy Thomas' that we now turn – that is, in relation to the film *Magic* (1978). Starring the Welsh-born Anthony Hopkins, *Magic* – quite often one of Hopkins' critically overlooked roles – is a psychological horror, whereby 'Charles 'Corky' Withers, a failed stage magician, attempts a comeback accompanied by a foul-mouthed ventriloquist dummy named 'Fats'. Suffering from mental delusions – facets of Fats' transposed personality – Corky commits murder (first, his agent Greene, then his high-school friend Duke). Eventually opting for suicide – in order to put an end to these possession-induced killings – the film ends with the audience aware of the impending death of both Corky and Fats (although unaware of which of the two will die first). So, looking, once again, at Taffy Thomas' partial appearance in Peter's festive photograph – with both Fats' demonic presence and Corky's eventual permanent adoption of his dummy's voice (with both of them now wearing identical knitted crew-neck

---

7   Peter has a particular nostalgic fondness for these home-made Christmas decorations. However, with the benefit of a more health-and-safety-conscious mindset – well aware that Peter's family were 'smokers' – such nostalgia is shrouded in sheer relief: 'Sadly, crepe mania died out around the end of the '70s and living rooms went back to being drab and featureless. This was probably due to the fact that the stuff was flammable as hell and probably responsible for burning loads of people's houses down' (Robertson, 2010: 40).

jumpers) – it is Peter's amateurish operating of Taffy Thomas that, suddenly, takes on an uncanny edge. No longer are Peter's 'Gottle of Geers' (that is, his clumsy attempts to replicate the ventriloquist's distorted 'Bottle of Beer') innocent alone. Indeed, Taffy Thomas' sideways glances, with slowly blinking glazed eyes, are, now, far more reminiscent of Fats' 'coming alive' than being as a result of Peter's awkward hand movements. In the wake of *Magic*, then, Taffy Thomas is a true example of the possessed childhood toy of the late-1970s.

Apart from a room to 'withdraw' into at Christmas, and the perennial home of an eerily perched 'Taffy Thomas', the parlour was – occasionally after school, but particularly during the afternoons of the weekends and holidays – the room where Peter and an invited friend would be expected to play. Indeed, with the room to themselves, it was often a site of quite boisterous, noisy indoor play.

With an 'Aaargh!!!' Peter Jones, jumping from the armchair, launches himself at me. We grapple, strain, and grunt; our underdeveloped bodies locked in mortal combat. He's got me in a Half-Nelson (his hand, under my arm, is locked behind my neck). But with an almighty push – and an almighty 'Uur-urgh!!!' – we separate, and, grabbing him by both legs, I straddle him, pinning him face down on the carpet in a Boston Crab. Half-an-hour of this, and we fall away from each other, gasping for breath, and laughing our heads off.

Peter and his friend (yes, another 'Peter') were, of course, emulating – upon the carpeted floor of the parlour, with the armchair (and, quite often, the sofa as well) as the 'ring' – one of the most popular televised sports of the 1970s: Saturday afternoon wrestling. Screened at 4 p.m., as part of ITV's *World of Sport*,[8] it was often broadcast live from such salubrious venues as Brent Town Hall, Wolverhampton Civic Hall, and Bletchey Park, and with its distinctive commentary by Kent Walton (English-born, but with an affected Canadian accent), it became one of the most popular televised sports of the late 1960s and 1970s. Much of its popularity was due to the whole host of flamboyant wrestlers that the sport offers – wrestlers that, despite being born and bred in the working-class areas of Britain's towns and cities, accentuated their adopted personas with exotic-sounding names. Amongst many others, there was Zoltan Bocsik, Big Daddy, Leon Fortuna, King Fu, Les Kellett, the Masked Madagascan, Mick McManus, Kendo Nagasaki, Jackie Pallo, Ricki Starr, Adrian Street, Terrible Turk, and so on. Indeed, '[t]hose of us who come from the 1970s mutter these names with nearly as much reverence as schoolboys of the 1950s talk about Denis Compton and Len Hutton, or Tom Finney and Stanley

---

8 Significantly, *World of Sport* began in 1965 in an effort to offer an alternative to the BBC's *Grandstand*. However, 'the fact that the commercial channel showcased such downmarket fare as wrestling merely emphasized the intrinsic superiority of the BBC' (Viner, 2009: 187).

Matthews' (Viner, 2009: 186) – furthermore, Jackie Pallo (most definitely as a result of him being a 'baddie'), 'was a name as powerfully evocative of the kipper-tie decade as Lord Lucan, Red Rum and Gilbert O'Sullivan' (Viner, 2009: 187). Pallo, who was loved to be hated by 'the brolly-wielding grannies at ringside' (Viner, 2009: 187), quite often faked – as did all the other wrestlers – many of their injuries,[9] biting his own lip 'when blood was called for to make a headbutt look real' (Viner, 2009: 187). Furthermore, '[e]veryone knew that it bore almost no kinship to the noble art of wrestling as depicted on ancient Greek urns', yet, 'by the 1970s we were hooked' (Viner, 2009: 188).

Despite the wrestlers 'faking it' and the sport's overall lack of 'authenticity', it was immensely popular, with both a live and television audience that truly believed in the 'violent' sport within which they willingly immersed themselves in the culture of. As, '[t]here were impressionable schoolboys and gullible grannies who refused to believe that a Boston Crab was anything other than the most painful physical predicament known to man' (Viner, 2009: 188).

Central to the perpetuation of their adopted personas (in relation to them being either 'goodies' or 'baddies'), many wrestlers displayed foibles that, in turn, allowed them to play to the audience. For example, Mick McManus 'used to pretend that his Achilles heel was his ears', whilst Jackie Pallo 'used to hate it when anyone grabbed his ponytail' (Viner, 2009: 189). Yet, amid these weird and wonderful displays of exaggerated machismo, some nurtured even more extravagant personas, such as 'the peroxided and mincingly camp Welshman Adrian Street'[10] (Viner, 2009: 190). All in all, this was a so-called sport which seemed to appeal to the very young (that is, boys – such as the two Peters) and the old (elderly, 'brolly-wielding' women). Fundamentally, though, the simple reason why – of an afternoon – Peter and his friend would attempt to sweatily emulate the on-screen, over-the-top antics of their wrestling heroes and villains such as Jackie Pallo was because '[t]here was certainly something childlike about the pantomime-style wrestling on *World of Sport*' (Viner, 2009: 190).

Richard Bowood's *The Story of Houses and Homes* (1963), one of the series *A Ladybird 'Achievements' Book*, provides an overview of the characteristics of suburban residential properties built during the twentieth century. In so doing, it insists that, like Ivy Cottage, they 'are withdrawn from the road which makes them quieter' (1963: 44). Whilst Ivy Cottage was already standing come the start of that century, it is both very much a twentieth-century house (as the majority of its residents have, so far, lived within its walls during those 100 years) and it is 'withdrawn from the road', as a result of its front gardens, and is, thus, 'quieter' than many a house and home. In many respects, silence was something which

---

9   As Viner makes explicit 'many of the others like to produce "the claret" by nicking themselves with a concealed razor blade' (2009: 187).

10   As to place emphasis upon the façade that was Saturday afternoon wrestling on ITV, Adrian Street's 'camp' persona was a sham: 'In reality, almost inevitably, he was emphatically heterosexual' (Viner, 2009: 190).

fundamentally defined Ivy Cottage during the time that Peter and his family lived there. Due to his mother's nervous disposition, Peter was forbidden to possess toys which made excessive noise, and music was kept to an absolute minimum (the kitchen radio was only put on for the news), meanwhile the parlour's record player only ever crackled into life at Christmas and the occasional Sunday – and, only then, with Mario Lanza's semi-operatic tones emanating from it at a minimal volume. The remainder of the time (certainly during daytime hours) the house was virtually silent. Many rooms of the house – for example, the two 'front parlours' – were devoid of any sound for days, even weeks, on end. Therefore, what characterised Ivy Cottage was silence. Even when the TV was on in the living room, it could not be heard in other rooms. So, generally, it was a silent, still house. Indeed, Ivy Cottage echoed with a deafening stillness.

This is all in keeping with David Toop's work to do with the appreciation of silence as audible, uncanny sound. For, in *Sinister Resonance – The Mediumship of the Listener* (2010), it is such silent, still spaces within the home that space itself becomes audibly tangible. Whereby:

> [s]pace itself is an instrument in which the background sound of subtle auditory shifts, singing resonance and dead echoes fills the air so completely that this peripheral sound seems to personify the place itself, a ubiquity of such familiarity that it fades into nothing (Toop, 2010: 147).

This 'peripheral sound', as 'it fades into nothing', with the rooms of Ivy Cottage such as the parlour, the entire house – as its overall uncanny silence combined with the day-to-day gentle cacophony of living – generated a homely sound year-in-year-out: As '[s]ound surrounds the home in their own air, a ring of familiarity, changing with the seasons and change itself' (Toop, 2010: 148).

In *Children and Spirituality – Searching for Meaning and Connectedness* (2008), Brendan Hyde highlights the necessity of providing children with contemplative spaces in order to 'nurture' the spiritual dimension of children's lives. Such 'appropriate spaces would also be characterized by silence'; in that, quite often, '[s]ilence, stillness and refection are qualities that are often absent from children's lives' (Hyde, 2008: 162). Hyde, noting that both schools and homes are places of constant, frantic activity (where 'working in groups', and endless usage of television, computers, mobile phones, etc., are given priority over silent individuality), positions such a tendency towards noise immersion as societal: 'In Western culture, people are uncomfortable with the quiet, and they try to fill the silence with noise of one kind or another' (Hyde, 2008: 162). This is all exacerbated – with noise equating productivity, and silence perceived of as a by-product of being unproductive – by institutional pressure against 'doing nothing' as it is merely 'time wasting'. Thus:

> [i]n the present classroom climate of Western education, many would argue that it is a brave teacher who puts the curriculum on hold to enable children to simply sit, to be, and to engage in the present moment (Hyde, 2008: 163).

Likewise, Hyde insists, 'it takes a wise parent to recognize that when, for example, her or his child is clutching at a small rock … that the child may be expressing her or his spirituality' (Hyde, 2008: 163). Both teachers and parents, then, should 'allow time for the child to engage in the present moment' (Hyde, 2008: 163). In essence, and according to Adams et al., in *The Spiritual Dimension of Childhood* (2008), '[w]hilst we rush around, however, many children are regularly encountering spiritual moments – ones which we easily miss' (Adams et al., 2008: 59).

One memory of Peter's is of such a 'spiritual moment' – whereby he was provided with the time 'to engage in the present moment' – amid the contemplative space of the parlour. It is Christmas evening, and Peter – having completed building a structure out of Lego (a present opened that morning) – switches off the light and stares at what he has just made.

Now in semi-darkness – with the only light in the room coming from the dying embers of the coal fire, and the bright twinkle of the tiny light-bulb at the top of what I've just built – I'm lying, on my front, on the carpet, and staring proudly at my Lego lighthouse. I can barely see it, as the side that faces me is in deep shadow; all I can really see is its silhouette, and its shiny plastic sides occasionally glinting with sparks from the fire. The light-bulb at the top is like a star (with the wire and batteries that power it – taken from Jeremy's tool box earlier that afternoon – hidden deep within the structure itself). I'm mesmerised – lost even – in the darkness that surrounds me as it gradually closes in upon this dimly lit scene before my eyes. Semi-darkness. Shiny plastic. Glowing, twinkling light. It's Christmas night, and I'm basking in my happiness.

Christopher Day (2007), whilst acknowledging that bright light is of benefit to older children (for example, teenagers), in order to stimulate mental tasks such as tackling homework, insists upon semi-darkness as a requirement of imaginative play for those younger. As '[s]mall children, however, aren't ready to be woken from their dreamy, fantasy-rich in-between world', as they 'need magic mood – twilight *quality*, though not as dark' (Day, 2007: 102–3). Indeed, with regards to children's development overall, 'access to the magically dark is as important as the upliftingly bright' (Day, 2007: 103).

As mentioned earlier in this chapter, Ivy Cottage – and its parlours in particular – did resonate with certain distinctive sounds (the record player, for instance). Indeed, during the 1970s it echoed with the analogue, synthesised sounds of the Dübreq Stylophone. Devised in 1967, and immensely popular throughout the 1970s, it was, arguably, the musical instrument of that decade's youth – all helped by its 'space-age' aesthetic. For, Richard Lewis – in *The Bumper Book of Fads and Crazes* (2005) – stresses its appeal: '[A]n iconic and futuristic piece of late sixties design, possibly the most beautifully crafted electronic instrument ever created, especially the woodgrain model', the Stylophone 'really did look as though it was from space' (Lewis, 2005: 249). Yet, the electronic shrill of the Stylophone was not the only music to be heard played in the parlour – as, against the wall that separated that room from the hall, was a family heirloom: an upright piano.

The piano within the parlour is an absolutely central aspect of *The Clifton House Mystery* (broadcast Sundays, 8 October–12 November 1978). According to Alistair McGown and Mark Docherty, in *The Hill and Beyond, Children's Television Drama – An Encyclopedia* (2003), '*The Clifton House Mystery* is to all intents and purposes a horror movie for those who would never be allowed to stay up late to see them on TV' (McGown and Docherty, 2003: 125). Indeed, committed to videotape (that is, rather than film) at HTV West's Bristol studios, this series aimed at children was obviously '[m]ade on a budget far lower than that of even the most low-budget horror flick' (McGown and Docherty, 2003: 125). Yet, despite its low-budget production values, *The Clifton House Mystery* is a genuinely scary example of 1970s children's television: where ghosts of solemn, moustachioed redcoat, and a candle-bearing elderly woman, mingle with a four-poster bed-ridden, rotting skeleton that has been discovered in a walled-up bedroom. Furthermore, the added presence of a plate-throwing poltergeist and spots of blood that drip from a ceiling, results in scenes that 'are very frightening for younger children' (McGown and Docherty, 2003: 125). Although, in order to adhere to the educational requirements of children's television programming – and to recognise the regulations to do with the franchising of independent television (whereby 'local' themes should clearly be reflected in regionally produced series) – a 'history lesson' of sorts forms the basis of *The Clifton House Mystery*'s storyline:

> To this end a mini-lecture is delivered, by a librarian no less, on the Bristol riots of 1831. The soldier ghost had been the commanding officer of the 3rd Dragoon guards on the night crowds of thousands had filled the streets of Bristol to protest against restricted voting rights (McGown and Docherty, 2003: 125).

To this end, the officer – a Captain Bretherton (a Bristolian) – agreed to allow his soldiers to retreat if the rioters did similar; however, those protesting failed to honour such an agreement, and widespread death and destruction ensued. Bretherton, as a result, managed to escape the carnage, and lay in hiding at the house of his mother. There, in order to avoid any chance of charges of cowardice, he remained until his death – at which point his body was bricked up in secrecy.

Yet, it is sound – or, more accurately, sparing use of sound alongside copious amounts of lengthy silence (again, a direct consequence of its low-production) – that provides *The Clifton House Mystery* with its inherent dramatic tension and horror. For the eventual exorcism[11] of the dead soldier's spirit involves the close-up of the ghost-hunter's contorted face, overlaid video footage, 'and thunderous

---

11 Significantly, and in keeping with the way in which 'the occult' tended to be portrayed in children's television drama, it is noteworthy that this scene in *The Clifton House Mystery*, totally avoids addressing the religious dimensions of a true exorcism – and,

use of horse and battle noise sound effects' (McGown and Docherty, 2003: 125). Thus, in effect, '[t]he limited amount of music that could be afforded is turned to positive advantage', with 'the long silences being used to create tension' (McGown and Docherty, 2003: 125). Although, when it is sparingly used, '[c]lever use of music is key to the serial, with the ghosts' appearances usually signalled by the music box rendition of the soldier's regimental march' (McGown and Docherty, 20003: 125). And it is music in the parlour, provided by the grand piano, which is the most effective – especially when the father, 'West Country pianist', Timothy Clare, gripped in moments of possession, plays the music box tune. In the series' final instalment, Episode 6 (12 November 1978), when the Clare family – post-exorcism – sense that their house is at peace once more (akin to, as mentioned earlier, the Manning household's relief 'as if a storm had passed'), their return to a calm stillness is emphasised through their patriarch's measured playing of the piano. With the episode beginning with their father's failed attempt to deliberately recite the music box tune at the piano (now seemingly unable to recall a note of it), Timothy Clare calmly plays as 'end of part one' approaches, whereby his wife and three children make themselves comfortable sitting at the kitchen table. 'Part two', in turn, opens with a tranquil scene, whereby Mrs Clare, sitting, reading a broadsheet in the parlour (all leather Chesterfields, and mahogany bookcases – all lit by soft table lights and the flickering flames of an open fire), relaxes to a classic piece played gently by her husband. After a short while, the family gather together in front of their television as hearth, to watch themselves being interviewed as part a pre-recorded local news report on their home and its now-passed paranormal goings-on. However, before it ends, their TV set loses its reception – just as the music box (the inherent theme of which had not been heard since the exorcism) comes to life once again. Thus, as far as *The Clifton House Mystery* is concerned, music – played in its many forms, but especially by that of both the music box and the piano – is not only evidence of a haunting, but it is a manifestation of the haunting itself; that is, the interplay between silence and music amid the domestic as characteristic of a paranormal condition.

The Kitchen

It's 1.30am, and me and Mammy have just finished watching the Saturday-night/Sunday-morning horror double bill. Daddy's already home from the pub, and he's been in bed an hour or so. Clearing away plates and cutlery after our cheese, crackers and Branston Pickle in front of the TV, Mammy empties the over-brimming contents of our living room's glass ashtray into the kitchen bin. I gulp; I hope that all of the fag-butts and matches are out? I turn to the chip

---

anyhow, 'in 1978 memories of the attendant fuss that had surrounded *The Exorcist* would still be fresh in the programme-makers' minds' (McGown and Docherty, 2003: 125).

pan on the gas cooker, its metal coated in a yellowing covering of grease. I peer inside, and the fat (a mixture of cooking oil, lard, dripping, and so on) is full of suspended over-cooked scraps of chips and unrecognisable 'black bits'. Making sure that each and every one of the cooker's knobs are off, I check them again, and again, and again. After turning off the kitchen light (Mammy already ahead of me, on the landing, and going into the toilet), I have one final nervous look, into blackness, towards the cooker – just to make sure that no glimpse of the distinctive blue of lit North Sea Gas can be seen. Nope, nothing. Still with some trepidation, I start to climb the stairs and, in my mind's eye, the chip pan bursts into flames, and the whole room – and, in turn, the entire house – is ablaze.

Peter's over-cautious checking and double-checking of certain rooms of the house (especially the kitchen) ahead of going to bed – it was part-and-parcel of his bedtime ritual – was evident of a collective cultural mind-set of fear that had set during that era:

> Moreover, there was a sense in the 1970s that everyday life was fraught with danger, and that one of the government's responsibilities was to save us from ourselves (Viner, 2009: 287).

The government had, by the 1970s, put in place a series of televised Public Information Films – produced by the Central Office of Information (COI) – that graphically depicted the many hazards of 'everyday life' – and it was such government-sponsored televised shorts that, quite possibly, were wholly responsible for Peter's rather paranoid disposition. Katy McGahan, a curator at the British Film Institute National Archive, insists that 'people of a certain age', having repeatedly viewed (during their childhood) such propagandist films of a 'nanny state', more than likely:

> bear some deep-rooted scars as a result of having been relentlessly subjected to footage of children their own age being fried alive whilst playing Frisbee near an electricity pylon, maimed by a firework, or crushed by a tractor whilst larking about in a farmyard (McGahan, 2010: 2).

It was those films that depicted the tragic consequences of poor fire prevention that, quite possibly, resulted in the greatest post-viewing trauma. For whilst the 45-second *Searching* (1974), with the camera panning across the burnt-out interior of a home, touched many an adult's nerve with 'primeval parental fear of their children predeceasing them' (Russell, 2010: 30), *Fire Routine* (1979), was a 90-second insomnia-inducing film to do with pre-bedtime safety:

> Putting out those cigarettes and placing a guard over the fire is surely just simple, common-sense advice. Yet imploring us to shut every door and unplug every

appliance before climbing the wooden hill to Bedfordshire did little to ease the lives of more obsessive-compulsive members of the populace. *Fire Routine* dealt another blow to the idea of the home as a safe haven (McCallum, 2010: 32).

In relation to Peter's memory of endlessly checking the kitchen for possible fire hazards ahead of bed, it is, though, both *Polystyrene Tiles* (1971) and *Fat Fires* (1973) that are to account for such obsessive-compulsive childhood behaviour. The former – an animated, contemporary take on the interior scene/double portrait that is Jan van Eyck's *The Arnolfini Marriage* (1434) – shows Mr and Mrs Arnold Finney showing off proudly their narrow kitchen, with its ceiling of polystyrene tiles, all freshly coated with gloss paint. Whilst the cautionary voice-over states that both polystyrene tiles and gloss paint are, on their own, 'safe', the viewers are then warned, 'But, together, they are a very serious fire hazard'. For, at this point in the short film, a pan on the cooker has not only burst into flames, but the flames – reaching the ceiling – then set the tiles (and, in turn, the whole house) alight. Meanwhile, the latter – *Fat Fires* – is an even briefer Public Information Film, that has a woman (we assume, a wife and mother), cutting up potatoes in preparation to make fresh chips; as, behind her, the pan is already on. With the telephoning ringing, she stops what she is doing, and leaves the kitchen. As she does, so, the camera shows a close-up of the chip pan as it erupts into flames. The narrator then, quite menacingly, states, 'Never leave a fat pan unattended'.

Peter's kitchen at Ivy Cottage during the 1970s had both an always-ready chip pan on the gas cooker, and a ceiling of polystyrene tiles coated in gloss paint.[12]

Two memories.

I'm sitting on the chair next to the kitchen table that is just in front of the doorway. Whiskey, our she-cat, comes plodding in calmly from being out in the garden; from the hall, past the foot of the stairs, she enters the kitchen, only – at 'that spot' again – to leap into the air as if she's trying to jump over something, and runs like a maniac towards the far side of the kitchen. In doing so, it's as if she's invigorated – as if, momentarily, she's a kitten once more.

I've just come home from school, and Mammy meets me in the hallway. Excitedly, she starts to tell me what an elderly visitor, that afternoon, had said to her in conversation: 'Ooh, you know Mrs so-and-so, don't you?', I nodded,

---

12   At one stage, in order to camouflage both the combined staining of excessive fried cooking and excessive tobacco usage, the kitchen's polystyrene tiles were coated in gloss paint with the commercial name of 'Tobacco'. In many respects, Peter's childhood paranoia of the kitchen bursting into flames at any given moment (as a result of the potentially lethal combination of polystyrene ceiling tiles, lit chip pan, and a family of smokers) is encapsulated in this paint entitled 'Tobacco'.

but the name means nothing to me to the extent that I instantly forget it. 'Well,
she popped 'round for a cuppa earlier, and, dew, do you know what she said?' I
shake my head increasingly bewildered by all of this. 'She said – and, well, you
know that she's a bit psychic, don't you?' Even more bewilderment. 'Well, she
was sitting in the kitchen, in the chair, next to the door and – pointing to 'that
spot' – she said 'My, what a cute little ghost dog you have there!' Mammy, now
convinced of what she has expected all along (that there is some sort of spirit
there, at 'that spot'), says, nodding sage-like, 'Well, there you are then!' Now,
with both of us standing at the entrance to the kitchen, me and Mammy stare at
'that spot': Now I can see (but can't really) a gossamer-like white Scottie, or
the hazy black-browns of a little Terrier, sitting there, wagging its tail, its bright
black eyes twinkling.

Stephen O'Brien, the Welsh-born medium who came to prominence during the
early 1980s (but whose psychic powers revealed themselves, when he was a child,
during the 1970s – something that is discussed in the next chapter) is explicit in
insisting that it is not only humans, but family pets and domesticated animals,
that haunt our homes, as 'I've lost count of the times spirit animals have returned
to their masters and mistresses through my mediumship' (O'Brien, 1989: 138).
Furthermore, and as possible explanation of Whiskey's leaping over 'that spot' in
the kitchen of Ivy Cottage, O'Brien further elaborates:

> People have often asked me over the years if pets are psychic: the answer is
> 'yes'. Animals' minds are uncluttered and free of prejudice and social etiquette.
> Even the most humble of pets possess a soul-ability of sensing of seeing spirit-
> people that most of us find difficult to register (O'Brien, 1989: 140).

In this case, though, Whiskey was not 'sensitive' to the presence of 'spirit-people',
but that of a 'spirit-animal'. As such, we now turn to James Herbert's fourth novel,
Fluke (1977).

James Herbert's *Fluke* (1977) is, in the context of his entire written output, an
anomaly. As Herbert is renowned – before and since the publication of *Fluke* –
as a 'horror writer', his 1977 work was met with surprise, resistance, and even
outright hostility both pre- and post-publication. The publishers, New English
Library – already notorious, by the early 1970s, for publishing countless pulp
novels that oozed copious amounts of sleaze and gore – were expecting Herbert
to have written something in a similar vein: 'Instead *Fluke* was a book about
reincarnation' (Cabell, 2003: 73). With little or no shocking content, it was,
instead, a story about a dog who was convinced that he was once a man. Sensing
that they now had a flop on their hands, the publishers – over a lunch – tried to
persuade Herbert, even at this late stage, of changing his book so that it contained
some element of horror. They suggested that the cover be amended to depict 'a dog
with fangs', and that the entire novel be turned into 'a rabid dog story' (Herbert,

cited in, Cabell, 2003: 73–4). But, Herbert refused to compromise, as he very much wanted this book to differ significantly from his previous ones, for with *Fluke* he was desperate to encourage his readers to be speculative, to contemplate such themes as reincarnation, and, in doing so, to ask themselves two fundamental questions: '[W]hat if there is something called reincarnation? And do we take the thoughts of one life into the next?' (Cabell, 2003: 74).

Upon publication and thereafter, and despite his publisher's serious reservations, *Fluke* – whilst, admittedly, failing to please all of his readers – became a favourite with many, as 'it's a gentle, amusing fantasy' (Fraser, 1988, cited in Jones, 1992: 156), with a narrative that unfolds to not only disclose that Fluke, a dog, was indeed once a man, but that – in his previous, human existence – a terrible crime was committed against him (a crime that, quite possibly, resulted in his death). Befriending a fellow dog, Rumbo (who is crushed to death mid-story), the first half of the book focuses upon Fluke's struggling to comprehend his life as a canine, while the second half is concerned with his dawning realisation that, yes, he was formerly a human, and, ultimately, the solving of the 'crime'. All-the-while, reincarnation and life after death is debated in, quite often, a philosophical manner.[13] Yet, for the majority of his readers, the novel is too different, too much of a fantasy, and, as a result, '*Fluke* is often overlooked by die-hard horror fans because they don't consider it a horror novel' (Cabell, 2003: 78).

Fundamentally a story that is being told by Fluke, telepathically, to a dying vagrant that he comes across, its closing pages are amongst the book's most evocative. Finally coming to terms with who – *what* – he is, Fluke finally embraces his canine self, knowing that his previous human form (again, in its multiplicity) was being remembered:

> Fresh flowers had been placed at the graveside, and I knew I had not been forgotten. The memory of the husband, the father, the friend, would dull with time, but I'd always be somewhere in a corner of their minds (Herbert, 1977: 189).

This remembering of his former human self was taking place, though, at a time when he knew that it was now time for him to *forget*:

> My emotions were fast becoming those of a dog, as though, now my search was over, a ghost had been vanquished. The ghost was my humanness. I felt free,

---

13   Any explanations of reincarnation and life after death offered, are multi-dimensional, as '[o]ne of the nicest twists in *Fluke* is when a fellow dog, Rumbo, dies and is reincarnated as a squirrel' (Cabell, 2003: 76). Furthermore, as a form of 'in-joke' for loyal readers of Herbert – and further demonstrations of the multi-dimensional nature of both Herbert's books and reincarnation itself – Rumbo eventually makes another appearance, as this squirrel, in *The Magic Cottage* (1986) and, then, once again – although, this time as a fox – in *Once* (2001).

free as any bird in the sky. Free to live as a dog. I ran for nearly a day and, when I finally dropped, the last remnants of my old self had been purged (1977: 189).

With his 'ghost of humanness' purged, Fluke is now able to observe life afresh, quite literally from a new perspective and with a sense of new-found freedom:

And by and large, I enjoy what I am. I see life now from a different level: knee level. It's surprising the difference it makes. It's like always approaching a place from the same direction, then suddenly coming from the opposite way: the familiar changes shape, looks different somehow. It's still the same, but has taken on a new perspective. Know what I mean?

I've travelled the country, swum in the sea. Nobody's ever owned me again, but many have fed me (1977: 189).

So, with the eventual relentless progress of life after death, he is now – at last – fully a dog:

And I've made love to seven different bitches.

Time's running out for you now; death's nearly here. I hope what I've told you has helped, I hope it's made some sense to your feverish brain. Can you smell that heavy sweetness in the air; it means I've got to go. It's a lady friend, you see. She lives on a farm three fields away and she's ready for me now ... (1977: 190).

Then, on the penultimate page, reincarnation's logical conclusion is alluded to:

One other thing before I go: I met Rumbo again the other day. I'd been sleeping under a tree when an acorn hit me on the nose; when I looked around I heard a voice call out 'Hello, squirt', and there he was above me, grinning all over his little squirrel face. He showered me with a few more acorns, but when I called his name he looked blank, then scurried off. I knew it was him because the voice – thought pattern if you like – was the same; and who else would call me 'squirt'? (1977: 190).

And, finally, with the novel's last page, the 'wish' of life after death is offered:

Excuse me now, my lady friend's scent is really becoming too much to ignore. You don't need me anymore anyway, the next part you have to do on your own. At least, I hope I've helped. Maybe we'll bump into each other again sometime.

Good-bye.

Hope you're a dog! (1977: 190).

… With one last painful shudder, the old man's breath left him and took his life with it.

He died. And waited (1977: 191).

The Living Room

The two photographs, opposite, are near-identical. They are the same photograph, but whilst one has degraded to the extent that much detail has been lost, the other (a slightly-enlarged copy of the original, when the original was in a less faded condition) still shows the pattern of wallpaper, upholstery, and so on. What they have in common is that they both show Peter lying on his living-room sofa, his form bleached by the late-morning blazing sun that comes through the window above him. Wearing house slippers, Peter's face is sad, and the overall mood of the snapshot is one of melancholy. The sofa, which has already been recovered by Peter's mother, has threadbare cushions with bursting zips, and white, painted arms that are extensively chipped. Indeed, this hardship is emphasised if we compare Peter's position with an image to be found in Geoff Dyer's meditations on photographs and photographers, *The Ongoing Moment* (2005). In particular, Dyer's inclusion of Dorothea Lange's *Skid Row, San Francisco* (1934), has two men, having hit hard times, sleeping on a sidewalk, their postures mirroring those of Peter. Whilst Peter is reclining in relative comfort, the run-down condition of the sofa, coupled with his wearing of hand-me-down clothing, allows us to draw parallels between this urchin-like boy of the mid-1970s and the two adult hobos of the mid-1930s. Furthermore, in discussing the works of Brassaï (*The Riviera*, 1936) and André Kertész (*Jeno in the Woods of Népliget, Budapest*, 1913; *Broken Bench, New York, 20 September*, 1962) – whereby the focus of their works are public benches (both pristine and broken) – Dyer highlights the resilience of the bench as an adaptive form of seating, as 'a bench weathers the storm, takes whatever life throws at it' (Dyer, 2005: 131). Yet, as a site of often only fleeting rest, '[t]here is something inherently sad about a bench' (Dyer, 2005: 133). With all of this in mind, we begin to appreciate what is behind the sad, melancholic mood of Peter's photograph: whilst the sofa has, indeed, 'weathered a storm' (worn and chipped, due to years of daily use), it displays – unlike the public bench – a certain lack of permanence. For, in just a few years – when eventually beyond further repair – it would be taken to the local tip and dumped there amid the detritus. To be left behind, and lost.

Jay Prosser, with *Light in the Dark Room – Photography and Loss* (2005), reiterates that, in surrounding ourselves with family photographs, we are often surrounding ourselves with images of relatives that are no longer with us. In doing so, we are making explicit the 'hidden truth' of the photograph, where they 'are not signs of presence but evidence of absence' (Prosser, 2005: 1). Photographs, in accentuating the absence of loved ones, 'contain a realization of loss'

**Figure 2.3   Peter lying on the sofa in the living room of Ivy Cottage –
Faded original**

Source: Author's own collection.

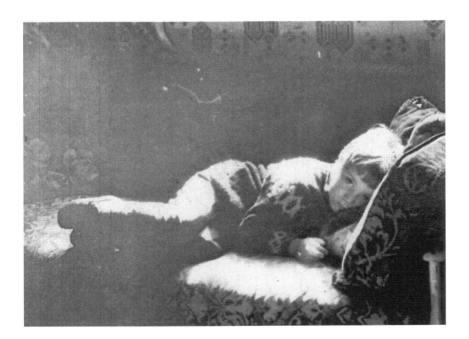

**Figure 2.4   Peter lying on the sofa in the living room of Ivy Cottage –
Enhanced copy**

Source: Author's own collection.

(Prosser, 2005: 1). In making us conscious of such 'loss', we should acknowledge that all photographs capture moments of reality – but, of course, those moments are now gone. Therefore, Prosser argues, '[i]t is a myth that photographs bring back memories', as they, fundamentally, 'show not the presence of the past but the pastness of the present' (Prosser, 2005: 1). In opposition to cinema and television, photographs – as isolated, fragments of time – not only record lived moments, but resist any form of cohesive narrative being applied to them. For, especially with their inclusion in any form of autobiographical text, 'photographs are increasingly used as shutes into something missing, pointers to a loss that can't be recovered in the text' (Prosser, 2005: 8–9). Indeed, it is the point at which photography and autobiography converge – where presence and absence exist side-by-side, and memory struggles with forgetfulness (and the perceptions of loss that these all, collectively, bring about) – that is key here: And, it is that point that photography and autobiography converge, that Prosser terms '*ph/autography*'. For, *ph/autography* is when the photograph, fracturing the autobiographical narrative, brings about a heightened engagement with the autobiographical text within which that photograph is to be found. Capturing 'the lens of photography and the mirror of autobiography in interplay', the conceptual application of *ph/autography* underlines 'how photography when we really engage it inevitably becomes autobiographical' (Prosser, 2005: 10).

Within popular television of the time, the ageing sepia photograph – as a site of paranormal activity – was utilised to great effect in Series Two, 'Assignment Four', of *Sapphire and Steel* (broadcast across four episodes, Tuesdays and Thursday, 27 January–5 February 1981). Investigating a 'time break' in a lost-and-found shop, the two 'agents' of the title, Sapphire (played by Joanna Lumley) and Steel (David McCallum), confront the faceless, bowler-hatted Shape, who has entrapped the property's landlord and one of his tenants in an old photograph (only to eventually kill both). Not only that, but the Shape exists within, and moves between, ageing photographs, all-the-while releasing sepia-tinged children from nineteenth century photographs to act as his young accomplices. Significantly, for the writer/series creator – P.J. Hammond – the key inspiration behind this malevolent dimension of photography 'was the Aboriginal belief that to have one's photograph taken was to have someone steal your soul' (Callaghan, 2010: 71). Furthermore, whilst in the series' opener it is established that the Shape exists 'in all photographs from the first photograph ever taken' (Callaghan, 2010: 73), as the episodes unfold the actual existence of the children in/from the photographs is brought into question. As, initially, Steel argues that they are 'not alive; they're not living … they're not ghosts, they're not images … something in between' (cited in Callaghan, 2010: 74–5), but, later on, Sapphire insists that, instead, '[t]hese are ghosts before death' (cited in Callaghan, 2010: 75). In this context, then, Peter's on-going sofa-bound existence – or, rather, entrapment – in a fading sepia photograph takes on a rather sinister dimension: Peter, here, is not only an 'image' and, in a way, a 'ghost', but 'something in between'. Indeed, considering the photograph's melancholic mood, the sadness in Peter's face, and the sense of loss that pervades it (both the loss of childhood and the childhood home), Peter is very much a 'ghost before death'.

I'm sitting on the living room sofa, and I have on my lap my new Rupert Annual. Well, it's from the jumble sale that Mammy has just come back from – so, it's not new, but new to me. I look at the cover, and there's Rupert, smiling, on a snowy hillside, his arms outstretched above him in joy. But, upon opening the book, I am in awe at what opens up before: Across two entire pages (the endpapers), is Rupert Country, Nutwood – but a view of it such I have never seen before. With Rupert and Willie Mouse in an orange helicopter that is flying over lush green fields and woods, there are the houses and church tower of the village, the old Professor's tower, the Chinese conjuror's pagoda, and the Wise Old Goat's castle. At the very top of the right-hand page I can even glimpse the sea. But it is the foreground – in its darker sage-green greys – that take my breath away. To the left, Edward Trunk, on all fours, is perched atop of a boulder that juts out from a cliff-face; to the right, Bill Badger and Algy Pub are clambering over rocks lower down the cliff-face. Like Rupert's on the cover, Algy's arms are outstretched – but, unlike Rupert's, outstretched both up and out: up, towards Rupert and Willie as they fly overhead in the helicopter; and out into the landscape. It's like Algy is about to leap; down and down – into this landscape that dwarfs them all – until he lands gently, cushioned by the soft greens of this wonderful landscape. I want to jump out into this expanse of Nutwood – into the pages, and out into the depths of the landscape.

By 1965, Alfred Bestall had stopped producing (that is, both writing and illustrating – as he had done since 1935) 'Rupert' stories for the *Daily Express*. Although, that is not to say that his characteristic artwork was no longer to be seen; as examples of his distinctive style was to still be found – and, as a result, continued to be cherished – amid the Rupert Annuals. Thus, every year until 1973, he contributed enchanting covers, endpapers, and title pages that were unmistakably his. Having now rid himself of the pressure of producing regular Rupert strips, these more one-off commissions are deemed to be those amongst his most outstanding output. Quite often meticulous, full-colour panoramic paintings, it was *Rupert's Own Countryside* (to be found inside the 1967 annual, as per Peter's memory above) that 'was the closest Bestall ever came to making a Nutwood map' (Robinson, 2010: 52). This 'map' of Nutwood bears great resemblance to the British countryside itself, as, when quizzed with regards the inspiration behind his expansive landscapes such as this, Bestall suggested that it was a 'place with undulating ground and plenty of foot-slogging', and 'I have seen that kind of country in the Severn Valley, but I think the Sussex Weald is one of the closest' (cited in Robinson, 2010: 52). With such 'undulating ground' as source countryside for Rupert et al.'s 'foot slogging', Bestall – employing exquisite, delicate brushstrokes – 'used the endpapers to paint more freely than he could for the cover pictures', coming up with 'atmospheric landscape pieces, where figures were incidental, rather than dominating the composition' (Robinson, 2010: 85).

Peter's appreciation of such an 'atmospheric landscape' – which made him want to dive into its depths – is in keeping with Gaston Bachelard's notion of the child as dreamer. With *The Poetics of Reverie – Childhood, Language, and the Cosmos* (1971), Bachelard – with an expansive form of prose that can be likened to landscape itself – elaborates upon such a tendency to dream as a child:

> Suddenly such a dreamer is a *world dreamer*. He opens himself to the world, and the world opens itself to him. One has never seen the world well if he has not dreamed what he was seeing. In a reverie of solitude which increases the solitude of the dreamer, two depths pair off, reverberating in echoes which go from the depths of being of the world to a depth of being of the dreamer. Time is suspended. Time no longer has any yesterday and no longer any tomorrow. Time is engulfed in the double depth of the dreamer and the world (Bachelard, 1971: 173).

Peter, as such a childhood dreamer sitting on his living room sofa – with the Rupert Annual endpapers before him – is a true 'world dreamer': Opening himself up, Alfred Bestall's world, in turn, opens itself up to him. In solitude, both his and Rupert's worlds have stopped – Peter's world and Nutwood as one; yesterday, today, and tomorrow, in unison. And, again, contemplative silence (that is, of both worlds) are essential, as '[r]everie can become deeper only by dreaming before a tranquil world' (Bachelard, 1971: 173).

In Anthony Burton's *Children's Pleasures – Books, Toys and Games from the Bethnal Green Museum of Childhood* (1996), there is a short section entitled 'Things in Little' (154–5). Whilst the term itself already helps us conceptualise the perspectives of children and childhood, it is Burton's words to do with 'smallness' and the 'miniature' which allow us to appreciate further the imaginative worlds within which the child exists. Whereby large, simplistic objects suit the handling capacity of babies, 'once children can control their movements, small-scale articles seem appropriate to them' (Burton, 1996: 154). It is 'scaled-down' versions of what can be found in the adult world that is of interest to children from the age of one and older – an interest that coincides with a growing realisation that they now have a certain control over such miniature objects. Furthermore, 'in relating to these smaller symbols, children can practise their relations with the world from a more advantageous position than that they usually occupy' (Burton, 1996: 154). In essence, then, children – once they are in possession of the miniature – transform these symbols 'into a private world which they rule' (Burton, 1996: 154).

One toy – which, upon holding, is to possess the miniature, and to contemplate private worlds – is the marble. Richard Lewis (2005), when questioning the enchanting qualities of marbles, insists that – not only are they a thing of beauty due to their colours – but that they are aesthetically intoxicating as a result of their roundness:

> [T]he sphere offers us so much. The very shape of our planet, the globe is at once terrestrial and preternatural. An object with no edges, brimming with potential energy (Lewis, 2005: 130).

It is their spherical density and weight, Lewis adds, that encourages their holding – and, with a rolling movement, their play. Furthermore, once a marble rolls it comes alive; spinning across carpet, linoleum, asphalt, and so on, it is pure delight 'to watch it spin across the floor, catching the light and casting its glow upon the ground' (Lewis, 2005: 130). It is their colours that have the power to mesmerize. For Lewis, these were to be found in the 'cats-eyes, with their edible-looking swirl of coloured glass encased in a clear ball', and amid 'the single-colour glass marbles that glowed deep ultramarine, warm orange and red or pale yellows like the sky' (Lewis, 2005: 131). Whilst Lewis' friends at school fetishised 'alleys', which were 'glass 'chinas' painted in opaque colours', he was most covetous of a 'china' called 'King Lois', 'a rich blue, white and red, rarer than any' (Lewis, 2005: 131).

I hold the marble between my thumb and forefinger and, bringing it right up to my eye so that its glass touches my lashes, it fills my field of vision. Looking up to the sunlight that is streaming in through the living room window, all in front of me is diffused and seemingly water-like. Inside the illuminated marble, a swirl of slightly out of focus oranges (the 'eye' of the 'cat') are at the centre – a centre that is now surrounded by countless clear bubbles that, frozen in both space and time, look like planets and moons. Staring into this timeless, lit-up mini-universe, it is like looking at a blinding version of outer space. But this is an outer space that is so close that it seems to be inside me. Right inside my eye and my brain.

Peter's memory of gazing into a marble as an inner astronomy of the imagination, is all akin to Bachelard's notion of 'cosmic reverie', where the 'dreamer' – in front of a captivating image – enters into an almost meditative state, and, in doing so, consciously acknowledges a bodily coexistence with the universe. And the key element to this coexistence is the image before us:

> It gives us the whole before the parts. In its exuberance, it believes it is telling the whole of the Whole. It holds the universe with one of its signs. A single image invades the whole universe. It diffuses throughout the universe the happiness we have at inhabiting the very world of that image. In his reverie without limit

or reserve, the dreamer gives himself over, body and soul, to the cosmic image which has just charmed him (Bachelard, 1971: 175).

Quite simply – especially in childhood, as experienced by Peter and his holding of the microcosm that is a marble to his eye – '[a] universe can be born from an isolated image' (Bachelard, 1971: 175).

Furthermore, Peter's meditative experiencing of the inner astronomy of his imagination, was of its time – as, come the 1970s, British science fiction shunned an outer space (of crass aliens and the like), as both source and setting, and, instead, embraced the more cerebral, and Freud- and Jung-derived, 'inner space'. Colin Greenland, in *The Entropy Exhibition – Michael Moorcock and the British 'New Wave' in Science Fiction* (1983), defined 'inner space' as not only a pragmatic term 'used to distinguish earth and its atmosphere from outer space', but as a new genre of fiction that tended to 'look inwards'. Thus, 'inner space' became:

> a psychological metaphor, denoting the landscapes of dream and memory; and, by extension, of the subjective world: that is, the external world as transformed and encoded by the individual consciousness (Greenland, 1983: 51).

However, the one toy of Peter's childhood – where an inner space (and associated inner anxieties) extended out into the depths of the universe itself (with its infinite dimensions a source of anxiety) – was the Viewmaster.

Peering into the inside of the Viewmaster 'binoculars', before me is a 3-D image: against a backdrop of the blackness of space, with countless stars beyond, is – suspended in this 3-d-ness – the 'U.S.S. Starship Enterprise'. This 3-D image is edged in blackness; a blackness that not only holds a three-dimension-ness within it, but possesses an additional 3-D quality of its own. With the Star Trek reels adding a further black depthlessness to the black depthlessness already in the Viewmaster itself, the image – that is, of deep space – is pulling me into the Viewmaster, through the Viewmaster, and out into the vast expanse of the universe. With a shudder, I whip the Viewmaster from my eyes, scared of looking any longer into its depths, its blackness.

Graham Kibble-White (2005a), touching upon the Viewmaster's space-age aesthetic, insists that '[t]he contraption itself resembled a 1950s NASA prototype of the kind of virtual reality goggles the boffins predicted we'd all be strapping to our heads any day now' (Kibble-White, 2005a: 207). Initially marketed towards adults as a means by which travelogue world vistas could be viewed in 3-D without having to leave the comfort of home, the GAF Viewmaster was, by the 1970s – especially in its vivid red casing – a children's staple as the company's reels were themed increasingly towards cartoon characters and hit TV shows (such as, with

Peter's memory, the William Shatner-era *Star Trek*, from 1966–1969). In an era of quite primitive screen-based media (that is, pre-home computer, etc.), such 3-D technology – termed 'stereoscopy' – provided its user with views that (even to this day) are beyond experiencing and even comprehension. To children such as Peter, then, the Viewmaster's three-dimensional version of Star Trek offered both a look into (what is now) the 'retro-future' and the unfathomable (and sometimes unnerving) depths of the universe – again, from the comfort of the living room.

Christopher Day (2007), in explaining children's relationship with, and experience of, their environment, states that, between four and seven years, children are preoccupied with how they can 'use' – and, thus, transform – adult spaces: Indeed, 'they make 'places' with fabric, furniture and other things we adults assume had other functions' (Day, 2007: 12). With this in mind, it is interesting to contemplate the possible answers to the following question posed by Robin C. Moore: 'What is going on when a small child fondles the fringe on the edge of a rug?' (Moore, cited in Goodenough, 2003: 57). For Peter, the edge of the living room carpet – where it met the underlying linoleum – was often a site of 'war play'. In particular, with the edge of the carpet itself acting as the parapet of a trench, Peter played – and, as a result, re-enacted – the battles of the First World War.

I've just spent over ten minutes placing my Airfix HO-00 scale British 'Tommies', with their characteristic knee to ankle puttees, along the trench (on the lino, against the edge of the carpet). Shouting out 'Charge!', I send them 'over the top', out into No Man's Land (the carpet proper, as it stretches out across the living room). With them all now spread out in front of me, heading towards the enemy, I start to knock them over – dead, wounded – with a flick of my forefinger as a bullet; again, again, again, and again, I do this until at least half of them are down. The rest, those that still survive, I move forward, one by one, inch by inch, making them struggle over swathes of barbed wire (that is sprue, the lengths of plastic that they were all attached to when still in their box). Finally, and with both my hands flattening them en masse as I go 'Boosh! Boosh! Boosh' in a hail of spittle, they are all felled by an artillery barrage. The battle is over, and my 'Tommies' have been massacred.

Peter's play with Airfix plastic soldiers – thus, his living room's small-scale re-enactments of such large-scale First World War battles as Passchendaele, Somme, Ypres, and so on – were, of course, childhood versions of 'wargaming'. Wargaming being, more often than not, an adult private pursuit that had, by the 1970s, become public group tournaments. As Harry Pearson, in *Achtung Schweinehund! A Boy's Own Story of Imaginary Combat* (2007), notes, by that decade, 'there were over two hundred wargame clubs in Britain alone and shops selling lead figures on every high street' (Pearson, 2007: 129). Moreover, the wargaming phenomenon was ushered in by seminal publications on the topic – such as *Donald Featherstone's War Games* –

Battles and Manoeuvres with Model Soldiers (2009, first published in 1962). In the introduction to the 2009 edition (edited by John Curry and with a foreword by Paddy Griffith), the social-cultural context of *War Game*'s original publication date is as important as the content of Featherstone's book itself. For, in an era when the Campaign for Nuclear Disarmament, the Cuban Missile Crisis, and the early years of American involvement in Vietnam had, collectively, declared war – that is, war as a patriarchal 'game' – to be an abhorration, Featherstone had 'provided a detailed manual on exactly how that game should be played on the tabletop' (Griffith, cited in Curry, 2009: 8). And, perhaps even more significantly, *War Games*:

> coincided with the 'Airfix revolution', whereby a few expensive 54mm lead soldiers could be replaced by whole battalions of cheap little plastic 25mm (or 20mm if you insist) chappies who are entirely within the financial means of any schoolboy (Griffith, cited in Curry, 2009: 8).

Following on from Featherstone's seminal 1962 text, a whole swathe of similar publications – including many more by Featherstone himself – further established wargaming as the pastime for both 'schoolboys' and retired military personnel alike. Pearson, as a child of the 1970s, borrowing all that were available for loan, provides a vibrant list of such titles:

> *Advanced War Games* had come from the village library. I had, by now, borrowed every book on wargaming they had: *Introduction to Battle Gaming* by Terence Wise; Donald Featherstone's *War Games* and the follow-up cascade of *War Game Campaigns*, *Solo War Gaming* and *Wargames Through the Ages Volumes I, II, and III*; *Practical Wargaming* and *With Pike and Musket* by Charles Wesencraft; *Charge!* By Brigadier Peter Young and Colonel James P. Lawford; and, my personal favourite ... *The War Game* by Charles Grant (Pearson, 2007: 128).

One such publication, that Pearson does not list, is Gavin Lyall's *Operation Warboard – Wargaming World War II Battles in 20–25mm Scale* (1976), which, touching upon the relationship between the wargaming environment and the real battlefield, insists that 'the actual landscapes over which you fight can only be symbolic of the real world' (Lyall, 1976: 16), to the extent that 'most wargamers end up with some form of tabletop structure' (Lyall, 1976: 33). In essence, then, the wargamer – whether the professional adult or the child at play – enters into, with the act of wargaming, a symbolic relationship with their environment; whereby aspects of the domestic (carpets, the tabletop, etc.) are transformed – both materially, and in the imagination – into sites of war. Lyall makes explicit the practicalities of such a transformation, and how the table-as-battlefield is limited by the dimensions of the home itself. Not only are the dimensions of tabletop wargames defined by the size of the rooms within which they are fought, but they take place in rooms that – during the everyday – are intended for very different functions. For, as Lyall admits, 'most of us have to settle for a warboard in sections that can be laid over a dining or kitchen table' (Lyall, 1976: 33). Furthermore, whilst Lyall asserts that '[w]here you set up your battleground must depend initially on what's available in your own home' (Lyall, 1976: 33), Featherstone elaborates that the 'novice' – due to both a certain ignorance, and financial limitations (conducting a small-scale wargame on the restricted space of the floor or a tabletop) – is little concerned about the realism of his 'terrain', to the extent that 'he uses books for hills and his houses are made of bricks filched from the children's toy cupboard' (Featherstone, 2009: 31). Finally, such a 'novice' is even denied permanence of any kind, as any floor- or tabletop-based wargame he conducts is 'one that is erected before the battle and laboriously packed away when his opponent has caught the last bus home' (Featherstone, 2009: 31).

Fundamentally, it is upon the wargamers' floor or tabletop that such domestic battlefields encourage transformation of their environment through careful consideration – and, thus, manipulation – of size, scale, and ratio. As the majority of figurines utilised in wargaming are 20–25mm in height – and, as such, are deemed to be approximately in 1/72 scale – one inch, to the model, equates, 72 inches to an actual soldier. Thus, 'a one-inch-high figure represents a six-foot-tall person' (Pearson, 2007: 125). Yet, it is when this 1/72 scale is applied to the domestic wargame battlefield that relative size becomes a problem. 'Ground scale' – that is, the measurement of the entire space over which the wargame takes place – is, within the domestic space, fundamentally flawed at 1/72 scale. As the actual battle of Waterloo was conducted on a front of nearly 4,000 yards, this would equate 55 yards at 1/72 scale: 'If you wanted to refight Waterloo in 1/72 scale you'd need to hire a football field' (Pearson, 2007: 125–6). In essence, then, ground scale has to differ to figure/height scale; but, none the less, the actual width of the model soldier still presents its own problems, as a single figure does not occupy the space of a single soldier, but, instead, 'the space that more than ten soldiers would occupy' (Pearson, 2007: 126). Thus, the problem of scale is now transferred to that of a problem of ratio. The answer to this problem is, of course, to acknowledge that one wargame figurine represents many actual soldiers on the battlefield – and, with regards the optimum ratio, '[f]or reasons largely connected with aesthetics and economics, 1:33 is the most popular' (Pearson, 2007: 127).

Taking into account this rather slavish attention to the minutiae of size, scale and ratio, Donald Featherstone, in *War Games*, touches upon the human dimension to these diminutive versions of real combatants. Indeed, their very construction out of man-made materials (first lead, then plastic) provides model soldiers with both an inherent dispensability and invincibility. They can be sent conscious-free into battle 'without causing a single wife to be made a widow or child to be rendered fatherless, because there is no braver than the lead soldier without any lead wives of lead children!' (Featherstone, 2009: 19). Yet, the model soldiers 'lifelessness' is, here, 'given life', and it is the wargame as giving life to the lifeless that we now turn.

First published in 1975, Donald Featherstone's *Skirmish Wargaming* is concerned with small-scale encounters. Hence, providing rules and tactics covering the historical (and future) period of 850AD–3015, there is one section, entitled 'First World War Trench Raid (1916)' (99–105). Significantly, this skirmish's narrative – as do all of the others within the book – adopts a filmic-come-novelistic approach. Thus, the 'cast' of the opposing sides, British and German, by means of introduction, are listed by both rank and name, with the wargame's accompanying text – that is, the description of the wargame as it is being played – taking on a rather visceral, narrative quality. For example, here is a paragraph which describes the pre-skirmish conditions to be found amid a section of the British trenches:

> Men lifted their heads to ask who was hit as others, splattered with the blood of their friends, picked themselves up to resume their crouched, dripping posture. Sometimes men disappeared completely, or, when the smoke had died away, could be seen lying yards away or even outside the trench. There was a constant procession of men making their painful way along the trench, some tightly holding parts of their body, their teeth clenched or moaning as their faces worked with pain; some smiled and even laughed in a semi-insane manner; others were carried in piggy-back fashion by a comrade, or were lying inert on stretchers (Featherstone, 1975: 99–100).

The 1999 film *The Sixth Sense* – described as a supernatural 'chiller' – focuses on a small boy, Cole Sear, and his claim to be able to 'see dead people'. Seemingly, then, 'Cole has knowledge beyond his years', as 'he can see things adults cannot' (Pile, 2005: 141). It is this uncanny ability that means he 'lives in a terrifying world of his own', but 'Cole himself becomes a creepy figure, embodying both intense childhood anxieties and also fearful contact with the dead' (Pile, 2005: 141). Thus, even during the film's more 'normal' moments – when, for example, Cole (in a deleted scene, made available as an 'extra' for the DVD release) plays with a small number of plastic toy soldiers – mundane aspects of childhood take on a spiritual dimension. As Cole, having covered up two of his 'dead' soldiers with a piece of red tissue paper, explains that they are 'Private Jones and Private Kenny – they got killed'. Tearfully describing their deaths and personal lives in great detail, it is now obvious to the viewer that Cole is able to imbue life (following their death) in these inert figures having been in conversation with these soldier's spirits. Thus, from this perspective, Peter's First World War re-enactments upon the carpeted floor of the living room of Ivy Cottage during the 1970s – especially his voicing of his figurines' speech – can be better understood as the wargamer giving life (and then death) to the dead of the battlefield.

'Charley's War', essentially an anti-war strip, was published weekly within the war comic *Battle-Action* from 6 January 1979 until 4 October 1986. Kibble-White (2005b) describes the way in which *Battle-Action* announced the arrival of Private Charley Bourne to their readership: "'He was a boy soldier pitched into the horror of the World War One trenches!" ran the billing on the cover' (Kibble-

White, 2005b: 39). The strip's first instalment tells the story of 16-year-old Charley, as an under-age volunteer, 'taking the King's Shilling' – that is, enlisting into the army. And so began *Battle-Action*'s most fondly remembered storyline, with this introduction to a believable, rounded, humane character.

The readers' anticipation of 'Charley's War' – as one of '3 powerful new stories' within Issue 200 – was whetted by the tantalising inclusion, on the previous week's back page (that is, Issue 199, as part of *Battle-Action*'s regular 'Big War Films' series), of Lewis Milestone's *All Quiet On The Western Front* (1930). In this issue of *Battle-Action* (published 23 December 1978), it is explained to the readers that Milestone's *All Quiet* is an adaptation of Erich Maria Remarque's novel, and that the film's main (German) protagonist, a patriotic schoolboy, 'is soon disillusioned as, in the wastes of the Western Front, he finds nothing but death and suffering on a massive scale'. Of course, *Battle-Action*'s readers would soon be able to draw clear parallels between the central anti-war theme of *All Quiet* (that is, both the novel and the film) and 'Charley's War'. So, in this respect, just prior to the inaugural episode of 'Charley's War', *Battle-Action*'s readership were being 'educated' with regards the cultural legacy of the Great War. And this 'education' not only continued, but gained momentum, as the 'Charley's War' strip gathered pace, often taken a seasonally topical turn. For, in the issue dated 22 December 1979, Charley, just a few pages after his appearance in that week's strip, is to be found atop of his own question-and-answer puzzle. Considering that this was indeed a 'Christmas issue' of *Battle-Action*, the single-page quiz shows a rather pensive Charley, in heroic pose, alongside a tank (its side-mounted gun blazing), with the words 'Charley Bourne's World War 1 Quiz' in snow-topped period lettering below. Even if the readers did not possess an extensive knowledge of the Great War (as they did, say, of the Second World War), they were encouraged – in such an environment of excited learning – to '[h]ave a guess at the answers if you're not sure!'. Stressing that 'Charley Bourne asks 7 tough questions from the battle-scarred trenches of the First World War', all of the puzzlements – adopting a dual questioning-informative tone – were concerned with December/Christmas-related aspects of that conflict. For example, Question 2 asked 'WW1 took place between 1914 and 1918. At Christmas time, in which year, was an unofficial truce called between German and British troops when they met and exchanged gifts in no-mans' land? 1914, 1926, 1918'. The answer informed the reader that it was, indeed, '1914', elaborating that '[t]he incident happened on the Western Front where the men exchanged chocolates, cigarettes and even played football matches'. Significantly, of course, here were the young boys of a peaceful post-war Britain, just days before the unwrapping of their Yuletide presents, being educated in the events experienced, around Christmas-time, by the young soldiers – quite often 'boy soldiers', little older that the average age of *Battle-Action*'s readership – during the Great War.

The editorial aim of 'Charley's War' to both educate and entertain was supported – as the readers' enthusiasm for the strip increased – by a related rear-page series, entitled 'Oh, What a Lovely War!'. Obviously, the title of this back-page serialisation was in homage to both the original Stratford stage production and its late-1960s cinematic adaptation of the same name. Although, any anti-war content of the original(s) – and 'Charley's War' itself – here was downplayed as a result of a return to a more traditionalist 'arms-and-armour' approach, as, under the subtitle 'Revealed at last! Amazing facts and stories about World War One!', aspects of the conflict were examined in a glorified manner (whilst, at the same time, the horrors of it all were glossed over). Thus, on the 19 May 1979, the rear page of *Battle-Action*, with the slogan 'Slay Ride' (the pun being intentional), noted that 'vicious spiked 'caltrops' were sometimes used to halt a cavalry charge'. But, at the same time, this full-colour page placed far more emphasis upon the various horse-mounted combatants' dashing uniforms, such as that of the sword-wielding 'Austro-Hungarian Hussar' and the 'Russian Cossack'. So, whilst that week's bloody instalment of 'Charley's War' ended with that strip's 'hero' running a German machine-gunner through with a coiled, spike-ended barbed-wire support, the rear page depicted, in a bloodless manner, 'Uhlans – the elite of the German Cavalry – clashing with French Dragoons'. Thus, both the horror and the glory of the First World War in a single issue of *Battle-Action*.

On the 12 July 1980, *Battle-Action* proudly announced the first of four 'cut out and keep' centre-fold instalments of 'Charley Bourne's WW1 Game'. Promoted on the cover by the enticement 'Inside: Part 1 of exciting war game in colour!', the centre pages found Charley – wearing a rather all-too-cheerful grin – explaining that this was 'an exact replica of a board game that was issued to British troops like me ... We played it in the trenches of the Great War! ... Believe me, you'll have fun playing 'From the Ranks to Fieldmarshal'!' So, collecting all 'four weekly parts' (the rules being included as part of the final instalment), the readers were, thereafter, not only able to continue to learn of Charley's exploits, but be dazzled by the completed board's pomp and circumstance (shoulder pips, military colours, and the King abounded) playing the game as either a winner ('A Gallant Act. Saves Colonel's life at very great risk. Receives Victoria Cross and Promoted 1 Rank') or a loser ('Placed on Half-Pay. Shake dice and miss as many turns as number thrown before resuming').

Significantly, within the 25 April 1981 issue, Charley Bourne is, once again, taken out of context of his own strip and, within a single-page spread that is driven by a dream sequence, utilised (exploited even) as a means of 'recruiting' more readers to *Battle-Action*. Awoken from his dream – within which, at a court-marshal, he is 'charged with failing to increase the circulation of the paper in which you appear' – Charley, in the final frame, back in the reality of his trench, fixes us with a steely-eyed stare and speaks directly to the comic's faithful, imploring them to 'do their bit' in fighting the war against falling circulation. Simultaneously reinforcing the homosocial bond between the reader and the comic, he pleads 'so I'm asking you, pals ... Place a regular order by filling in one of the coupons below and hand it to your newsagent! The other coupon is for a friend! Encourage *all* your friends to buy *Battle-Action* weekly'. Significantly, the use of the term 'pals' here (not only as an oblique reference to the 'pal battalions' of Tommies that characterised the early stages of the war), suggests an intimate male-male friendship – not only between Charley and the regular reader, but between that reader and his immediate circle of friends.

Jay Winter, in *Sites of Memory, Sites of Mourning – The Great War in European Cultural History* (1997), takes the reader on a journey 'past a number of "sites of memory"' (1997: 7). And this is how Winter defines such sites:

> The physical, emotional, and artistic artefacts we pass testify to the catastrophic character of the Great War and to the multifaceted effort of the survivors to understand what had happened both to their lives and to those who had died in the war. These facets of cultural history are no more than that: they are neither representative nor exhaustive; instead they are meant to suggest the dimensions of the disaster and the search for a language within which to try to find some meaning in it (Winter, 1997: 7–8).

I very much agree with Winter that the sites of memory of the Great War are, indeed, 'neither representative nor exhaustive', as I would insist that the plastic soldiers that Peter, during the early-to-mid 1970s, and, the comic strip that Peter read towards the end of that decade – 'Charley's War' – can both be understood as 'physical, emotional, and artistic artefacts' relating to the First World War. In essence, akin to monuments to the Unknown Soldier, they are Great War sites of memory that are to be found amid children's culture of the 1970s.

The Stairs

Bill Bryson (2010), rather precisely and mathematically, instructs us that any form of stairs comprise of three aspects of geometry. These are 'rise', 'going', and 'pitch', whereby:

> [t]he rise is the height between steps, the going is the step itself (technically, the distance between the leading edges, or nosings, of two successive steps measured horizontally) and the pitch is the overall steepness of the stairway (Bryson, 2010: 333).

Thus, with this scientific explanation in mind, it is almost a relief to find out that, in fact, '[d]escending a staircase is in a sense a controlled fall' (Bryson, 2010: 334). For, plunging down a flight of stairs, step-by-step, you are actually 'propelling your body outwards and downwards in a manner that would clearly be dangerous if you weren't fully on top of things' (Bryson, 2010: 334).

Having repeatedly climbed up the stairs only to jump straight back down again many times already (gradually increasing the number of steps that I take up each time I have jumped), I'm now half way up. This is it. I daren't do any higher, this is high enough. I jump, and – with my right hand on the bannister – I push myself out with all my might. Mid-flight, from the kitchen doorway to my left, my grandmother appears, 'Mam', and she's carrying a mug of tea. She stops, and looks at me startled as I crash to the floor just in front of her slippered feet. I miss knocking into her and scalding us both with her hot drink by an inch. Clearly not happy with any of this, she passes me and, walking along the hallway, she shouts over her shoulder 'Mind yourself now, Peter. You'll twist your bloomin' gut doing that, you will! And then where will you be!?!' I stand solemnly at the foot of the stairs, and, in my mind's eye, I imagine myself, crumpled on the floor, my body contorted into an horrific, mangled posture – the result of me having 'twisted my gut'.

With this memory of propelling himself in a somewhat reckless 'controlled fall' down the stairs (whereby, according to his grandmother, he was risking life and limb – and she was most probably right), Peter lands with a thud and, catching his breath, he turns, and runs upwards, leading us to the upstairs of Ivy Cottage.

The Front Bedroom

Terence Conran's *New House Book – The Complete Guide to Home Design* (1999, first published in 1985), when discussing the manner in which surfaces such as walls can be covered, and, as a result, a room's sense of space can be altered, implores: 'Use mirrors to create the illusion of space, increase light alter a room's perspective' (Conran, 1999: 159). Conran, in *The Bed and Bath Book* (1978), notes that four sections of mirror-glass, when placed around a wash-basin, for example, 'provide an infinitely repeated reflection' (Conran, 1978: 183). It is such an 'infinitely repeated reflection' that engrossed Peter as a young boy in Ivy Cottage.

I walk into the front bedroom. It is midday, and as there is no sunlight in this room until early evening, it is dim, and chilly. I approach the dressing table. It is painted white, and has a fixed central mirror atop of it, and, attached to either side of this by hinges, are a pair of side mirrors. I stare at my face in the mirror before me. Then, leaning forward, I simultaneously angle the two side mirrors so that they are opposite one another. I then – with a growing sense of unease – look sideways. And, there I see it: That endless corridor of reflections that stretch on and on and on. Wanting to look – but, at the same time, not wanting to look – I wonder what is at the very end of this 'corridor'. Does it even end? Seeing myself – my face, and the back of my head – over and over again, I now start to panic ... Throwing myself backwards, I manage to pull myself out of this vortex – pushing both side mirrors back to their original positions as I do so.

Peter's deep-rooted anxiety of staring into mirrors – and, thus, being lost in his infinite reflection – taps into an age-old human angst that predates the mirror's general introduction into the home, whereby 'reflections were a cause of deep, widespread alarm', as they conjured up 'superstitions about doubles, or 'fetches', uncanny spectres who call the living into the land of the dead' (Warner, 2006: 173). Mirrors as portals to other worlds – those of the living as well as the dead – is a common motif, of course, in children's literature. For example, with both Lewis Carroll's *Through the Looking Glass and What Alice Found There* (1871), and Philip Pullman's trilogy *His Dark Materials* (1995–2000), 'children's fiction tackles the doubled, or multiple, worlds opened by mirrors' (Warner, 2006: 208). Anthony Browne's first picture book – entitled *Through the Magic Mirror* (1976) – combines the child's wonder of the mirror with an uncanniness of ultra-realism. Browne, employing an 'effective use of clear, bright outlines, often against blank white backgrounds that give a cut-out effect' (Townsend, 1987: 324), along with a nostalgically imbued 'meticulous craftsmanship', demonstrated his skill in 'getting under the emotional skin of situations' (Powers, 2003: 128). For, in *Through the Magic Mirror* (1976), the reader is introduced to Toby. Spiky-haired, with bottle-green shirt collar protruding over the crew neck of a Fair Isle patterned pullover, brown flares, and green, stack-heeled shoes, he is well and truly a boy of his time – the drab and dreary mid-1970s. However, as his world and adventure unfolds, his surreal 1970s existence is one which harks back to the Victorian child's 'looking-class' and before:

> Toby sat in the big chair. He was fed up.
> Fed up with books, fed up with toys,
> fed up with everything (n.p.).
> He went into the living-room.
> Nothing was happening there (n.p.).

The fact that 'nothing was happening here', in the living-room, was emphasised by Toby's father, can of beer on his armchair, asleep in front of the TV, whilst his mother, hair in curlers, was reading the paper whilst scoffing chocolates.

> Going back upstairs he saw himself in a mirror.
> Something looked very strange. What was wrong? (n.p.).

For, what Toby saw in the mirror, was not his face, or even the front of himself, but his Magritte-esque reverse. Browne himself was to admit – in his autobiography *Playing the Shape Game* (2011: 62–3) – that the inspiration for this picture book, was not only Magritte's mirror-fixated 'Not to Be Reproduced', but Miroslav

Holub's poem 'The Door' – both of which, when combined, resulting in Toby's stanza-like mirror-as-door surrealist tale:

> He put out his hand to touch the mirror –
> and walked right through it! (n.p.).

Browne explains that Toby 'steps through the glass and enters a strange world', where '[t]he setting is the same dull street that he has known all his life, but everything is peculiarly altered' (Browne, 2011: 63). Once 'outside':

> An invisible man passed by (n.p.).

Those very words appear on the page where the man's head should have been visible, between his trilby and pinstriped collar and tie. Meanwhile:

> On the corner was an easel.
> On the easel was a painting
>   of a painting
>   of a painting (n.p.).

Thus, Browne's canvas shows an on-page painting: That is, a painting on an easel, which, within it, contains the same painting on the easel – which, within that, the painting on the easel, again and again, ad infinitum. Then, more Magritte-like imagery:

> Suddenly the sky became dark as a flock of
> choirboys flew overhead (n.p.).

And, several more surrealist-inspired pages on, and Toby finds the mirror once more, where:

> Toby stepped through, back into his own house (n.p.).

As Toby does so, his right leg, from the knee down, can be seen to be coming through the mirror. Having re-entered his house, he is now home, and – having left the surrealism of the streets outside behind him – he is now no longer 'fed up':

> He turned around and looked at himself in the mirror. When he saw his face, he smiled (n.p.).

Despite being back amid the drab and the dreary, he is quite clearly content with the fact that, once again, 'nothing was really happening'. As, finally, on the last page:

> Then he ran down to tea (n.p.).

Mammy's Bedroom

The Usborne World of Electronics, published in 1982, contains two pages that depict 'Inside a radio' (Hawkins and Meredith, 1982: 76–7). On the left-hand page, there is a cut-away illustration making visible the internal circuit board, showing capacitors, diodes, transformers, transistors, and resistors. To Peter, it was the latter – along with glass-encased valves – that held the wonder of such a 'world of electronics': that is, quite literally, miniature worlds of colour (resistors in particular) and seemingly microscopic precision engineering (vales). For, with his brother, Jeremy, employed as a TV repair man, Ivy Cottage was chock-a-block with amateur electronics magazines, and a number of bulky television sets – all in varied states of working order – to be found throughout the house.

I am in Mammy's bedroom, and I'm standing to the side of the TV that's up against the wall to the side of the window. I push the 'On' button, and I wait for it to warm up. Eventually, a picture appears out of the fuzzy haze of the screen. But, I'm not interested in what's on TV, I want to look down the back, and peek inside. On tip-toes, I strain to see through the vents at the top, and stare down into its gloomy depths. A number of valves are beginning to glow in the dim, dusty, cobwebbed interior. I breathe in a feint smell of warm circuitry. I touch the rear, moulded casing, and I feel an electric warmth. A world within a box within a room.

This particular memory of Peter's underlines the notion that children – through imaginative play – always enter into a state of mind that is of the in-between, where '[t]he outer – material, 'real' – world gains primacy over the inner – child-created, imagined – world only slowly, with much overlap' (Day, 2007: 14). With the child's outer world constantly overlapping with their inner world, it is such nest-nook spaces that provide perfect play-nest places within the home. These – like the inside of an analogue television set – are 'child-scaled, (almost) adult inaccessible, dark and a bit magic, but in the middle of domestic life' (Day, 2007: 125). Such an appreciation of everyday household electronic appliances – with their ability to emanate a certain presence amid the domestic sphere – is central to the notion that there exist forms of haunted media. For, from the moment that radio was introduced, the home was then said to be 'haunted' as it introduced the voices of other into familial space. Then, with the development of television, such a 'haunting' of the home progressed to a higher plane as a result of those voices now being accompanied by hazy, flickering versions of the human form. Furthermore, such TV-detained viscous corporeality, came to very much characterise the nature of such 'hauntings' of modernity – that is, 'the paradox of visible, seemingly material worlds trapped in a box in the living room and yet conjured out of nothing more than electricity and air' (Sconce, 2000: 126). Moreover, whilst the 'ghosts' of radio merely spoke through the electronic apparatus, those of the television set 'seemed to actually reside *within* the technology itself' (Sconce, 2000: 127). Thus, from the early years of its broadcasting onwards, television not only took on such a sinister, spectral dimension within the home, but – in the psyche of the viewer – it became 'a sentient entity brooding in the corner of the living room', whereby '[m]any reported a certain uneasiness around the new medium' (Sconce, 2000: 131). Whilst some appreciated the TV's ability to transport them to 'other worlds', there were paranoid others that interpreted this 'new medium' 'as a zone of suspended animation, a form of oblivion from which viewers might not ever escape' (Sconce, 2000: 131). This, then, was the TV-derived 'twilight zone' of the Cold War, where even the comforts of home offered no respite from feelings of fear and dread. So, it is vital to stress that, as well as the living room having now taken on such an uncanny dimension, the 'original 'twilight' space, however, was television itself' (Sconce, 2000: 133). Furthermore, television's ability to 'haunt' was something which transcended the temporal limitations of its time of broadcast, as even when an evening's programming was over, and all was switched off, 'the television set itself still loomed as a gateway to oblivion simply by sitting inert and watchful in the living room' (Sconce, 2000: 166).

The history and development of the television imbued many other elements of the paranormal, especially that of 'psychic communication', with the mind – as already an 'organ' of 'projection' – enhanced by its interaction with the screen. For, noting the prefix shared by both teleportation and television, the latter 'was to take its place in society as the culminating mass medium of mind-voyaging in the modern era (Warner, 2006: 269). Furthermore, all 'smart' electronic objects – and televisions in particular – are perceived to have a cognitive dimension in themselves, with a number of theorists highlighting apparatus's ability to 'dream', 'in the sense that they leak radiation into the space and objects surrounding them, including our bodies' (Dunne and Raby, 2001: 8). For, these 'dreams' – electromagnetic radiation that seeps into our bodies – creates its own invisible, yet physical, dimension: 'Hertzian Space'. Indeed, I would insist that such 'dreaming' by electronic objects amid 'Hertzian Space' not only permeates our bodies in a broad manner, but that these 'dreams' invade our brains specifically – and especially the imaginations of children. Fundamentally, though, '[t]hinking of them in terms of dreaminess rather than smartness opens them up to more interesting interpretations' (Dunne and Raby, 2001: 8). 'Hertzian Space', then, is where 'the secret life of electronic objects is played out, secret not only because we rarely glimpse it, but also because we are only just beginning to understand it' (Dunne and Raby, 2001: 8). Yet, as it permeates or bodies (and despite our inability to sense or feel it, doing so), 'Hertzian Space' is not just that which exists within close proximity of a television screen, 'it is part of the space our bodies inhabit' (Dunne and Raby, 2001: 12).

So, Peter staring into the 'Hertzian Space' that was the enclosed back of an analogue TV set allowed him not only to see what was happening inside the object, but, in turn, it allowed his body – through his imagination – to inhabit that space. As our inhabiting of 'Hertzian Space' – whereby, in doing so, we humanise such a space – is not reducible to a mere form of representation or visualising, 'but as a catalyst, encouraging the poetic and multi-layered coupling of electromagnetic and material elements to produce new levels of cultural complexity' (Dunne, 2005: 121). That this happened when he peered into the back of the television that was in his mother's bedroom – when, of course, she was not there – is highly significant, as '[o]nce children become aware of separateness from mother, they inhabit a world *between* self and environment, between fact and fantasy' (Day, 2007: 14).

Daddy's Bedroom

Like the 'looking-glass' of the mirror, the humble wardrobe – in children's literature – has been presented as yet another portal to other realms. Most famously, the initial instalment of C.S. Lewis' 'Narnia Chronicles', *The Lion, the Witch, and the Wardrobe* (1950), has the four children, Peter, Susan, Edmund and Lucy, 'enter the imaginary land of Narnia through the back of a wardrobe' (Townsend, 1987: 232). Thus, as such otherworldly portals, the wardrobe was also a means by which the medium, Matthew Manning, was – quite startlingly – confronted with the physicality of the spirit world. As he outlines in his autobiographical *The Link* (1974), on 17 July 1970, just as his boarding school summer holidays had begun, his parents brought home a newly purchased antique wardrobe and duly placed it in his bedroom. Made of sturdy oak, and of massive dimensions, Manning immediately felt an overwhelming sense of unease. For, '[a]s soon as it was placed in my room I got an odd feeling from it; I liked it and at the same time I felt there was something very wrong with it' (Manning, 1974: 27). Upon hanging up his clothes, and his bolting and locking of its two doors, Matthew left his room momentarily. On his return, just moments later, both doors were found to be open. This occurred several times that day, and continued to happen across the coming weeks. Then, about a month later, when Manning was home from school for a weekend, similar happened – albeit, this time, in a far more shocking manner. Entering his bedroom, the wardrobe doors, he noted, were shut tight. Then, leaving the room for an hour or two, he returned later to discover both doors open. So, closing them, he sat down to listen to a record, with his back to the wardrobe. All of a sudden, a boot flew past him, hitting the window in front of him. Spinning around, and to his alarm, both wardrobe doors were wide open, and he realised that 'the boot had come from the cupboard' (Manning, 1974: 28). With the wardrobe, then, as an entry point to other worlds, and a means by which the afterlife can make its physical presence felt, here is a memory Peter has of the large wooden wardrobe that stood in his father's bedroom. It is a sunny morning, late August 1982, and Peter's father has just died the evening before.

It's 10am, and the sun pours in through Daddy's bedroom window. Mammy is downstairs in the kitchen; sobbing, her wails, every now and again, echo up through the ceiling below me, and even through the very floorboards and carpet that I stand upon. I'm in front of Daddy's wardrobe, and – with a slight hesitancy – I turn the key, opening its creaking door. The smell hits me first; a heady mixture of musty wood combined with a man's aftershave. In front of me, all on hangers, are suit jackets, and ironed shirts. Although, it is only the edge of each sleeve that I really see: all side-by-side, they form a concertina of cloth and multiple patterns. But, it is the sight of his paisley shirts and ties that strike me the most – for, they are the patterns that are Daddy. I start to cry ... The sense of loss is not overwhelming. It's just a void. An empty feeling. But, it is a strange thing to feel – emptiness – as I stare into such a chock-a-block wardrobe. A wardrobe so full of clothes. So full of patterns.

The children's picture book author-and-artist, Anthony Browne, declares what he does visually – that is, to produce an illustration – as 'playing the shape game'. Following the death of his father when Browne had only just started Art College, aged 17, it was the memory of staring helplessly at his father's writhing, dying frame that obsessively influenced his artwork for the next few years. As such, upon eventually entering the world of publishing, Browne often considered producing a book in which his father was to be the main character. Yet, Browne was seemingly unable to, as he just could not think of a suitable visual approach as a starting point. However, several decades later, having discovered an old suitcase of his mother's – within which was his father's dressing gown – he knew now how to tackle such an emotive task:

> I took the dressing gown out of the case and held it, and was instantly transported back to the age of about five. For the first time in decades I remembered what it was like to be a young boy who thought his dad could do anything. It was a breakthrough, for I suddenly knew exactly how to make the book. The nostalgic effect of the dressing gown inspired me to write a story specifically about my own father and the way I felt about him as a young boy (Browne, 2011: 114).

The result was *My Dad*. Published in 2000, it was not only the point at which, perhaps, Browne truly came to terms with his father's passing, but where his concept of the 'Shape Game' reached full maturity. For, as Browne himself readily admits:

> [t]he dressing gown – or at least its distinctive pattern – is the visual key that links every picture and I play the Shape Game with it throughout the book (Browne, 2011: 115).

Thus, the distinctive brown, window-pane check of his father's dressing gown – as well as being something that the paternal figure wears constantly, whether he's walking a tightrope or playing football – is something which adorns the book's surrealist representations of his father's prowess. Hence, when it is exclaimed that Browne's father is able to 'swim like a fish', the scales of the aquatic form are replaced by the gown's geometric pattern. Furthermore, this adherence to such a tender repeat reproduction of a patterned item of clothing that Browne readily associates with his childhood years and with his father, is maintained right until the final two pages, which bear the following epitaph: 'I love my dad. And you know what? He loves me! (And he always will)' (cited in Browne, 2011: 115). Thus, with the very last page showing a father holding his child in a loving embrace, as bleached sunlight is being cast over the two, Browne – in an almost confessional-like statement of true achievement and pride – claims that '[i]t is probably the happiest picture that I have ever painted' (Browne, 2011: 115).

Hardy Amies, in his *ABC of Men's Fashion* (2007, first published in 1964), contains the following musing over ties and their design: 'Ties have the biggest opportunity of displaying pattern and, like other garments, are usually better without it', as 'you will perhaps agree that there is enough pattern (and colour) in your face without introducing any more into your costume' – indeed, '[m]any women and nearly all men forget how complicated a piece of design is a face' (86–7). Considering Amies' assertion that ties should be pattern-less, as to not detract from their male wearer's facial features, it is significant that Peter's memory places so much of an emphasis upon the busy pattern of his father's ties that sunny, autumnal morning. For, as the years have gone by, Peter has – to his dismay – struggled to even remember what his father actually looked like. However, Peter can – to this day – recall each and every patterned tie, shirt and suit to be found in that immense, musty, wooden wardrobe of his father's. Thus, it is with at least some consolatory relief that he is still able to successfully engage in this particular exercise of mental recall. In cognitively 'playing' such a 'shape game', Peter – like Browne, reunited with his father's dressing gown – is his younger self once more.

Peter's Bedroom

The woman walks slowly down from upstairs, turning, from the hallway, into the front room, and from there – via the 'knocked-through' opening – into the dining-room-come-kitchen. All the rooms are bare, except that the latter contains a stark wooden tale, upon which is a glass with some form of drink poured into it. The woman, upon spotting it, picks it up, and starts to swallow. Suddenly, and even before she has finished drinking, she starts to float – her feet, at first, hovering just inches from the floor. Then, rising, and rising, and rising, she is now distraught: her mouth and her eyes wide open in terror. Eventually, with her back pinned to the ceiling, she lets out a blood-curdling scream ... Then, I wake with a jolt. Quickly sitting up straight in bed, I stare at the drawn curtains, the morning light beginning to seep through. It had been a dream. Was she dying? Did she die? It felt as if she had. It had been a nightmare.

With Peter's memory of such a vivid childhood dream – which has stayed with him since – we will now consider children, dreams, and spirituality. It is important to do so, as Adams et al., in *The Spiritual Dimension of Childhood* (2008) – in the chapter entitled 'Unforgettable Dreams: The Impact of Spiritual Dreams upon Children's Lives' (2008: 131–43), note that, quite crucially, '[c]hildren's dreams received relatively little attention compared to adults' dreams until the late twentieth century' (2008: 132). Acknowledging that both adults and children encounter 'dead people' in their dreams – and bearing in mind Peter's dream, and the feeling of dread it left him with in his waking state – we should also note that '[s]ome dreams can be an intensely spiritual experience' (2008: 63). Whilst initially disturbing, such 'spiritual' dreams – that include 'going to heaven' and/or being reunited with deceased family members and pets – often, far from being entirely disconcerting, 'bring comfort to the dreamer' (2008: 64). For, such spiritually comforting dreams are examples of what Carl Jung defined as big dreams; that is, dreams that seem significant for long periods thereafter – as in Peter's case, with this particular dream/nightmare, decades – and, as a result, 'are often remembered for a lifetime' (2008: 133). Often incomprehensible (either at the time, or thereafter), such life-long remembered 'big dreams' – which are centred upon, amongst other experiences, 'flying' (or, in Peter's case, that of 'floating') – attain great significance, 'often impacting upon spiritual life' (2008: 133). Thus, bearing in mind the potential impact of such 'big dreams', they tend to, thereafter, act as day-to-day 'spiritual landmarks', whereby '[t]hey can also motivate people to develop greater spiritual self-awareness, leading them to ask questions about what is real and what is illusion' (2008: 135).

What Dreams May Come is a 1978 novel by Richard Matheson, which tells the story of Chris Nielsen and his wife Ann – with the former dying in a car accident, and the latter, unable to cope with the grief of losing her husband, taking her own life shortly after. With its title taken from Shakespeare's *Hamlet* ('For in that sleep of death what dreams may come, When we have shuffled off this mortal coil, Must give us pause' (Act III, Scene 1, cited in, Schwartz, 2000: 3)). Matheson claimed that his work was founded upon established research to do with life-after-death. As such, Matheson – with *What Dreams May Come* – offered 'a proto-New Age fable with an afterlife scenario adapted directly from the mythologies of South Asia, that is, India and Tibet' (Schwartz, 2000: 2). Yet, it is the 1998 film adaptation – more so than the original book – which is perceived of as being 'fictitious', as the big-screen version, for some, is 'a work of the imagination (a film) about a work of imagination (life and death), which constructs a western illusion about an eastern illusion' (Schwartz, 2000: 2). Nineteen years in the making, and employing state-of-the-art cinematography, the big-budget adaptation – in rejecting many of the novel's bleaker moments – was, without doubt, 'a stunning visual cornucopia' (Schwartz, 2000: 2). Indeed, in a film where, as some critics observed, the visuals are far more convincing than the actual plot, it is the former which 'lifts that story from an overtly romanticized tale about the power of love to transcend death to a display of graphic wizardry' (Schwartz, 2000: 2).

With the book and the film, at times, differing from each other quite significantly, it is with their respective endings that any such deviation is at its most glaring. For, whilst both endings deal with the notion of intra-existence karmic issues being engaged with, and overcome, through life-after-death trauma, in the film Chris and his wife – after their reunion in the afterlife – are empowered to return to Earth together, meeting as similar aged children playing with toy boats upon a pond. However, in the novel, the couple are unable to reunite in Heaven (Ann's suicide precludes this), and are, instead, forced to be reincarnated separately, only to lead unrelated lives on Earth thereafter. Indeed, Chris' realisation that this is to be the case, occurs when, in conversation with his afterlife 'guide', Albert, he is told that Ann will be reborn in India:

India?

'It was immediately available', he said, 'as well as offering a challenge to her soul; a handicap to overcome which can counterbalance the negative effect of her suicide'. 'Handicap?' I asked uneasily.

'The body she's chosen will, in later years, contract an illness which will cause severe sleep deprivation'.

Ann had taken her life with sleeping pills. To balance the scales, she'd acquire a condition which would not permit her to sleep normally (Matheson, 1979: 279).

Having shared such dire news, Albert's words now attempt to comfort Chris:

'The rest is good', he said. 'In compensation for the pain she endured and the progress she achieved in her last life. Her new parents are intelligent, attractive people, the father in local government, the mother a successful artist. Ann – she'll have another name, of course – will be given much love and opportunity for creative and intellectual growth (Matheson, 1979: 279–80).

Finally, Chris is made aware of what will be his destiny upon reincarnation:

I will become a doctor.

At first, I considered being born in India as well. The difficulties of doing so and ending up a doctor, however, are close to insuperable and I have had to alter the idea. Being born in India is not the objective anyway. Ultimately reaching India to help Ann is.

Which is why I've chosen who I have as parents: Dr and Mrs Arthur Braningwell of Philadelphia. They are young and well-to-do and I will be their only child. I will have a comfortable upbringing, attend medical school and believe I am to follow in my father's footsteps.

At the age of thirty, that resolve will change entirely, for reasons I will not go into, I will leave the path of comfort to practice medicine in the deprived areas of the world.

Eventually, I will arrive in India, take care of, fall in love with and, finally, marry a young woman whose soul will be Ann's. Whether we will ever know or even sense what is really happening is not important. We will be together again.

Nothing else matters (Matheson, 1979: 290).

Ultimately, Chris is informed that his future human form has already been born:

The infant body chosen by me is four and a half weeks old now (Matheson, 1979: 290).

And, it is this notion – that the bodies of newly-born children are 'soul-less', but are eventually occupied by the spirits of those who have lived before – that we engage with in the following section.

The Bathroom

Akiko Busch, in *Geography of Home – Writings On Where We Live* (1999), admits that, in most houses, the bathroom is a relatively small space, but that human desire for moments of solitude is suited to such small, secluded places. As such, '[t]he bathroom – this outpost of privacy – is the only place in the house where we are justified in being alone' (Busch, 1999: 136–7). Although, Busch insists that there is more to the bathroom than just 'being alone', as it is the place in the home where the running of water provides both a sensory and cognitive tranquillity which enhances such feelings of 'being alone': 'Privacy and running water are a beautiful combination. Call them the two essential ingredients for clear thought' (Busch, 1999: 142). Also, it is often the sounds generated by 'being alone' amid the enamels and the ceramics of the bathroom that add further to the experience, as 'the acoustic qualities of hard surfaces in this room, and the aural privacy they create, serve to heighten the sense of solitude' (Busch, 1999: 142). Thus, the bathroom 'makes contemplation a realm you can float on, drift across, or plunge into completely' (Busch, 1999: 142).

It's mid-morning, and only me and Mammy are in the house. I've been playing in the garden, and I've touched something, so I'm up in the bathroom to wash my hands. With the water turned down low to a mere trickle, I wet my hands, rub them around the bar of soap, and begin to lather them. After a minute or so, I rinse them under the tap. Then, I do it all again. And again. And again. In all, now, I've washed my hands seven time. I always wash them seven times. Seven is my favourite number. If I don't wash them seven times – every time – something bad will happen, I just know it! Then, as I dry my hands on the towel, Mammy walks in, startling me. Frowning at me, she sternly asks 'You're not washing your bloody hands again, are you? You're always washing your bloody hands! You must have been Lady MacBeth in your last life!'. I'm in shock. She's caught me washing my hands. Was I once Lady MacBeth? I go cold with the thought.

The suggestion that children are the reincarnated souls of the deceased is something which anthropologists have historically encountered. Heather Montgomery, with *An Introduction to Childhood – Anthropological Perspectives on Children's Lives* (2009), notes that within both Buddhist and Hindu cultures it is sometimes claimed that a reincarnated child merely resembles someone who has died. Amongst many tribal communities such an understanding of 'pre-existence' is 'central to people who believe in reincarnation', and who, as a result, 'attempt to see, in their children, reincarnations of parents, family, or other ancestors' (Montgomery, 2009: 95). For, among one particular Inuit whaling community in Canada, a child was thought to be a reincarnation of his dead uncle, where even what he had to say was scrutinised for the 'passing on' of wisdom. So, '[i]n this case the identity of the child, and the way that he was raised, depended on who he was believed to be in a former life', whereby, '[h]is daily life therefore would be influenced by his existence in a previous one' (Montgomery, 2009: 96). Thus, in instances like this, we have to acknowledge 'that there is no such thing as a new person being born or that a child is a new addition to the community' (Montgomery, 2009: 97). For, as with the Ndenbu of Zambia, new-born children are considered already 'known', and are, for the rest of their upbringing, 'watched for signs of who they once were' (Montgomery, 2009: 97).[14] With all of this in mind, then, the child can no longer be understood as a true 'individual', whose everyday experiences can be interpreted solely upon the grounds of 'individuality', but that, instead, 'his or her existence needs to be conceptualized as part of wider cosmologies which look at how and why ancestors return to earth' (Montgomery, 2009: 97).

---

14   However, Montgomery also notes that, depending upon a culture's beliefs, '[i]n some cases children are the reincarnation of complete strangers and are born thousands of miles away from where they died' (Montgomery, 2009: 97).

This is all similar to when Peter's mother mentioned to him (when he was 10 years old or so) her disbelief, when he was a toddler, that he was able to verbally repeat the mixture ratio for making concrete ('Four of sand, to one of cement'). As, to his mother, the obvious 'explanation' for this was that his great-grandfather's knowledge – that of 'Dad Evans', a stonemason – had been 'passed on' to Peter through reincarnation. This phenomenon – again, familial belief in ancestral reincarnation – manifested itself many a time during Peter's childhood whereby his mother (and other female members of his family) would often equate any familiarity of his looks or physical/mental development or dexterity with ancestors as a by-product of reincarnation rather than a result of genetics or socially or culturally transferred behaviour.

In *At Home – A Short History of Private Life* (2010), Bill Bryson – in outlining the development of porcelain enamels c. 1910 – notes that it is when baths became both hardwearing and aesthetically pleasing to the eye. Indeed, such a durable and attractive bathroom surface, is achieved by applying certain powders to cast iron and exposing all to very high temperatures several times. As such, this porcelain-like sheen that such enamels achieve, is neither one of porcelain or of enamel but that more akin to the qualities of glass: Thus, '[e]namel bath surfaces would be quite transparent if whiteners or other tints weren't added to the glazing compound' (Bryson, 2010: 398). Crucially, the introduction of such hard, gleaming, and readily cleanable, surfaces within the home – and the bathroom especially – was not only part of the continuity of the already established 'purity and hygiene' discourse, but it coincided with late-nineteenth-century science-based revolutionary notions that whilst there were linkages between 'cleanliness and whiteness', such 'whiteness' did not always equate true 'cleanliness'. For, as the 'medical-hygienic' school of thought entered into the public sphere, people's understanding of what was 'dirty' and what was 'clean' suddenly became divorced from what they could see. In this era of the microscope, it was realised that '[p]hysical health was influenced by processes that were not perceptible at all' (Laermans and Meulders, 2006: 120). Thus, with the knowledge that silent pathogenic organisms (bacilli, microbes, protozoa and viruses) – that could not be seen by the naked eye or detected through smell – the '[s]triving for cleanliness became an unceasing struggle against an invisible but omnipresent enemy that could be perceived only by scientists' (Laermans and Meulders, 2006: 121). Hence, the bathroom at Ivy Cottage (a house, of course, built during the late 1800s), was a place where microscopic elements of 'filth' were – across the decades of the twentieth century – supposedly banished from.

With this dual understanding of the existence of microscopic dirt still able to lurk amid the hard, gleaming confines of the bathroom, a short story that Peter read during the late-1970s had a particular impact upon his imagination. George MacBeth's 'Birth' – in Giles Gordon's *A Book of Contemporary Nightmares* (1977), which belonged to his mother, but was illicitly read by Peter – is, essentially, a Radical Feminist text that suggests that the protagonist – 'Valorta Primavera. First Lieutenant. Uterus Probe Advance' (MacBeth, 1977: 115) – is a sole survivor of an all-female crew of a spacecraft (the '*Black Pearl*', referred to as a pinkish, dirigible 'airship') that has crash-landed on a bleak, nigh-on featureless 'ice planet'. Following a first line in which Primavera, still lying face-down, acknowledges her survival, she remembers the moment of impact:

> The wet, slapping sound as the envelope struck the frozen surface returned to her
> at full volume, echoing in her brain from the sloping tub-line walls of the crater
> (MacBeth, 1977: 115).

Furthermore, opening her eyes, she notes that around her resembles 'Glossy snow. White nothing. Sound, nothing' (MacBeth, 1977: 115).

With further memories of an on-board pornographic film (involving disturbing scenes of violent, male-on-female, anal rape) being screened, each evening, in order to encourage a continued hatred of men upon post-landing settlement of their planned target planet, 'Uterus', (a film accompanied by the warning voice of the 'mother' of the 'mother-ship' – 'Leander Vagina'), Primavera's clearing senses bring the planet's surface more into focus:

> The hard white surface she had first seen six inches from her opening eyes now
> stretched away as far as she could see, rising towards some high horizon. The
> ship must have landed in one of the enormous bath-like craters in the Artic side
> of the planet Uterus. In the distance she could vaguely make out a remote dark
> area, perhaps some kind of oasis or well (MacBeth, 1977: 118).

Focusing further:

> The hard white surface continued unbroken for as far as she could see. On
> all sides it seemed to stretch away towards the same vague steamy horizon
> (MacBeth, 1977: 118).

The surface of the planet Uterus is continued to be described, throughout the rest of the short story, as a 'white crystalline surface', a 'white smoothness' that is 'as hard as enamel' (MacBeth, 1977: 119), whereby:

> Uterus, she said. You are indeed the snow-planet we aimed for. Here no infection
> of male atrocity could ever soil the clean elegance of your lakes and hills
> (MacBeth, 1977: 121).

Exploring further, the well-like break in the surface is eventually discernable, as 'it was a clearly defined circular area, apparently bordered by some bright metal, and flanked by a shimmer of light' (MacBeth, 1977: 121).

However, such hopes of all-female utopia are, quite literally, drenched, as the ice planet's surface seemingly starts to thaw with the gradually increasingly flow of water all around. Indeed, it all ends with Primavera's realisation, upon drowning, and being swept along by the increasing current down into the 'well', that:

The myth of her life as a space explorer with Leander was all a fantasy. There was no airship. No snow-planet. All that was real was the pornographic film that had made her vomit.

Uterus, she thought. You finally betrayed me.

As Valorta was swept away, she heard through the echoing waters what seemed to be the true voice of her destiny, a far-off human sound that sealed her in horror.

John, it said. I wish you wouldn't throw your used Durex in the bath. I hate flushing spunk down the plug-hole.

It was the voice of a woman, the only one Valorta had known.

Leander, she breathed (MacBeth, 1977: 126–7).

So, whether perceived of as a sci-fi tale of the fate of Feminism, or a damning condemnation of a sordid decade and its preoccupation with pornography, 'Birth', ultimately, is the story of semen in a bath that is washed away down the plughole. Significantly, though, as an adult text read by a child, it offers yet another insight into the microscopic-as-cosmic aspects of the childhood home, where even the bath – let alone the bathroom itself – has the potential to be planetary in both scale and scope.

The Attic

It's late at night, and the wind is howling. I can hear slates – which are, one by one, being blown off the back of the roof – smashing on the concrete just below the kitchen window. I run into the bathroom, and look up at the open loft hatch, and peer up into the dark of the attic. Mammy and Kathleen are already up there. Having climbed up there on the stepladder that's in front of me, they had tottered across the rafters to the growing hole in the roof. With high-pitched whoops, they are trying to hold down the tiles. The rain is lashing in, their perms are flying everywhere. I'm scared that there won't be a roof left by the morning. I'm scared.

With *Environment and Children – Passive Lessons from the Everyday Environment* (2007), Christopher Day makes connections between home's 'mood' at its very apex, the elements, and the child's sense of wonderment. For, whilst the cellar is seemingly independent of the emotional effects of the weather, '[i]n contrast, attics amplify it', as, Day insists, 'heat or rain-beat on roof, frost and draught, sunlight chinks or bare bulbs and deep shadows' (Day, 2007: 124) can all be encountered at the top of the house. Furthermore, 'full of past clutter, they're *above* the world – places from which imagination can fly' (Day, 2007: 124). Thus, amid the storm-lashed attic at the top of Ivy Cottage, in a place where the 'imagination can fly', perhaps it is time to recall one of the most traumatic tales to be set in such a space: Virginia Andrews' *Flowers in the Attic* (1979). Author Virginia Andrews 'is today best remembered as the author of choice for 12-year-old desperate to express their developing maturity' (Kibble-White, 2005a: 76). For Andrews most infamous work, *Flowers in the Attic* (1979), is a disturbing tale of four children who – following the death of their father – are locked away at the top of their family home (their grandparent's mansion) by both their demented mother and grandmother. An immense literary success (especially amongst teenage girls on the cusp of puberty), *Flowers in the Attic* was:

> much talked about in girls' toilets, [where] those excited exchanges usually concentrated on the volume's theme of incest and whether or not you would ever actually do that with your own brother in real life (Kibble-White, 2005a: 76).

Perhaps on a more serious note, we should acknowledge that *Flowers in the Attic*, as its core, highly controversial theme (especially for a novel that sold 40 million copies), was one of incest. Indeed, the four Dollanganger children – teenage Chris and Cathy, and five-year-old twins Corry and Carrie – are subjected to starvation and poisoning (the latter, by arsenic-laced doughnuts given to them by their mother Corrine – after initially suspecting poison was being administered by their grandmother, Olivia). Imprisoned for three-and-a-half years in a bedroom, where their only respite is a more spacious existence – via a secret stairway – in the mansion's attic, Cory eventual dies (his body being placed into a hidden room in the attic), and the true extent of incest is revealed: Not only do Chris and Cathy enter into such a relationship, but all four children are the offspring of an incestuous coupling – as Corrine and her late husband were actually uncle and niece. *Flowers in the Attic*, though, was an end-of-decade adult text which was bookended by two girls' comics which – whilst nervously steering away from themes of incest – certainly tapped into the chilling mood of abusive adults, traumatised children, and houses and homes of incarceration: *Spellbound* and *Misty*.

Spellbound was published by D.C. Thomson between 1976 and 1978, lasting just 69 issues. Launched on 25 September 1976 (with its run ending 21 January 1978), and available in the newsagents every Thursday, the first issue came with a give-away 'mystic sun pendant', and was '[a]n occult-tinged weekly that specialised in spine-tingling tales of terror and featured willowy heroines with a tendency to go heavy on the mascara' (Kibble-White, 2005b: 215). Thus, and despite its relatively brief print run, amongst *Spellbound*'s dozens of eventual spooky strips that appeared – and, as swiftly, disappeared – were: 'Beware the Mystery Dolls', that was to do with waxworks who came to life; 'Hetty in the House of Secrets', involving governesses and ghosts; 'The Strange Ones', where three new arrivals at a ballet school unleash their evil psychic powers; and 'Zodiac Girl', which – perhaps the most of its time, the mid-1970s – manages to blend together '[f]ashion, boutiques and astrology' (Clarke, 2008: 39). Whilst some of *Spellbound*'s strips were vaguely paranormal in both their tone and content, others were outright terrifying. For instance, there was 'The Haunting of Laura Lee' –

which told the tale of a girl possessed as a result of wearing a ring that once belonged to a (now long dead) concert pianist – and a whole host of other stories offering a 'relentless parade of ghosts, ghouls and ghastly old geezers' (Ingram, 2008: 7).

Misty, however, set out to scare from Issue 1. First published on 4 February 1978 (actually published 1978 – 1980, and out every Monday), *Misty* was full to its rafters with black cats, vampire bats, haunted houses, and gothic, virginal, teenage girls. Indeed, despite *Misty* being a publication in which a post-Punk Britain was often reflected in its pages in a vacant-eyed, 'children of the damned' manner – and one which, at the same time, steadfastly ignored the gore that was oozing out of the late-night cinemas and home video 'nasties' – *Misty*, overall, was more akin to 'an ethereal child in a flowing gown that owed more to the literary sensibilities of *Wuthering Heights* and Mandalay than it did to Thatcher's Britain' (Sweetman, 2007a: 30). Published by IPC, the associate editor, Pat Mills, gathered together an all-male team of writers, artists, and so on, to produce this – what was to be – revolutionary comic aimed at an all-female readership. Containing timeless ghost stories that had an otherworldly air of unreality about them, '*Misty* dared to offer a metaphorical world that explored nascent and emergent sexuality', as '[i]t bridged the leap into the world of womanhood, revealing it as fearful and thrilling, deadly and liberating' (Sweetman, 2007a: 31). As, for its pre-pubescent female readers coming to terms with their emerging sexuality, *Misty* offered 'agony aunt'-style help, support, and advice that was shrouded in a non-patronising gossamer-thin veil of gothic. As, '[t]he sinister subtleties of the stories centred on troubled girls who were often becoming aware of strange feelings and did not quite know what to do about them' (Sweetman, 2007a: 31).

With the first issue coming with a free 'lucky charm bracelet', it introduced the reader to the editorial character of 'Misty', 'an escapee from a Roman Polanski nightmare with long black hair, lush eyelashes and an impassive expression' (Kibble-White, 2005b: 170). Meanwhile, one of its most memorable strip was 'Moonchild', which 'brought us an abused and friendless girl who had "*the power!*"'. With puberty derived 'power' being an extremely potent form of telekinesis, 'Moonchild' was clearly the comic-strip daughter of the on-screen *Carrie* (1976) – 'with its central character Carrie White replaced by the enigmatic Rosemary Black' (Sweetman, 2007: 33). Indeed, Rosemary Black's true 'power' was to instil in the comic's readers that – instead of tactics such as bullying – positive thinking was at the heart of true feminist empowerment. Jenni Scott – in 'Female identities and socialisation in the 1970s wave of British girls' comics' (2008) – examines the feminist-era impact of popular culture upon such publications as *Misty*. Indeed, in conversation with Pat Mills, it is quite obvious that the adult 'horror market' was behind the genesis of many of *Misty*'s strips:

> 'Moonchild' was quite deliberately based on *Carrie*. When I talked about starting *Misty*, I said we should look at all the kinds of female adults' fiction that were around at the time, and we should do girls' comics versions of that. It was a deliberately calculated policy to do *Carrie*, to do 'Audrey Rose', which I did as

'Hush, Hush, Sweet Rachel', we never quite got around to doing *Flowers in the Attic*, but it was definitely on the list – but most of those female mystery books that were around, we did good girls' comic versions. When *Misty* moved away from that, and got caught up in silly traditional stuff, that's when it lost its way' (Mills, cited in Scott, 2008: 8–9).

It is such a shame, then, that *Misty* did not have the longevity to bring to its cobwebbed pages a version of Virginia Andrew's classic, *Flowers in the Attic*. For, despite 'billing itself as 'a different world' and 'not to be read at night'' (Kibble-White, 2005: 172), and lasting 100 issues, *Misty* sadly folded as a publication in its own right on 12 January 1980. Yet, when combined, *Flowers in the Attic*, *Spellbound*, *Misty*, and the like, allow us to investigate the links between children and spirituality more generally – and 'spirit children' specifically.

Heather Montgomery, in *An Introduction to Childhood – Anthropological Perspectives on Children's Lives* (2009), suggests that the starting point for any culture-based study of children and childhood is problematic, as it is often difficult to ascertain where the 'anthropology of childhood' starts, or what it should entail. As, in the case of 'spirit children', their existence – or, indeed, multiple existences – fall into notions of both the yet-to-be-born and, even, those who have lived before. As a starting point, then, any study of the 'spirit child' should incorporate those 'children who are believed to exist in the supernatural world' and who, as a result, are 'waiting to be born as embodied children' (Montgomery, 2009: 87). Additionally, any understanding of such a childhood existence, should refute any form of divide between 'spirit children' and the embodied child, as 'they are part of the same continuum which links the supernatural and the natural world' (Montgomery, 2009: 89).

Noting that previous studies of Aborigines and certain West African societies hold central such beliefs of 'spirit children' within their cultures, Montgomery highlights a particular study carried out during the 1930s of the indigenous population of Western Australia, where any perceived boundary between 'spirit children' and 'embodied children' was, at best, blurred, and, in most cases, non-existent. From the moment of conception until many months after being born, these 'spirit children' were understood of as otherworldly rather than human. For, '[i]t was only when they began to laugh and respond and manifested a personality that they were no longer referred to as spirit children' (Montgomery, 2009: 88).

Significantly, and with specific reference to Phyllis Kaberry's study of the Australian Kimberleys of the late 1930s, even the 'spirit children' themselves were conscious of the inter-related nature of 'their lives as spirit children and their current existences' (Montgomery, 2009: 89). As, indeed, this particular study noted that – as separation between the spirit world and the mortal worlds was considered non-existent – such 'spirit children' 'are seen as belonging, and having allegiances, to both worlds', and, as a result, 'as being constantly torn between the two' (Montgomery, 2009: 90). Furthermore, the anthropologists who combined ethnographic studies of West African societies and their indigenous literatures, claim that 'spirit children' were also, at times, the result of reincarnation, whereby they 'are believed to be those who die and are reborn several times into the same family and whose time in the world of the living is very short' (Montgomery, 2009: 90). Significantly, the relationship between the 'spirit child' and its parents, siblings, and other children, can often be hostile, malevolent, and capricious, with 'spirit children' often perceived of and described – that is, amid an environment of jealousy – as cruel, dangerous, and deadly. Either way, though, such an unquestionable co-existence with 'spirit children' – be they 'good' or 'evil' (especially if they die in childbirth, or shortly thereafter) – is often understood as a means by which mothers cope with a high infant mortality.

Stephen O'Brien, a Welsh-born medium, is someone who claims not only to have communicated with such 'spirit children', but who, personally, enjoys great personal comfort from doing so. For, he has this to state in his autobiography, *Visions of Another World – The Autobiography of a Medium* (1989):

> Spirit-children often visit me and it's always a great joy to see them. They bring feelings of light and energy, a quick, fine vibration of youthful enthusiasm. Their eyes are bright and open wide, and yet behind them there seems to be an inner-knowing that very few earth children possess (O'Brien, 1989: 114).

The ways in which the spirituality of children manifest itself varies, of course, from child to child. According to Brendan Hyde, in *Children and Spirituality – Searching for Meaning and Connectedness* (2008), more emotional-led forms of spirituality occur almost every day, and are bound up with the child's general inquisitive behaviour, where – in attempting to come to terms with what is happening around them – they will casually ask a number of, what are (to all intents and purposes) quite deep, philosophical questions. However, on another occasion, a certain, more 'receptive', child, may reveal a far deeper spirituality, as they begin to display an affinity with both barely perceptible levels of reality and unreality. Indeed, this is where they claim to be 'perceiving energy around people, hearing voices or perhaps seeing visions', as '[s]ome children are able to tune into these intuitive capacities, and these types of experiences are more common than many believe' (Hyde, 2008: 15). For, one such person who, as a child, was highly 'receptive' to 'hearing voices' and 'seeing visions', was Stephen O'Brien, and it is to his life as a 'spiritual child' – that is, the child as medium – that we now turn.

Adams et al., in *The Spiritual Dimension of Childhood* (2008), note that spiritually attuned children enquire, on a regular basis, about existential matters – such as death and dying – but may also express themselves freely about their interaction with the dead. Indeed, they will often do this in such a precise manner, that such children 'report seeing or having conversations with the deceased person just as they would have done prior to the death' (Adams, et al., 2008: 63). Communication with the deceased – as something that was quite, everyday and normal – was a childhood experience that Stephen O'Brien encountered from an early age, but it was still a phenomena which those around him, especially those already active in public psychic activities, had yet to convince him of with regards their full extent and meaning. For, a 10-year-old Stephen O'Brien, after a night of hearing 'ghostly hands' hammering the front door of his family's small South Wales' terraced house, was told, the following evening, by an elderly neighbour – Mrs King (whom he had befriended, referring to her as 'Gran') – that he would be, as an adult, a medium. Mrs King, herself, was a self-proclaimed spiritualist, often taking part in the 'open circle' at the Spiritualist Church in Oxford Street (Swansea). As evidence of her prophecy that O'Brien would be, as an adult, a fully fledged medium, she – alerting him to his already-ever-present spirit-guide – stated: 'There's a North American Indian behind you, telling me this' (cited in O'Brien, 1989: 13). O'Brien then claims that, amid an out-of-body experience later that night, he sensed the presence of his spirit-guide – only, this time, with female companion, or – to quote O'Brien – 'squaw', alongside. Furthermore, when a little older, and living at another address following a slum clearance programme, O'Brien was now well aware that, at all times, he seemed to be accompanied by 'spirit-people' – insisting that, occasionally, he could even catch a glimpse of them:

> One morning, glancing through the window, I saw a small girl sitting on our garden wall. She wore a party frock and as I idly admired it she suddenly stood up and jumped from the wall. I shot out of my chair, fearful that such a small child would injure herself with the six-foot drop. But before she reached the ground, she vanished. I was quite taken aback because she had looked so very real to me (O'Brien, 1989: 26–7).

However, still unconvinced of his true psychic abilities, he often 'dabbled' in the paranormal, as, when he was 16, O'Brien visited a school friend at home one evening, and, instead, of revising for their forthcoming exams as planned, they engaged in a practice of the occult: the Ouija board. This was to not only initiate a contact with the spirit-world, but was a key moment in his life as an eventual medium. For, eventually in communication with a 'friend' from the 'Other Side', both boys were told, through a message provided by the board's pointer, gradually going from one letter of the alphabet to another, that – in their forthcoming examinations – they would pass six exams each. Knowing that they had not studied hard enough, they rebuked such a message, and, come the exams, O'Brien passed only three exams, whilst his friend had passed only one. As such, they were now convinced that the 'message' was nothing but nonsense:

> But the spirit-people had the last laugh. When Mark and I re-sat the examinations, he obtained a further five and I added three to mine. That meant we both had gained six passes each. SIX – just as my unseen 'friend' had accurately foretold. But how on earth could the Other Side have known? How could *anyone* have

known? Yet, there was no doubt about it, they were right. As strange as it seemed, somehow

they knew my pathway;
they were watching;
they were waiting (O'Brien, 1989: 35–6).

His, pathway, though – despite being watched upon by waiting spirits – was, on an everyday level, similar to that of many young South Wales boys as they entered manhood during the 1970s, where, as a result of high unemployment, O'Brien entered into a succession of poorly paid, menial jobs. Although, shortly after enrolling at the Welsh College of Music and Drama, Cardiff, O'Brien briefly found work as an Assistant Stage-Manager at a theatre. Then, in a bout of automatic writing, he made contact, once again, with his spirit-guide: Declaring himself to be his 'Guardian Spirit', he explained that his name was 'White Owl', and that he had died at the age of 21, and that his 'woman' was 'Running Deer'. He also explained that had a 'white stallion', 'Silver Cloud'. Indeed, 'White Owl' claimed that he had been instructed to 'guide' O'Brien's spirit approximately 100 years before O'Brien had even been born. Thereafter, their relationship developed to the extent that – when O'Brien became a practising medium – 'White Owl entranced me to deliver an inspired address, lasting from 15 to 45 minutes, to the people' (O'Brien, 1989: 83).

Conclusion

Whilst ghostly silent the majority of the time, Ivy Cottage's downstairs occasionally resonated to the deafening cacophony of a multitude of sounds: ITV wrestling, the Stylophone, the piano, and Mario Lanza on the record player. Meanwhile, its front door, hallway, and kitchen offered thresholds into both material and spiritual worlds. At the end of each day, though, it was the place in the home that Peter played in both in the light and in the dark, voicing the lives of both those that were alive and those that were dead. With Ivy Cottage, then, thought – by Peter and his family – to be haunted by a number of spirits, it is worth noting that, according to Peter Ackroyd, in *The English Ghost – Spectres Through Time* (2010), '[n]oises are often the first inklings of a haunting' (Ackroyd, 2010: 9). Indeed, as evidence of a more extensive spirit presence, 'there are the voices' (Ackroyd, 2010: 10). However, we should also remember that 'many spectres cannot speak' (Ackroyd, 2010: 10). Thus, Ivy Cottage's ghostly silence is itself the noise of a haunted house; that is, the spiritual resonance of a haunted home. Yet, we should also acknowledge that despite its soundless quality of its spectral presences, any notion of the spirituality of childhood being merely one of a comforting experience is wrong. For, Adams et al., in *The Spiritual Dimension of Childhood* (2008), in a section that touches upon 'the darker sides of spiritual experience' (2008: 68–70), refer to a particular case study – that of nine-year-old 'Joe', who, one night, glimpsed the ghost of his uncle, and, as a result, was traumatised thereafter. Indeed, Joe – in conversations with both his family and those conducting the research – attempted to justify his sighting of his dead uncle by insisting that his spirit was somehow 'trapped' between 'Heaven' and 'Earth'. Thus, 'Joe's story highlights the potentially frightening or unsettling nature of some spiritual experiences', where, for some children, whilst 'these darker moments will be forgotten … often they can have a lasting effect upon children's thoughts and views' (Adams et al., 2008: 70). Meanwhile, the upstairs of Ivy Cottage – as well as offering portals to other worlds (via mirrors, wardrobes, and the like) – was one not only of electricity-derived 'Hertzian Space', but that of hard, white, enamelled surfaces to be found in the place of solitude that was the bathroom.

Overall, though, as Ivy Cottage was deemed a family home – indeed, Peter's childhood home – to be haunted, it is time to contemplate the fundamental notion of what we mean by 'haunted'. For, in Matthew Manning's *The Strangers – My Conversations With A Ghost* (1978), the medium – in a final analysis of his haunted childhood home, and his psychic communication with the 'ghost', Robert Webbe – contemplates what exactly is our true relationship with those that are dead:

> The most powerful question asked by Webbe at any time was,
> 'Are you a ghoulle of Tomorrow?'
> Although I regard Robert Webbe's story to have a moral to it, maybe it raises a more interesting question:
> Are we already ghosts to somebody else? (Manning, 1978: 125).

Thus, with Peter's family – and Peter himself – engaging with the notion of reincarnation, the skills and practices of mediums, and the belief of spiritualism on a daily basis, as the banal, the mundane, as the everyday, Manning's question should, perhaps, be asked once more. For, in relation to Peter and his family's existence at Ivy Cottage, are they already ghosts to somebody else? If the upstairs of Ivy Cottage was, quite possibly, a space where 'spirit children' roam, does the spirit of Peter's childhood of the 1970s still reside there?

Chapter 3

The Childhood Spaces of the Garden

Frankie painted back porch ... and making fences for back garden (Millie's diary, Tuesday, 30 May 1978).

Sun, but very sad day for us all. Llantwit New Cemetery. House and gardens looked lovely in the sunshine. Frankie would have been very pleased if he could have known that his workmates and his Polish friends, who he had not seen for years, saw his house and gardens looking so lovely (Millie's diary, Saturday, 28 August 1982).

Introduction

As with the previous chapter, this will be a consideration of Peter's childhood home – in particular, the wastelands and gardens of Ivy Cottage – in relation to, not only the cultural texts of the time, the 1970s, but both adult and childhood texts predating Peter's mid-1960s birth (often by many, many decades). This will not only demonstrate both the longevity of such texts, but stress that childhood of a particular decade does not exist in its own cultural bubble: for every decade of childhood is a cumulative reinterpretation of what it is to be a child. Additionally, and as with Chapter 2, we will appreciate that Peter's childhood of this era, the 1970s, took place in a family home within which there were constant reminders of the age of the house. In the case of this chapter, then, it is the wastelands and gardens themselves – through our cultural analysis of them – that will offer a number of reminders as to their age, and, in turn, the age of the house.

Imaginative Play and Other Dimensions

In Chapter 2, I talked at length about Peter's warplay with Airfix soldiers within the 'small spaces' of the house. But, amid the far more 'open spaces' of the Ivy Cottage's wastelands and gardens, Peter's warplay – quite literally – entered another dimension. Journalist, Andrew Collins, in his autobiographical *Where Did It All Go Right? Growing Up Normal in the 70s* (2003), is at pains to elaborate that his childhood warplay was not to be mistakenly conceived as, literally, one-dimensional. When differentiating between his play with Airfix-made 'little soldiers' and 'big soldiers', this is '[a] distinction worth making clear: 'little soldiers' were HO/OO scale, and 'big soldiers' were 1/32 scale' (Collins, 2003: 90). This distinction mattered to the young Peter as well, for whilst Peter's 'little soldiers' suited the smaller spaces of the house, they were often, outside, victims of not only the elements (occasionally being blown over by the 'friendly fire' of a gust of wind) but of the garden itself (especially when going 'AWOL' for ever in the undergrowth). This vulnerable fragility of such 'little soldiers' is in keeping with the perception that their plastic composition enhanced such tendencies. Harry Pearson, in *Achtung Schweinehund! A Boy's Own Story of Imaginary Combat* (2007), gives his reasons for his eventual preference for playing (and, then, 'wargaming' proper) with lead rather than plastic miniature figurines:

> As a boy I loved my Airfix figures. Why, then, did I grow to dislike plastic soldiers so much? … The problem was they were, literally, lightweight. There was a sense of impermanence about anything made of plastic, of built-in obsolescence (Pearson, 2007: 64).

All things considered, then, out in the gardens – and amid the wastelands in particular – 'big soldiers' were, for Peter, the toy of choice (although, still of the plastic sort – as the lead versions were far beyond what was available to him and his meagre pocket money). So, on the residual patch of sand next to the coal shed, 1/32 scale 'Afrika Korps' soldiers faced the 'British 8th Army' in a renewed El Alamein. Where the swathes of gravel (that is, the beach of some distant 'Pacific island') met the banks of nettles (that island's inland 'Jungle') same-scale 'US Marines' faced equally-sized 'Japanese Infantry' in an endless battle for 'Iwo Jima'. Likewise, amid the blossoming flower beds and the neat lawns, isolated 'sticks' of 'British Paratroopers' were 'dropped' to fight entire divisions of 'German Infantry' in a re-enactment of 'Operation Market Garden'.[1] Indeed, in the latter scenario, the 1/32 scale soldiers were scattered (as in the actual battle) far and wide – with, in Peter's imagined version, Ivy Cottage's flower beds and lawns now the vast open fields of a German countryside.

This type of imaginative play is, of course, common within such fertile, outdoor environments of the home and its surroundings. Christopher Day, in *Environment and Children – Passive Lessons from the Everyday Environment* (2007), notes that:

> [a]dults live (mostly) in a world of material facts – 'known' and unchanging. For children, the 'real' world is often servant to an imaginary world. Even single rooms, gardens or behind-the-shed forgotten places can be whole palettes of mood, whole geographies of mountains and jungles, harbours and shops – places to live out fantasy through action (Day, 2007: 4).

Wastelands

Walking along the hall, then, and leaving the house through the back porch, we, like a young Peter, run down the flight of stone steps, and – missing the last

---

1   The botched Allied attempt, in 1944, to quickly take bridges over the Rhine.

few – we jump! Smack! Our breath exhaled with force, we have landed on the bare concrete floor that is in front of the cellar window. Looking around, it's late September, 1970, and Peter is a four-year-old 'dwt'.[2]

A fleeting memory. Are we viewing a house that is for sale? Is this the day we enter our new home? Is this a day or two after we have moved into Ivy Cottage? I'm in the so-called 'garden', and, as an overgrown madness, it is as high as the sky. The actual cobalt blue of the sky is only occasionally glimpsed, along with blinding shafts of sunlight, through the arching, thorn-wielding bramble branches, and the dense, dry clumps of towering, seeding grass. Am I alone? I feel alone. Quick as it came, the memory is gone.

Half-remembered, fragmentary, and short-lived, this very early memory of Peter's (quite possibly one of his first), is remarkably akin to Laurie Lee's that opens his classic autobiographical tale of a country childhood, *Cider With Rosie* (1959). The moment that, like Peter, Lee enters the overgrown surroundings of his family's new home:

> I was set down from the carrier's cart at the age of three; and there with a sense of bewilderment and terror my life in the village began.
>
> The June grass, amongst which I stood, was taller than I was, and I wept. I had never been so close to grass before. It towered above me and all around me, each blade tattooed with tiger-skins of sunlight. It was knife-edged, dark, and a wicked green, thick as a forest and alive with grasshoppers that chirped and chattered and leapt through the air like monkeys (Lee, 2002: 9).

When Peter and his family first moved into Ivy Cottage, all of the land that surrounded the house could best be described as wasteland, as all was overgrown, and strewn with refuse, rubble, and the like. Even the enormous, rectangular, red-bricked warehouse situated next to Ivy Cottage was in danger of being engulfed by this all-consuming wasteland. Initially owned by the Church (above its front entrance, in raised brickwork, was the Cross), it was, for the first couple of years that Peter and his family occupied Ivy Cottage, empty, and nigh-on derelict.[3] Furthermore, the majority of the extensive land to be found behind Ivy Cottage actually belonged to the warehouse plot, and not to that of the house;

---

2   An example of the Welsh-English dialectic hybrid that is Wenglish, 'dwt' refers to 'A little one, especially a little child' (Lewis, 2008: 99).

3   During this time, a flat-capped, overall-wearing man would occasionally be spotted working on the warehouse, repointing walls, repairing the corrugated roof, replacing broken windows, and so on. Eventually, after a number of years, and refurbished proper, it became

for it was only through eventual and prolonged authorised use that the 'back garden' of Ivy Cottage was reclaimed by the house itself.[4] Indeed, this particular mutual agreement of use was brought about by the fact that any meaningful access to that land (that is, by car or van) was impossible, as there was only a narrow concrete path that separated the two properties at their nearest point, and, with that same path continuing around, hugging the warehouse's right-hand side, there was no physical barrier (such as a wall or fence) between that path and the land behind Ivy Cottage. Furthermore, the overgrown nature of all of the lands that surrounded both Peter's family home and the adjacent business meant that (certainly for the first year or so of the occupation of Ivy Cottage) any possible discernible boundaries between the two properties were totally obscured (and, thus, rendered meaningless) by weeds, etc. This, then, was an example of what Richard Mabey termed, in his 1973 ecologically aware, manifesto-like book, the 'unofficial countryside', a 'countryside' of sorts, to be found in towns and cities, where even the cracks in a stretch of concrete would eventually become wild habitats, where 'the labels "urban" and "rural" by which we normally find our bearings in a landscape, just do not apply', and where '[b]uildings and greenery alike are liable at any moment to be levelled, trimmed, landscaped, incinerated, modernised, or just vaguely "redeveloped"' (Mabey, 1974: 12).

Slowly but surely, month by month, year by year, the wastelands that surrounded Ivy Cottage (and the warehouse next door) were cultivated – tamed as it were – bit by bit. So, for the entire time that Peter and his family lived there, the gardens and the wastelands existed alongside each other – to the extent that, only a year or two before they actually moved out, the gardens at Ivy Cottage were to dominate as the wasteland dwindled to a sole triangular-shaped plot at the very bottom of the back garden.

Let us be clear on one thing, though, that any labelling of land seemingly lacking in use as a 'wasteland' is to underestimate its potential usage by a child. That is, it is a wasteland's intrinsic characteristic of apparent 'lack-of-usage' that instils that space of its magnetism as a space of imaginative play – a characteristic that is, of course, often lost on adults. As Robin C. Moore makes explicit, in *Childhood's Domain – Play and Place in Childhood Development* (1986), a wasteland's appeal to a child is all to do with the degrees of 'quality' it adds to that child's sense of place within their imagination:

> We wandered around a piece of undulating, weedy wasteland, part-way through
> a trip around 12-year-old Heather's favourite places in Notting Dale – a central
> London neighbourhood ... This was no wasteland, I began to realise, but a

---

a wholesalers purveying, as the shiny new sign at the front (just below the brickwork crucifix) boasted, 'Toys, Gifts, and Fancy Goods'.

4   I use the term 'reclaimed' as, later on in this chapter, it is explained how, earlier on in Ivy Cottage's history, the land upon which the warehouse was to stand eventually formed part of a much larger gardens that belonged wholly to the house.

peaceful haven ... [as] the more she talked about this fertile land, the more it began to acquire a rich significance invisible to me moments before (Moore, 1986: 2).

Indeed, what Moore realised was that a 'wasteland' – as it appeared no longer to belong to the adult world – was a 'quality' place of play that was now 'owned' by the children that played upon it, as '[t]here was a real sense of childhood possession there, in a place temporarily abandoned by the adult world' (ibid.). Children, then, through play, transform 'wasteland' (land seemingly lacking purpose) into a piece of land with a clear purpose, a 'use' – a space of play.

Ruth M. Arthur's novel *On the Wasteland* (1975), citing the *Shorter Oxford Dictionary*, defines 'wasteland' as 'Land in its natural uncultivated state'. Set amongst a Suffolk marsh known as the Wasteland, it is a tale of Betony Craig, a lonely orphan in her early teens, and not only her emerging relationship with both a boy slightly older than her (Lionel, or 'Linney'), but her dream-like immersion in the area's mysterious Viking past:

> The Wasteland lay across the salt marsh, around the Pool, a great wilderness of emptiness and silence, wild territory lost and forgotten, but for me it held a world of magic.

> From the beginning when I first saw it, long before I had claimed it for my own, I had a strange feeling of belonging there, a queer kind of recognition, an impression half-remembered of having been there before (Arthur 1975: 3).

Betony's summer-long adventure on the Wasteland maintains its magical allure right through until the end of the book:

> Although my dreams were finished, the spell of the Wasteland seemed as potent as ever, its magic as enchanting.

> ... I saw my future spread out like a carpet before me, patterned with bright designs, I saw opportunities, achievements, successes and disappointments in the interesting work ahead of me, and somewhere along the way a husband, a home, and children, the promise of happiness enough to last a lifetime. Here on the Wasteland was where it had all began (Arthur, 1975: 158).

Thus, for Arthur, the 'wasteland' – whilst 'uncultivated' – is not an expanse of land that is devoid of form and content. Far from it – it is a place of high emotion; a romantic vista where romance itself can be found. Whilst the wasteland areas of Ivy Cottage's gardens and its immediate surroundings lacked these aspects of both romanticism and romance, they were, for Peter, places of early contact with the opposite sex.

Having regular liaisons with the (slightly younger) girl from a few doors further along the terrace, our secretive meetings in my garden – like today – involve her smuggling out of her home (having been ripped out of her dad's copies of The Sun*) a number of 'Page Threes'. So, we make our way sneakily down to the sunken, unused, side entrance of the warehouse. There, amongst the broken glass, and hidden by the surrounding weeds, I am being encouraged by the girl to peek at this fleshy contraband. In order to display keenly my yet-to-truly-emerge heterosexuality, I – in emulation of what 'real men' (such as Sid James in the* Carry On *films) did – 'phwoar' incessantly, as my gurning face contorts in a leering manner.*

Wastelands of the 1970s, then, were not only places of intense emotional attachment (as with Arthur's novel), but a place where even children, like Peter, engaged in what Leon Hunt, in *British Low Culture* (1998), terms 'permissive populism'. With specific reference to the '*Sun*-sational 1970s', Hunt details a decade whereby a 'pornification of Britain' took place: phenomena ushered in, in part, by the very first 'Page 3 Girl' (November, 1970). Indeed, Peter's illicit consumption of such low cultural production is reinforced – justified even – through his choice of proletarian comic role model to emulate: Sid James. As James, 'the lusty and resourceful man of the people' (Calcutt, 2000: 120), connected with Peter, through humour, at the level of 'us'. As with the distinction between 'me' (the witty individual or outsider) and 'us' humour (escapist laughter borne out of necessity) in mind, Sid James 'was the *Carry Ons*' most consistent invocation of a more traditional "us"' (Hunt, 1998: 36).

Most of the time, though, Peter ventured into the garden, and the wasteland areas especially, on his own, and for no apparent reason than to occupy his lonely imagination.

Armed with a bread-knife secretly smuggled out of the kitchen draw, I sneak down and out into the back garden. With my 'machete' at the ready, I creep warily down the garden path, past the shirts and pants flapping in the breeze high up on the washing line, towards the fence that Daddy has nailed together, painted Lincoln Green, and erected in order to separate the garden proper from the wasteland beyond. Through the opening that still allows access into the initial, less dense, area of the wasteland (where, of late, our bonfires are held), I approach, across a floor of grey-black ash, the virulently-growing jungle of Japanese Knotweed. Lashing out, from left to right, and right to left, grunting primordially, my machete slices through their hollow stems with ease. After what seems hours, I return home, drenched with their watery discharge, and green with their fibrous chlorophyll.

What is significant here is that Peter, as a boy, wasn't necessarily engaging in imaginary play. He wasn't even consciously attempting to contribute, in any meaningful way, to the proactive clearing of this stretch of wasteland. No, this was purely getting lost in a destructive act for destruction's sake. Yet, more positively, Peter – denied any form of real control over the gardens flowers, shrubs, etc. – felt a certain ownership over the wasteland's weeds. They were his, and he felt he could do with them what he willed. Indeed, Mabey insists that plants that grow in the wild (such as buttercups, daisies, dandelions, ratstail plantains, and so on) 'are part of children's lives precisely because they are weeds, abundant and resilient plants that grow comfortingly and accessibly close to us' (Mabey, 1974: 109).

Yet, the wastelands of Ivy Cottage were to eventually become ordered gardens – and this, more often than not, was as a result of fire, and the burning, by Peter and his family of not only household rubbish, but objects retrieved from the local rubbish dump.

The Rubbish Tip

Clive King's *Stig of the Dump* (1976, first published 1963) was – and still is – a perennially popular book for children, to the extent that it 'had been reprinted 16 times by the late 1970s' (Carpenter and Prichard, 1995: 497). The opening two pages begin with a boy, Barney, on the precipice of a deep chalk-pit, contemplating its creation, its age, and – now – the accumulation of rubbish at its bottom, the 'dump':

> They must have dug and dug for hundreds of years. And then they got tired of digging, or somebody had told them to stop before they dug away all the hill. And now they did not know what to do with this empty hold and they were trying to fill it up again. Anything people didn't want they threw into the bottom of the pit (King, 1976: 8).

Peering down:

> Barney could see strange bits of wreckage among the moss and elder bushes and nettles. Was that the steering wheel of a ship? The tail of an aeroplane? At least there was a real bicycle. Barney felt sure he could make it go if only he could get at it (King, 1976: 8).

Going too close to the edge (as he had been warned not to), the ground gives way, and tumbling downwards, Barney (quite literally) stumbles upon the Stone-Age, grunting Stig amid the dump, who has constructed a home out of the rubbish:

> with bottle-glass windows and a tin-can chimney, and has done all the marvellous things that small boys are sure *they* could do with what you find on rubbish dumps, if only their mean old parents would let them (Townsend, 1987: 246).

Thus, this classic text – that Peter himself read as part of his school curriculum – has acknowledged generations of children's preoccupation with the multitude of places that people (both officially and unofficially) discard their rubbish: dumps and tips. For Peter and his family, the local 'tip' was a site of regular outings.

Out of the front door, and out of the gate; that is the way on to New Road, and to the shops. But, out of the back porch, down the steps, and turning left along the garden path (past the outdoor tap), continuing along the concrete at the front of the warehouse, and, right, down the gravel track that skirts its far side, you find yourself on Old Road. Over to the other side, and crossing the railway lines (through wire fencing along the way), across an access road, and you are into the tip.

The Old Road, and the tip beyond, seemed, then, like an extension of Ivy Cottage's back garden – as, quite simply, that was the way Peter and his father went to, and came back from, the tip. Also, the very fact that Peter and his father accessed the tip in such an illegal way (through wire fencing, over railway tracks) and, even, entered the tip without permission, resulted in this regular joint escapade being something akin to Colin Ward's study of 'unofficial playspaces' as shared by both children and adults in Bute Town, Cardiff. Through twisting alleys, the children mischievously took Ward into a district which the local council had condemned and, as a consequence, seemingly forgotten about. Yet, the boarded-up houses were still populated by 'the inebriates, the junkies and some bewildered homeless people' (Ward, 1978: 41). It was this unauthorised use of this wasteland, by both adults and children in unison, which resulted in it becoming an 'unofficial playspace', where play itself was founded upon this landscape of dumped items – 'a place where anything might be discovered', such as 'decomposed furniture and old gas ovens, timber for bonfires and bricks for improvised buildings' (Ward, 1978: 41).

Having been similar child-adult 'unofficial inhabitants' of the local tip, Peter and his father set about placing items they had 'discovered' upon, back home, a bonfire.

Having carried the heavy copper wiring back from the tip, and still sweating (and our clothes reeking of the tip's detritus), we quickly amass cardboard boxes, old newspapers, bits of wood, and dried lengths of bramble. All piled up at the very bottom of the back garden, and lit at various points with a few tossed Swan Vestas, it soon becomes a teetering, roaring bonfire. Daddy and myself heave on our booty from the tip onto the flames, and, within seconds, the wire's plastic coating starts to blister and melt, turning into flaming drips of molten blues and greens. The bonfire belches acrid black smoke into the grey sky. Mesmerised,

I watch as the wire begins to glow white hot. Staring into the very heart of the fire, I see the flames licking the charcoaled embers as they seem alive in a dance of intense red, yellow, and orange flashes. An hour or so later, with our faces and hands still stinging with the nigh-on unbearable heat, all that is left is smouldering white, grey and black ash. The wire, now dusty and naked, will – by tomorrow – be cool enough to retrieve. The whole garden, our clothes, and even the house stink of the bonfire and the burnt plastic for the rest of the day.

Christopher Day, in *Environment and Children – Passive Lessons from the Everyday Environment* (2007), insists that children are inherently drawn, particularly through their play, to fire. Referring to children as 'natural pyromaniacs', he also warns that, to children especially, '[i]ts drama can be overpoweringly seductive' (Day, 2007: 229). Yet, in a world increasingly 'smokeless', where fire is constantly guarded – even hidden – the child who is not exposed to fire in its natural state is denied the opportunity to develop particular aspects of their imagination, as 'there's something magically transfixing about open fires', where, for children, often engrossed for hours, 'whole stories unfold in flame pictures' (Day, 2007: 230). Indeed, fundamental to the child's imaginative engagement with fire is as a result of its almost magical ability to transform substances, 'through burning, melting and smelting' (Day, 2007: 230). And, for Day, the child's witnessing of a substance being transformed through fire is a key lesson in life, where a child is taught 'that nothing is permanently bound by its composition and form' (Day, 2007: 230). Furthermore, Day insists that such 'combustion-transformation processes' are so central to life – the lives of children in particular – that failing to appreciate fire and its effects leads to 'intellectual – not to mention soul – impoverishment' (Day, 2007: 230). Thus, in Peter's memory, there is that moment of epiphany detectable, a discernible moment of genuine mental enrichment, when he is watching hypnotically the transformative effects of his and his father's bonfire – namely, when the plastic that coats the wires begins to melt.

Furthermore, it was actually through the constant lighting of bonfires that the garden at Ivy Cottage, plot by plot, over a number of years, was cleared and transformed. Thus, the garden arose, quite literally like a phoenix from the ashes, as a result of 'combustion-transformation processes'. Furthermore, this was no Guy Fawkes' Night extravaganza. This was no middle-class excuse to roast chestnuts and the like. This bonfire was out of necessity. Peter's father, Frank, had to supplement his meagre blue-collar wage somehow. Collecting scrap metal, ounce by ounce, pound by pound, until it became nearly a hundredweight (and then carrying it all, in a canvas sack, over his shoulder, to the scrap metal merchant), was the way in which he ensured that – for him and his family – Christmas was one of the few times of the year when scrimping and saving wasn't an issue. Thus, and the very opposite of 'mean' parents not allowing their children to visit dumps and bringing back rubbish, for Peter and his family going to the tip was an essential element of daily life in a decade of particular hardships that was the 1970s.

Self-Sufficiency

The Wombles (BBC) was 'one of the most enduring children's animations of the 1970s' (Lewis, 2006: 325). Not only broadcast in the form of two highly-popular television series (1973, 1975) and a feature-length film (*Wombling Free*, 1977), these diminutive, pointy-nosed, furry creatures released a string of singles and albums between 1973 and 1977 (with their 1974 album *Remember You're A Womble* spending 31 weeks in the UK album charts), and found themselves marketed by a plethora of associated merchandise (totalling 150 licensed products). No doubt, then, that '*The Wombles* was an intrinsic part of 1970s British culture' (Johnston, 2010: 163). Inhabiting a burrow below Wimbledon Common, they steadfastly occupied their time cleaning up the litter left on the common by its human visitors and, in doing so (and according to the lyrics of the show's theme tune), 'making good use of the things that we find, things that the everyday folk leave behind' (cited in Turner, 2008: 55). Indeed, Elisabeth Beresford's original novels underline this ecologically focused trait of the Wombles further, as here is an extract from *The Wombles at Work* (first published 1973), with Tobermory's attitude towards refuse:

> [F]or like all the Wombles he can't abide waste and the way in which Human Beings throw away, and leave lying about, so much litter constantly amazes him.

> But then it astonishes all the Wombles, for they are the tidiest and the most careful creatures in the world and one of their favourite sayings is, 'What a human being throws away in a *day* a Womble can live on for a *month!*' While Great Uncle Bulgaria, over a sip of nettle juice syrup, has often said:

> 'If it wasn't for us Wombles clearing up all the mess that the Human Beings leave behind them, the world would be covered in rubbish, rats, flies, and pollution and all kinds of illnesses by now. It's an absolute disgrace the way they dump their litter!' (Beresford, 1976: 12).

Prioritising family and community above all else, they are a mainly fraternalistic grouping (as the lone female Womble is the kitchen-bound French maid, Madame Cholet), and are led by Great Uncle Bulgaria, a 'tottering patriarch in a tartan hat' (Lewis, 2006: 325). The *Wombles* are (simultaneously) conservative yet liberal, nostalgic but progressive – but, ultimately, adopting a 'global outlook akin to the 1960s or 1970s' (Johnston, 2010: 163). So, all of this would tend to link *The Wombles* with not only the Keep Britain Tidy campaign of the time, but – as they also display an ethos of hard work at a time of unemployment and strikes, and grow their own food when self-sufficiency was all the rage – their underground existence placed them alongside the communal attitudes to living that were to be found within Britain's alternative 'underground' of the time: Thus, '*The Wombles*' characters are a self-sufficient and tight knit community that exists slightly outside the bounds of normal (human) society' (Johnston, 2010: 154).

Of course, attempts to live beyond the means of a 'normal' society increasingly unable to sustain itself – especially through the adoption (either wholly or partial) of a self-sufficient lifestyle – was a characteristic trait of the 1970s as promoted through such alternative lifestyle guides as John Seymour's *The Complete Book of Self-Sufficiency* (1976). Indeed, even sitcom, with *The Good Life* (BBC, 1975–1978), attempted to both parody and promote such a radical societal shift. Sympathetically depicting the comic escapades of Tom and Barbara Good in their efforts to embrace 'the good life' of self-sufficiency in Surbiton, Surrey, it is John Esmonde and Bob Larbey's novel (1977, first published 1976) that pinpoints the moment at which 'growing your own' equates the break away from the 'rat race'.

In conversation, Tom and Barbara attempt to tackle their 'vague malaise' and incorporate into their lives 'the elusive "It"' – essentially, Tom turning 40, and him being stuck in a dead-end job at the drawing office at 'J.J.M. Ltd'. Indeed, Barbara asks:

> 'You want to sell up and buy a small-holding in the country to do this?'
> 'No', was his definite answer. 'This isn't meant to be the full going back to nature bit. Anyway, we love this house too much to get rid of it'.
> 'Self-sufficiency in Surbiton?'.
> 'Yes. I know it'll make the road look a bit unusual, but-' (Esmonde and Larby, 1977: 18)

> Tom flung his arms around her. He was not 40 any more – he was no age at all. He was happy (Esmonde and Larby, 1977: 20).

> They danced happily on, shouting 'Free, free!' to the night sky of Surbiton (Esmonde and Larby, 1977: 21).

Of course, such full-on, full-time self-sufficiency was only a dream for many. Although, its values did trickle down to many a dissatisfied white- and blue-collar worker and their families. Thus, at Ivy Cottage, Peter and his family – out of necessity, really, rather than any commitment to a 'personal is political' stance in support of 'green issues' – gave over almost their entire back garden to 'growing your own'. Soon potatoes, carrots, cabbage, etc., were being dug up. Across the glorious summers of 1976 and 1977 especially, bumper crops of sprawling strawberries lined the garden path that, following the direction of the washing line, led down from the house to the distant, remaining patch of wasteland beyond the fence. Moreover, this partial immersion in self-sufficiency at Ivy Cottage was something in which all the family, and Peter in particular, were actively encouraged to participate in. This holistic, all-in-this-together approach is, of course, integral to such a communal way of life that is self-sufficiency, where children are treated – and, as a result view themselves – on par with adults. For, as John and Sally Seymour's daughter, Anne Sears, reflects:

> When we were children we joined in with all the daily activities which were part of the life of a self-sufficient family. We had to look after the animals, milk the cow, and help to make butter and cheese. We worked as hard as the adults on the land, with sheep shearing, hay making and all the other harvesting and preserving activities (Sears, cited in Seymour, 2007: 8).

Furthermore, with Peter being included within his family's attempt to 'grow their own' in the mid-1970s, he found himself within, what Catherine Burke (2005) terms, an 'edible landscape' where the beneficial qualities of non-processed food are learnt. Peter's experience as a child is, of course, now at odds with the majority of today's children who 'are widely considered to be out of touch with the origins of the food they consume and have little awareness of the nutritional value of what they eat' (Burke, 2005: 246).

Eventually, Peter's mother would turn her hand to home-made food and drink all derived from their collective toil in the garden – with elderflower and elderberry wine particular family favourites. Indeed, in the kitchen, on top of the fridge-freezer, was perhaps *the* spot where the gentle plopping fermentation of two semi-cloudy demi-john's that encapsulated Peter's family's embrace of a slightly-inebriated 'good life' in Skewen.

Yet, such a 'good life' for the Seymours had not always been 'days of wine and roses', as their tentative, early engagement with this lifestyle, in a Suffolk cottage ('Broom') during the mid-1950s, was trying to say the least, where '[e]verything was hard work, a toil, a culture shock' (Peacock, 2005: 89), and the day-to-day drudgery of self-sufficiency was, quite often, a debilitating and demoralising experience:

> But life did begin to wear them down. If on Monday you walk a round trip of three miles to get your milk, it might be an adventure. If, three weeks later you are still having to walk that far each day for milk I bet it would be just about driving you mad! It certainly did John (Peacock, 2005: 92).

And, yes, similar testing aspects of self-sufficiency are aligned to Peter's memories of his family's efforts to sustain even their partial embrace of the lifestyle – often fighting a losing battle with the elements in the process.

––––––––––––––––––

It shouldn't have come as a surprise at all, for this storm had been long forecast. All morning we watch from the kitchen window as the winds gradually pick up, and the rain slowly comes in. But, then, all of a sudden, it hits. The garden begins to be battered. The trees sway, and the plants rattle back and forth. The grey sky and the hoed black earth become one in a swirling maelstrom. At the centre of all of this, is our plastic greenhouse. A flimsy aluminium structure, with clear polyurethane all around, it grips the ground with a bare number of metal pegs. It shakes and shakes and shakes. Then, suddenly, as the wind inflates it, it begins to shift, lifting itself off the ground, and across the garden. With both of us, by now, staring in disbelief, my mother runs out of the kitchen, along the hall, through the porch, and down the steps, in an effort to save the fragile plants within, darts for the now doomed greenhouse. Having struggled to unzip the entrance in the lashing rain, my mother is now inside, and desperately attempting to hold the structure down as it begins to disintegrate around her. Running out into the garden myself, I am in time to see what is left of it lift itself free of the earth, and, at a scarily increasing pace – with my mother still inside, her feet now wriggling in mid-air – being propelled across the garden by the merciless gale. Terrified, we shout, in unison, 'Woah! Woah! Woah!' as the winds, in a moment of triumph, wrench the tattered structure above and away from my struggling mother. Finally, like some form of prefabricated convulsion, it soars ever upwards, twisting and turning, only to come crashing down into the depths of the wasteland at the foot of the trees in the distance.

Ivy

Ivy Cottage was aptly named. Whilst, at the time that Peter and his family lived there, the ivy that once enveloped it completely had long been cut down, photographic evidence of its existence still remains. For, in Stephen Absalom and Robert King's *Around Neath* (2005), the version of Ivy Cottage that is covered, in its entirety, in this dense, green shroud is still to be seen (if only partially). As one of the book's black-and-white, fading photographs 'shows the Neath Corporation gas tram, close to the Terminus Hotel, Neath Abbey' (Absalom and King, 2005: 86). With the tram virtually filling the shot, and both the driver and conductor, at its shadowy rear, glowering into the bright daylight and the lens, Ivy Cottage is just about visible as a narrow strip of ivy-clad front wall on the far right-hand edge of the photograph.[5]

Yet, even when Peter and his family were residents of Ivy Cottage, ivy was still to be found in abundance all over the garden and its surrounding wastelands: For, ivy dizzily climbed the vast wall of the warehouse (this was at its far end, where the ivy, had, at the base of the wall, already meshed itself with the sprawling vegetation that covered the triangular-shaped wasteland at the very bottom of the garden). The ivy had also parasitically encroached upon the trunks of the trees that lined the bottom (Old Road end) and the side (the (lower) Terminus Road end) of the garden.

---

5   This picture can be dated – albeit rather vaguely – as taken sometime between 1897 and 1920, as gas trams, purchased from the Blackpool Corporation, were in service with the Neath Corporation during that period only (Absalom and King, 2005: 86).

Such a tendency for the wastelands of Ivy Cottage to encroach constantly upon its cultivated areas was tempered by Peter's family's maintenance of the garden's most suburbanly ordered elements – especially their sculpting of the many privet and box hedges that both defined and intersected the garden's plots and lawns. For Paul Barker, in *The Freedoms of Suburbia* (2009), the term suburbia itself equates 'sunrise garden gates and privet, privet, privet' (Barker 2009: 10). Thus, in many respects, Ivy Cottage asserted itself, at this time, as the epitome of a 1970s suburban garden through its proud display of squarely-trimmed hedges. Furthermore, these hedges provided Peter, his family, and Ivy Cottage itself, with a buffer of privacy from prying eyes from the pavement, New Road, and the neighbourhood beyond. Yet, it was a privacy that simultaneously denied and encouraged intrusive looks from passers by, for '[i]n suburbia, decisions about the hedge matter most: not merely privacy, but the right sort of privacy' as '[t]his is the garden as seen by the public and the neighbours' (Barker, 2009: 155).

Topiary

The Brotherhood of Ruralists (Sir Peter Blake being a one-time founding member), 'a group of seven British artists who had expressed a similar feeling for nature, realism and the past' (Rudd, 2003: 64), optimistically declared their loose manifesto as an artistic collective over dinner on 21 March 1975, and, thus, set about making a united stand against both the vortex-like nature of London as artistic capital of Britain, and the increasingly abstract nature of contemporary art. Sharing a passion for Elgar, Blake, Palmer, Wordsworth and the nineteenth-century Pre-Raphaelites, they rejected life in the metropolis and, having re-located to various parts of the West Country (thus, becoming 'ruralists'), they set about producing and self-promoting their highly stylised versions of Arcadia through a process of semi-communal living, co-operative creativity and self-protectionist exhibitions.[6] Typical of their output is, perhaps most famously, David Inshaw's *The Badminton Game* (1972–1973) which adorns the cover of *The Penguin Book of Modern British Short Stories* (Bradbury, 1988). Indeed, *The Badminton Game* (painted, admittedly, prior to the actual formation of the Brotherhood) displays many of the characteristics of the collected works of the Ruralists. Hyper-real in its detail, it depicts two longhaired, pale young women (possibly teenage girls), wearing almost identical burgundy-coloured dresses. They are totally engrossed in their game which takes place within a rather surreal self-contained world

---

6 For a full (retrospective) account of The Brotherhood of Ruralists, see: Anderson et al. (2008); Arnold (2003); Martin (ed.) 1991; Moore et al. (n.d.); Moore (2007); and Usherwood (August 2004). For more contemporaneous accounts, see: Moynahan (3 October 1976); Neve (4 October 1984); Odgers (23 April 1981); Usherwood (1981, June 1981, and October 1984). See also, John Read's 'The Lively Arts "Summer with the Brotherhood"' (broadcast 15 January 1978, BBC2).

that seems to consist of an English stately home (that manages to dominate the painting) and its immediate surroundings of lush, green lawns, shrubs and trees. Yet the painting – despite its dynamic content (informal play/exercise; breathtaking flora) – exudes both a dream-like claustrophobic stillness and a pubescent feminine purity. The Ruralists' artistic portrayal of young femininity often blurred the boundaries between pre-pubescent childhood innocence and the awakening of female sexuality. As such, the most significant feature of the Ruralists' work is its eroticism, whereby young women are placed dreamily, and seductively, within landscape settings.

Inshaw's *The Badminton Game*, meanwhile, with its slightly disturbing feminine presence, comes across, due to its oddly static content, 'as if this were some sort of ghostly coloured photograph' (Humphreys, 1990: 30). Furthermore, with *The Badminton Game*, women are not merely passive participants in a compositional landscape, they are, instead, distinctly sinister silent sentinels. Thus, the painting captivates us with its spatial intensity, that offers both geographical scope and suffocating claustrophobia. Yet it also offers momentary relief through the sensuous stillness of movement of its two gracefully feminine central figures. For Inshaw himself:

> [t]he moment, with the shuttlecock poised in mid-flight and the two young women held in statuesque poses, is a repository for many thoughts and moments, 'happy thoughts as well as sad, full of waking dreams and erotic fancies' (Inshaw, cited in Humphreys, 1990: 30).

Indeed, David Inshaw recently admitted that he views landscape as an inherently feminine, highly-sexualised environment: 'Landscape for me has always been a sensual experience … It's soft, curvy and round – it has a lot of feminine attributes' (David Inshaw, bbc.co.uk, 'Wiltshire – A Sense Of Place').

Against this cultural canvas of Ruralist art of the 1970s – where trees and topiary take on vital symbolism – we will now consider such artistic renderings of the garden within a particularly curious example of children's animated TV of the time, *Crystal Tipps and Alistair* (1972). Often referred to – in a knowing, post-Hippie manner – as 'Crystal trips with Alistair' (Lewis, 2006: 84), this is an unsettling piece of children's television that is not only 'of its time' but '[f]lower power, in a very literal sense' (Lewis, 2006: 84). The blue-haired, mini-skirted, ever-so-slightly spaced-out young girl of the title, Crystal Tipps, lives alone (well, alone apart from her faithful companion, Alistair the dog) in an ornate cottage that exudes Middle-English tweeness. Despite being a children's text, such a hyper-real version of Englishness was clearly in keeping with strikingly similar, and equally disquieting, painterly versions offered by the Brotherhood of Ruralists – Inshaw's meticulous depictions of red brick work, trees and sculptured shrubs as the 'uncanny English garden' especially. Taken together, these unsettling versions of the English garden were very much in tune with a society in which many suburban gardens were also decidedly odd in their homely-yet-unhomely conservative tweeness. As the celebrity gardener Joe Swift comments, the 1970s garden was characterised by such conservative tweeness:

> In those days, the 1970s, everybody's garden was unbelievably traditional. There was a lawn, cottage-style plants and traditional climbers around the outside. I remember thinking it was a bit twee and dull (cited in Murphy, 2 April 2011: 82).[7]

Yet, whilst reflecting the twee and the traditional, *Crystal Tipps and Alistair* is also a prime example of the psychedelic style of animation that seemed to accompany the heralding in of colour television into British homes. Thus, *Crystal Tipps and Alistair* merged retina-burning colour with fragmented collage realism to bring about, for the children watching, a *heimlich*-yet-*unheimlich* version of the English cottage and its garden.[8] For, the gentle antics of both Crystal and Alistair begin with a panned view of their home (again, a suburban idyll of a red-bricked cottage) supported on either side by walled gardens, and fronted with neat lawns, straight paths, orderly trees, and sculptured shrubs. Indeed, the never-ending maintenance of this perfect cottage garden is a central theme of many of the series' episodes. For example, in 'Sowing Seeds' (Episode 9), the multi-coloured 'Birdie' brings along the rain clouds, whilst the 'Butterfly' brings sunshine. All, of course, facilitates the germination of Crystal Tipps' newly-planted seeds and the (eventual) growing of them into mature plants. Yet, eventually (and quite crucial to this odd, and, in reality, far-from-idyllic version of the English garden), the dark side of nature materialises in the form of seed-eating, black crows.

In 'Gardening' (Episode 29), Alistair's attempt at sleeping in a hammock fastened between two trees is thwarted by Crystal Tipps' noisy use of a petrol mower. Indeed, the entire episode sees them busy themselves around the garden using various implements such as shears, hose, hoe, etc. Furthermore, the gardening theme is finally pursued in 'Topiary' (Episode 49), where the blazing sun (followed by menacing, dark rain clouds, and yet more sun), results in the garden's plants growing uncontrollably; to the extent that, eventually, they cover the house. So, with Alistair sweeping up the cuttings, Crystal Tipps – armed with the shears – enters into a frenzy of topiary. Indeed, producing green doppelgangers of Alistair and Birdie, the latter comes alive in an uncanny display of aerobatic foliage.

---

7   Entitled 'All about my mother', this article in the *Guardian Weekend* colour supplement (Saturday, 2 April 2011), in interviewing three celebrity gardeners and their mothers, illustrates how gardening knowledge was passed down (or, indeed, ignored) from one generation to the next via the familial maternal.

8   Another typical example is *The Magic Ball* (BBC, 1971). As a post-psychedelic form of childhood *Heimlich*-yet-*Unheimlich*, this series is discussed proper in Chapter 4.

Trees and Dwelling

Whilst Ivy once overgrew the entire house, and privet and box were being kept constantly in check, it was trees that dominated the garden majestically during the years that Peter and his family were at Ivy Cottage. The trees of Ivy Cottage's garden, by their very existence, defined both the garden and the house as places. As the interwoven relationship between trees and notions of place are multiple and varied, whereby '[t]rees can construct places and vice versa' as 'their size, rich materiality, their interconnectivity, their longevity, their life cycles and seasonal cycles all offer qualities which are readily and vividly drawn into the concepts of place' (Jones and Cloke, 2002: 86).

There is yet another fading photograph of Peter (Figure 3.1) within which, on this occasion, he is dressed up as a cowboy, standing alongside a sprouting fir tree. The fir tree, grown from a cutting (a cutting taken, by his brother and father, from a tree near Jersey Marine sands), barely comes up to his sheriff-badged chest. A few years later, there is another photograph of Peter (Figure 3.2) in his comprehensive school uniform. With the late afternoon sun bleaching this snapshot, Peter, grinning rather gormlessly for the camera, has his back against the fir tree – which, by now, is as tall as he. These two photographs, taken together, reinforce the role of trees amid our sense of dwelling in such a place as the garden

Figure 3.1   Peter, the cowboy, alongside the sprouting fir tree, Ivy Cottage
Source: Author's own collection.

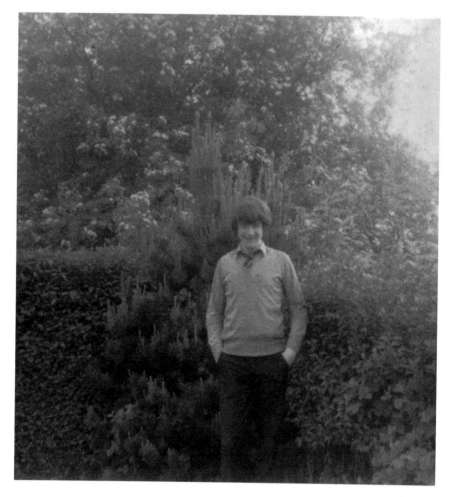

Figure 3.2   Peter, dressed in his comprehensive school uniform – The fir tree is now as tall as he is

Source: Author's own collection.

of our childhood home. Quite fundamentally, in such a place '[d]welling suggests a perspective which is about *being in the landscape*, about moving through it, in all the (perhaps) repeating yet various circumstances of everyday life' (Jones and Cloke, 2002: 140). Yet, dwelling in such a familiar, 'everyday' landscape does not equate to a predictability of vista, as 'it will often be unreadable from any one given position, and your orientation may be constantly or frequently, even habitually, shifting' (ibid.). Thus, as evidenced in these two photographs – taken just a few years apart – the fir tree especially presents itself as the focal point of

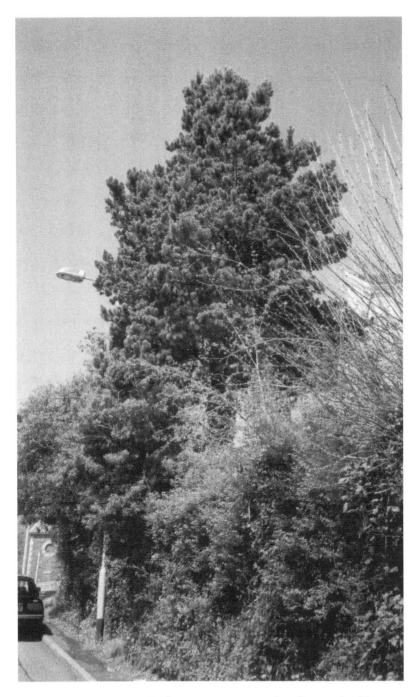

Figure 3.3   In 2005, and the fir tree towers over Ivy Cottage itself
Source: Author's own collection.

Figure 3.4   Winter – Peter, in his parka, in front of some of the trees of Ivy Cottage

Source: Author's own collection.

the familiar, yet constantly 'shifting', landscape of dwelling. It is present in both photographs, and it grows as Peter grows.[9]

Many years later, at the height of summer 2005, Peter returns to St. John's Terrace. Approaching Ivy Cottage from Old Road, and coming up (lower) Terminus Road, he photographs that same fir tree (Figure 3.3). This time, piercing the cobalt-blue sky, it is taller than Ivy Cottage itself. Then, just a few years later, Peter once again returns, and, now, to his dismay, the fir tree has been chopped

---

9   More contemporaneously, such a notion of a child growing up alongside the growth of a tree situated next to the family home is also the theme of 'To Build a Home', the opening track of The Cinematic Orchestra's 2007 album *Ma Fleur*.

to a dying (or already dead?) stump. Indeed, the garden of Ivy Cottage itself has been built upon: with newly erected houses and developments, having already swallowed up the garden, are seemingly about to gorge themselves upon the house itself. Jones and Cloke (2002), referring to the work of David Ley (1995), and the felling of two sequoias in a garden of a house in upper-middle-class suburb of Vancouver, commenting upon both the content and tone of a resultant protest letter, note that 'these trees, as such potent material presences, soaked up the complex social constructions of this place – for some people – and thus became key place markers', yet, '[w]hen felled, by others who did not share or care about such associations, it is as if the place itself is being unwoven' (Jones and Cloke, 2002: 93). Thus, upon visiting Ivy Cottage, and seeing the fir cut down (and over-development of what was once the garden), Peter felt as if Ivy Cottage, and his memory of it – which, together, amount to his sense of childhood place – had been 'unwoven'.

Although, the dead tree was also something which defined Ivy Cottage as a place, as, at the very bottom of the garden – standing resolutely as a stark silhouette in front of the views over the River Neath, Britton Ferry, and the hills further on – was a dead Elm, a recent victim of Dutch Elm Disease. Death and the English Elm are, historically, interwoven, as the tree produced wood of such durable nature that is was the wood of choice 'for furniture, floorboards and coffins' (Sterry, 2007: 182). Of course, a significant aspect of all trees – seen all year around, but far more visible once the leaves are shed – is lacking in life, and it lacks life due to its vital role in life preservation: bark. For, according to the Puffin *Trees in Britain* (n.d.) '[t]his bark is 'dead' skin but gives protection to the new skin forming underneath' (Badmin, n.d.).

If we consider the photograph of Peter, parka-clad, in the depths of a snowy mid-winter (Figure 3.4), the bare trees that line his garden are more than a mere backdrop of branches; instead, they seem to nestle his younger self. Indeed, as Roger Deakin, in *Wildwood – A Journey Through Trees* (2007) reminds us, trees – and woods more generally – are 'the guardians of our dreams of greenwood liberty, of our wildwood, feral, childhood selves' (Deakin, 2007: xii). Thus, the trees that surround Peter are, quite literally, 'guarding' his childhood self. Fundamentally, though, trees serve to raise the terrestrial plane so that it is in touch with the wild blue yonder and all that is above and beyond: 'Trees have the capacity to rise to the heavens and to connect us to the sky' (ibid.).

Shadows and Walking

Suburbia, according to Paul Barker (2009), is seemingly lacking in any form of visual coherence – especially when viewed from an elevated perspective:

> Most forms of suburbia create no special aesthetic pattern, seen from the air. They have a randomness you find in nature, rather than in art. Their main

attraction, from that high angle, is their greenery: all those garden and trees (Barker, 2009: 212).

Any attempt to view suburbia from the air is to engage in the form of geology-fixated historiography that is 'aerial archaeology'. 'Aerial archaeology' was pioneered by Alexander Keiller and Osbert Crawford in 1924, who, flying over Berkshire, Dorset, Hampshire, Somerset and Wiltshire, photographed and catalogued the landscapes below, eventually publishing all as *Wessex from the Air* (1928). Such aerial photography becomes an archaeology from the air as it makes visible vast ancient indents in the landscape – what Kitty Hauser (2007) terms 'shadow sites' – and, in doing so, it makes available 'an unknown country'.

Admittedly, not on any 'vast' scale – in fact, as its opposite, at the level of the 'intimate' – even Ivy Cottage's gardens, in certain respects, can be understood as 'shadow sites' – in particular, the many lawns that, when Peter and his family lived there, surrounded the house. 'Shadow sites' have a predilection for revealing themselves very rarely, and only then when the elevated angle of view is in harmony with both a complementary and adequate light source and suitable conditions of soil and flora – thus, the ability to discern such 'shadow sites' 'is contingent upon the time of day and even the time of year' (Hauser, 2007: 165). Generally, 'shadow sites' are most visible in low sun (hence, as they cast their longest shadows), and as a result of contrasting soil colour – and the slight varying shade of crop (even grass) growing upon that soil – as a result of cultivation or building having taken place in the past. Indeed, it is rainfall upon such a site – or, rather, the lack of it – that, eventually, will exacerbate such markings in the relief of these 'shadow sites', for:

> [w]here crops are stunted because of subterranean remains, during a drought they will dry out more quickly than the surrounding crops, and will thus draw pale lines on the surface of the land (Hauser, 2007: 170).

Just a few years ago, Peter purchased a bound volume entitled *My House History – The Historical Researcher's Map Portfolio*, which, offering a 'mapped history of 19 St. Johns Terrace' (Ivy Cottage) from 1854 until 2006, contains 'historical maps and [a] recent aerial photograph specially centred on your house'. Whilst the 'aerial photograph' very much reveals Ivy Cottage, and its immediate neighbourhood, as a (mainly) green, leafy, tree-smattered suburban sprawl of gardens and minor roads with, yes, 'no special aesthetic pattern', it is the enclosed '25 inches to 1 mile' Ordnance Survey 'County Series' maps that offer revealing insights into the history of Ivy Cottage – its gardens especially. Indeed, the 'reading' of such maps is, according to the Ladybird book *Understanding Maps* (1967), akin to the reading of a history of the area mapped, as:

> [o]nce you have become familiar with the various symbols and devices used in these Ordnance Survey maps, you can pick up a map of any part of the country and read it as you would the page of a book (Scott, 1967: 12).

The first map, then, from '1876' shows (especially when compared to the recent aerial photograph) Ivy Cottage amid a far more rural (rather than suburban) setting, with an extensive formal grounds (its formality defined by several paths that dissect these grounds – more on this later) and a number of attached extensions and detached outhouses. Indeed, upon examining the later same-scale maps included, one particular outhouse (a WC?), whilst all others gradually disappear, remains steadfastly until, come the map dated '1940', that too vanishes. Yet, of course, it fails to vanish completely. During the parched summer of 1976 that particular outhouse – demolished many years before – was to make itself visible once more, however fleetingly, as a 'shadow site'.

Mid-afternoon, and the searing heat thickens the air. Stepping out of the porch, the near white sunlight dazzles me. Standing on the top stone step, I – through squinting eyes – survey the garden from this heightened vantage point, and, in particular, the pitiful, parched excuse of a lawn ahead and below. Thinking that my eyes are playing tricks with me in such blinding light, I squint even more in an effort to concentrate my vision. No, they are really there. Feint straight lines – just the merest of a shade of lighter dried grass – are there. Just three sides of a square (the missing side presumably beneath the bushes that mark the side edge of the garden, with the steep drop down to the side road below beyond), it is most definitely there.

The 'it' that Peter perceived, was a barely detectable impression in the grass – Ivy Cottage's 'shadow site'. Indeed, this 'shadow site' betrayed the existence of – to Peter's eyes, in that harsh sunlight – just-about-buried foundations, the remains of a small building, of an out-house that no longer existed. Thus, at that moment, Peter began to appreciate that, indeed, 'the past is all around us'; sometimes visible, most of the time not.

The 'shadow site' of the levelled, and long gone, out-house, where its foundations were visible as an 'impression' below the grass, only now barely discernable as a result of the scorching of the earth during the heatwave of the century.

As with the 'aerial photograph', another version of Ivy Cottage 'from the air' is the Ordnance Survey view, and that changing view, over time, provides an 'overview' (quite literally) of how Ivy Cottage's gardens have morphed across the decades – indeed, over the centuries even. Thus, we return, now, to the '1876' map, and its depiction of Ivy Cottage's gardens at their most extensive (as there is, of course, no warehouse), with their criss-crossing network of paths. Indeed, with each path denoted as parallel broken lines, they form a geometric pattern that both skirt the edge of the gardens and dissect their expanse into orderly squares and rectangles. Bearing in mind that 'the art of map reading can be highly developed and a considerable knowledge gained of the nature of the country and life of its inhabitants' (Lockey, 1968: 15), a 'reading' of the '1876' map suggests that the 'life' of the 'inhabitants' of Ivy Cottage at that time revolved around their gardens and their walking of the paths that both surrounded and cut across them.

Come the late 1600s paths – or, rather, walks – had become vital elements of gardens and the appreciation of gardens. Suggesting the importance of walking within the confines of a garden, a 'walk' during this period referred to a path that was broad enough for two people to walk side by side one another – indeed, facilitating an ability to talk, such a 'walk' could, in turn, 'be called a conversational route' (Solnit, 2002: 88). Then, come the early eighteenth century – especially amid the English estates – the walk became something which, quite literally, revolved around aesthetic considerations that shunned a pure static vantage point in favour of a point of view based upon a leisurely, circumvention of the grounds, with such a 'circuit' becoming the socially acceptable way in which gardens and parks were viewed for the rest of that century. Indeed, by the late 1700s, with strict etiquette resulting in an enforced occupation of a country house's rooms by both residents and visitors in order to pass the time of day, come the afternoon, or early evening, 'the garden walk provided relief from the group, either in solitude or in tête-à-têtes' (Solnit, 2002: 99). Similarly, the gardens of Ivy Cottage – indeed, the detached nature of the house itself – facilitated such familial 'tête-à-têtes', as Peter's father – of a long summer evening with him – used to often joke that they should take a stroll around 'the grounds'.

Early evening, and I'm upstairs in my bedroom. The cooling four walls soothe me further as the day's intense summer heat begins to subside. 'Peter-o! Peter-o!' my father calls from the garden. 'Come out, and let's walk around 'the grounds'' he pleads, as I hear him laughing hoarsely. So, down and out, I am at his side and, with my occasional admiring glances up at him, we begin to both slowly amble along the pathway that circles our house. 'Round and 'round we go, chatting about everything but nothing in particular (his work, my schooling, the beauty of the flowers and shrubs that we pass). As we do so, the sun lowers ever further, and the light gradually dims. Then, as the Evening Star begins to twinkle bright, I look up at my father, and notice that his features are now in the process of being obscured by the encroaching twilight, whilst his voice becomes a comforting, disembodied drone high above me. A Polish-heavy Welsh accent, it is a drone that, I'm sure, will stay with me year after year after year. For it is a drone, I'm positive, that will remind me forever of these walks around our home, our garden, such summer evenings, as father and son.

Peter's memory of his father's voice taking on consoling-yet-surreal tones resonates with Ray Bradbury's fantastical evocation of a childhood summer *Dandelion Wine* (1975, first published 1957). Essentially semi-autobiographical, Bradbury's novel tells an often strange tale of a 12-year-old boy, Douglas

Spalding, and his experiencing of the rather uncanny Green Town, Illinois in the year of 1928. With many chapters previously published as short stories, it is Chapter 7 – previously known as 'Season of Sitting' – which draws parallels with Peter's memory of summer nights spent walking and talking with his father. Concerned with one of Douglas' family's summer rituals, the setting up of a hammock on the porch as a prelude to evening time conversation, the chapter makes explicit the comforting nature of the drone of the adults' voices (in particular, those of his father and grandfather), and, in doing so, moves from a relatively straight-forward realistic account to a more sensory-loaded dreamlike one – eventually concluding with a fantasy-tinged suggestion that the voices of the adults collectively drift on into the future:

> Douglas sprawled back on the dry porch planks, completely contented and reassured by these voices, which would speak on through eternity, flow in a stream of murmurings over his body, over his closed eyelids, into his drowsy ears, for all time (Bradbury, 1975: 22).

For, finally, 'the voices moved on into the coming years' (Bradbury, 1975: 23). Thus, in many respects, Peter – like Douglas Spalding, and his childhood home, and his family's conversations – made the connection with both Ivy Cottage's and his family's intertwined pasts/presents/futures through his father's voice becoming more than a sonic backdrop to their walk around the house.

Detached Politeness

Come the early years of the twentieth century:

> the affinity between the detached suburban house and its garden, within a low-density Arcadian landscaped setting, was affirmed by the middle-class garden- and romantic-suburbs in England and the United States (Clapson, 2003: 68).

Ivy Cottage was, by this time, such an 'Arcadian' landscaped setting. Furthermore, by the middle of that century, the garden performed a vital role in the external presentation of this middle-class house, where creative expressions of the self were pursued through cultivation and landscaping. So, whilst 'a neatly tended front garden allowed the house-proud suburbanite to impress the outside world, the back garden was a private family or household space' (Clapson, 2003: 68). Thus, the garden – and the back garden in particular – was cherished increasingly as 'defensible space'. Indeed, such 'defensible space' has, itself, been a 'contested space' as far back as the eighteenth century when '[g]ardens took European landscape painting as a key source' (Farley and Roberts, 2011: 101). So, the question has to be asked, '[d]oes all managed urban green space aspire to the

Figure 3.5   Peter and his family pose in the garden of Ivy Cottage
Source: Author's own collection.

condition of an eighteenth-century landscape garden?', as '[i]t still seems to be the default setting' (Farley and Roberts, 2011: 104).

With Thomas Gainsborough's *Mr and Mrs Andrews* (1748–1749), a painting that was commissioned by the Andrews family not only to celebrate their marriage, but was an attempt to advertise their prosperous lifestyle, the 'landscape is ordered and regulated' (Raw, 1997: 116). Through such displays of 'order' and 'regulation' the artist depicts not only 'human beings dominating the landscape' but he has placed a particular emphasis upon 'human control of the landscape' (Raw, 1997: 116). With *Mr and Mrs Andrews* in mind, if we look at the photograph of Peter and his family sitting together on the stepped path that ran along one side of Ivy Cottage (Figure 3.5), they are quite clearly amid a 1970s 'polite landscape'. Significantly, whilst Peter's gentile family garden portrait draws immediate comparisons with such examples of eighteenth-century 'polite portraiture' – a family posing in front of the land that they own – the viewer's eye is led, not to a distant hillside, but, along the path, to the house's front lawns, where stands the hand-powered rotary mower. Thus, as well as their proud ownership of a suburban house and its garden, the object of Peter's father's labour in the maintenance of that garden is also displayed as backdrop.

The metallic clanking, and steady whir of the blades, has drawn me from my play in the back garden. Walking along the flagstones of the side path, I see him: stripped to the waist, olive skin glistening with sweat, he grunts as he pushes the hand-powered rotary mower, backwards and forwards, backwards and forwards, backwards and forwards, in the blazing sunshine. The heady smell of freshly cut grass increases and increases and increases as he goes, grunting, back and fore, back and fore, back and fore. It is a sound and a smell that is my Daddy at work in the garden.

Of course, it has to be remembered that – despite Peter's father's considerable physical exertion upon mowing the lawn with such a manual device (and in such a blue-collar manner – stripped to the waist) – a well-kept lawn 'was a way of announcing to the world that the householder was prosperous enough that he didn't need to use the space to grow vegetables for his dinner table' (Bryson, 2010: 305). Their Gainsborough-esque sense of new-found prosperity, then, was clearly constantly underpinned (undermined, even) by such betrayals of Peter's father's non-professional, working-class status.

Mammy's Melancholia

The garden at Ivy Cottage was, of course, not just a masculine defensible space. As, in many respects, it was a feminine space of insecurity and uncertainty. Written by Carla Lane, *Butterflies* was a BBC2 sitcom that ran for four series as the 1970s entered hesitantly into the following decade (1978–1980, 1983). Indeed, such societal hesitancy was evident amid the sitcom's examination of the 'malaise' of middle class, middle-aged motherhood, where suburban housewife 'melancholia' was the situation of this situation comedy. Starring Wendy Craig as Ria Parkinson, she has been married for 19 years to dentist and lepidopterist Ben (i.e. a butterfly collector, hence partly explaining the series' title), yet spends the entire four series entangled in a platonic, guilt-laden affair with wealthy businessman Leonard Dunn. Thus, '[t]he central theme in *Butterflies*, indeed, was the temptation of adultery' (Lewisohn),[10] and, as such, 'her journey through mid-life crisis made this one of the most popular and resonant sitcoms of its day' (Hamad).[11]

The first series of *Butterflies* was screened at a moment in time when the positive effects of second-wave feminism were being felt by the ordinary housewife, whilst the last series was being watched by those very same housewives as, come the mid-1980s, the 'backlash' against feminism began. Against this shift of engagement with feminism from female consciousness raising to an identity bashing of the 'bra-burners', 'her misty-eyed yearning and wistful demeanour make for one of the most triumphant yet forlorn central characters in sitcom history'.[12] No surprise, then, that such a bitter-sweet comedy embraced this downbeat mood; and, in doing so, not only marked itself out as one of the most intelligent British sitcoms of the era, but allowed it to deal with such (for prime-time television) taboo subjects as teenage pregnancy and suicidal moodswings. Although, in contrast to such dark themes, all was lifted by the series' setting amid the light of the suburban home and its garden. With its sun-dappled location filming amid wide, sweeping, suburban avenues, Ria, throughout, comes across as slightly hysterical, seemingly constantly on the verge of a breakdown. And this sense of Ria, all-the-while, being borderline certifiable, was as a result of *Butterflies*' 'inclusion of an edge-of-surrealism, achieved by the use of dream sequences and voice-overs' – both of which (when taken together) were 'then still very much experimental narrative device'.[13]

This rather surrealist, unsettling mood is set in the opening episode of Series 1 (1978) amid the sitcom's suburban outdoor setting. Striding purposefully along a paved footpath (semi-detached houses, fronted by neat lawns, and low brick walls to her right, a quiet, tree-lined road on her left), Ria contemplates, in her mind (her thoughts made audible to the audience), a radical change to the appearance of her family home and garden:

> I think I'll paint the house purple this year. Yes, purple! With orange paintwork, and yellow, nylon nets. And I'll have naked gnomes and a rude door knocker. And I'll grow flowers in a hat. Maybe I'll form words with them. A sentence! [Out aloud] A vulgar sentence! And I'll hoist my knickers up on the television aerial. Dash about naked with the lawnmower. Yes, that should liven things up a bit!

Later, in Series 1, Episode 4, Ria is – in a rather unhinged manner – tending the roses in one of the garden's borders, telling the man who is delivering the family's bread from the baker's that, 'In fact, I'm trying to pretend that it isn't today, and that I'm dead. Her husband then pulls up in the car and, referring to the wrapped bundle on the roof-rack (actually a tent for a surprise weekend away for them both), she asks 'What are they?', to which he drolly retorts 'A couple of my patients,

10   See http://www.carlalane.com/butterflies.php
11   See www.screenonline.org.uk
12   See http://www.bbc.co.uk/comedy/butterflies/
13   See http://www.televisionheaven.co.uk/butter.htm

I've come to bury them in the garden'. As such, *Butterflies* demonstrates that even 'polite' middle-class suburban families – as expressed through the overly-meticulous presentation of their homes and gardens – are almost always on the verge of breakdown, and, as a result, are capable of homicidal acts. Thus, to Peter, his 'Mammy' addicted to prescription 'mothers' little helpers' such as Valium and sleeping tablets, and, quite often, capable of flying off into spectacular rages, Ria Parkinson was more than a mere sitcom character, she was the embodiment of the mother who was, quite clearly, suffering from a melancholic malaise, and on the very edge of breakdown.

Vandals

According to Mark Clapson, in *Suburban Century – Social Change and Urban Growth in England and the USA* (2003), the steady growth in the popularity of gardening in the latter half of the twntieth century, resulted in a dramatic increase in the number of garden centres, gardening magazines and journals, and was responsible for the rise of the gardening programme as a television genre. For, '[t]he BBC's long-running *Gardener's World*, for example, began as *Gardening Club* in 1955, and it stimulated many copycat programmes and series' (Clapson, 2003: 69). Indeed, *Gardener's World* was responsible for the emergence of the gardener as TV celebrity, with such lead presenters as Percy Thrower (1969–1976) and Geoff Hamilton (1979–1996) and assistants such as (the aptly named) Clay Jones, Geoffrey Smith (1980–1982; also, *Mr Smith's Vegetable Garden*, BBC, 1976), and Peter Seabrook (1976–1979). Quite often, Peter and his mother would end a hard day's gardening with the watching of Gardener's World; with both the theme music and the West Country, or Northern, drawl of the presenters' voices providing a particularly soothing end-of-the-day TV watching experience. But it was Percy Thrower who, during the 1970s in particular, crossed over from such 'evening gardening', to 'daytime gardening' for children, with his regular appearances on the BBC's long-running, and highly-popular, magazine programme for children, *Blue Peter*.

Following a guest appearance on the programme in November 1973 (with a slot on bulb planting), Percy Thrower became *Blue Peter*'s official, high-profile gardener. A recognisable television gardener since the 1950s, Percy Thrower coped with ease with incorporating even the most mundane aspects of gardening into engaging, yet narrow, time slots offered by the programme's makers, as, ultimately, 'he was enthusiastic about translating his passion for a young audience' (Marson, 2008: 84). On 21 March 1974, accompanied by two of the *Blue Peter* presenters (John Noakes and Peter Purves), the plot was dug out, with Percy Thrower revelling in 'the idea of showing children how much could be grown in a small space, 3.5 by 3.5 metres to be precise' (Baxter and Barnes, 1989: 135). Indeed, the 'plot' – thereafter known simply as 'The *Blue Peter* Garden' – was a 'small, secluded green space in front of the BBC restaurant block' (Marson, 2008: 84). Yet, in order to instil a constant sense of excitement in this gardening slot (with its often laborious focus upon planting, weeding, digging, and so on), significant new projects had eventually to be entered into – with the design and building of the *Blue Peter* Italian sunken garden – with its paving stones, urns and mini cypress trees – being the show's major gardening project of 1978: 'The result, with its pond, benches and the footprints and handprints of the pets and presenters of the day, defined the whole space' (ibid.). Although, on the 17 April of that year, the programme announced rather solemnly that the garden had been vandalised – with the garden, in fact, eventually being damaged by vandals three times (1978, and then, again, in 1980 and in 1983). Each time the garden was vandalised, *Blue Peter* presenters would appear on-screen and, entering into highly emotive and earnest speeches, lambaste publicly the vandals responsible. Indeed, one of the presenters who took part in one of these memorable broadcasted 'telling-offs', Janet Ellis, defended such an aloof approach: 'It sounds really smug and pompous to say it was very important to a lot of people, but it was' (Ellis, cited in, Marson, 2008: 85).

Vandalism, a perennial societal 'youth problem', arguably reached its peak during the 1970s. In Colin Ward's edited text *Vandalism* (1973), those that produce social spaces (amongst others) were asked to provide contributions on how vandalism could be prevented. Thus, Alan Leather and Antony Matthews' chapter, 'What the architect can do: a series of design guides' (Leather and Matthews, 1973: 117–72), offered practitioners' advice on how vandals can be dissuaded from their wanton acts of seemingly mindless destruction. One rule laid down by Leather and Matthews, with regards the building of particularly vulnerable, high-profile public places, was that '[c]are should always be taken over the provision and design of anything which may be considered to be of a novel, pretentious or prestigious nature' (Leather and Matthews, 1973: 166). Thus, admittedly 'smug' and 'pompous' (criticism levelled at both the BBC more generally, and *Blue Peter*, as a children's programme, in particular), the *Blue Peter* Italian sunken garden was not only 'novel', but, arguably, 'pretentious' as well. Indeed, being, at that time, one of the most televised gardens on British television it could not have been of a more 'prestigious nature' to wanna-be vandals in search of their '15 minutes' of infamy. Yet, with regards the 'symbolic impact' of crime, as, listing many forms of anti-social behaviour and vandalism, even the academics were adopting emotive terminology at this time. For example, John Lea and Jock Young, asking (almost in vain), with the title of their book, the question *What is to be Done About Law and Order?* (1984)], implored that '[c]rime is the end-point of a continuum of disorder' and, furthermore, 'it is a symbol of a world falling apart' (Lea and Young, 1984: 55).

Percy Thrower made over 200 broadcasts from the garden that he helped design, build, and maintain for *Blue Peter*, and, ultimately, in doing so, 'his enthusiasm and expertise inspired a whole new generation of gardeners' (Baxter and Barnes, 1989: 135). Eventually, though, this gardener for all ages, after several bouts of illness, was to die, aged 75, in 1988, having made his final appearance in the *Blue Peter* garden on 9 November 1987. Still a tranquil spot of televisual gardening history, '[a] plaque in his honour can be found in the garden to this day' (Marson, 2008: 85).

Midnight Secrets

On a more ethereal level, gardeners have often become preoccupied with the establishing of a 'secret garden' – especially within the context of such a garden being a form of 'rural seclusion' amid what would otherwise be the claustrophobic confines of an urban garden of very limited space and scope. Thus, for example, in *The Small Garden* (Brookes, 1985), Geoffrey Smith offers (with 'In a secret garden', 132–5) what was formerly two separate plots as one, where '[p]art of the old wall has been retained and, with its archway and the rustic steps at the end, now provides both division and link between the two gardens' (Brookes, 1985: 132). Indeed, with high brick walls on all sides, the entirety of this 'secret garden' is contrived in order to place emphasis upon its 'attachedness' yet 'detachedness' from both its house and wider surroundings:

> The atmosphere of the garden is that of a country retreat, remote from the pressures of the world: in fact, it is in the heart of a bustling town. It is completely self-contained and detached even from the house; the approach is along a walled passageway. The enclosed, private feel of the garden is emphasized by trees overhanging some of the walls from outside and by a big old pear tree inside the smaller plot (Brookes, 1985: 132).

Such a walled 'secret garden' – where access to it seems to be via some form of 'passageway' (whether an actual one, or one as a more spiritual pathway) – has long been a central element of children's cultures. Most famously, the setting of Frances Hodgson Burnett's classic children's novel *The Secret Garden*, first published in 1910, was inspired by the back garden of her family's home in Manchester. In her 1892 account of her childhood there, she rather breathlessly asks herself 'Was it always Spring or Summer there in that enchanted Garden which, out of a whole world, had remained throughout a lifetime the Garden of Eden?' (Hodgson, 1892, cited in Carpenter and Prichard, 1995: 89). A childhood space of enchantment, *The Secret Garden*, then, is concerned with Mary Lennox, who is (at first) a disagreeable, selfish child, who, having lived a privileged existence in India, finds herself having to live with her uncle on an isolated estate in Yorkshire. Wandering the house, and then the grounds, she eventually discovers a locked inner garden which, having been neglected for countless years, is reinvigorated through her nurturing (and that of Dickon's, a local boy she befriends). In doing so, not only does Mary display a more humanitarian side to her nature, but, eventually bringing along her young, bed-bound cousin Colin to this 'secret garden', its powers (alongside the collective emotional warmth that the children now generate) cure him of his supposed affliction. As such, '[i]n healing the garden they heal themselves, and indication of Burnett's belief in the importance of nature and its therapeutic effects' (McGown and Docherty, 2003: 85). Furthermore, *The Secret Garden* (the original novel and subsequent adaptations) – and the concept of the 'secret garden' more generally – somehow connects totally with children's imaginative yearnings that is, in turn, coupled 'with their instinctive feeling for things that grow' and 'with their longing for real, important, adult-level achievement' (Townsend, 1987: 71).

It is, though, the BBC's third adaptation of Burnett's work that we are concerned with here. Broadcast between the 1 January and 12 February 1975, the series' seven episodes were not only the BBC first colour adaptation of *The Secret Garden*, but they possessed a production aesthetic of its time (the mid-1970s) that, at times, was somewhat off-putting. Whilst continuous editing between studio-based videotape, location filming, reserves of stock footage was commonplace at this time (especially within children's programmes), 'its often illogical use here rests uneasy on the eye of the viewer, particularly when the key setting of the Secret Garden itself is rendered in a studio that seemingly exists at the centre of filmed locations' (McGown and Docherty, 2003: 85). Additionally, and rejecting totally an adherence to the frenetic traits of much of children's film and television (before and since), this adaptation in particular accentuates the novel's more contemplative passages, 'with long scenes containing either large chunks of dialogue or much meandering through the grounds of Misselthwaite Manor' (McGown and Docherty, 2003: 85), to the extent that 'on some occasions the viewer could be forgiven for thinking that nothing had happened by the end of an episode' (McGown and Docherty, 2003: 85).

Yet, despite these valid criticisms, it was precisely these aspects of this particular BBC adaptation of *The Secret Garden* that appealed to a young Peter. Brought up to appreciate the relatively large garden that surrounded Ivy Cottage as 'grounds', around which you strolled of an evening: spaces within which (as well as imaginative play) contemplative conversations took place whilst walking. Then, the 'long scenes' of 'large chunks of dialogue' whilst 'meandering through grounds' all made, to Peter, perfect sense. As, to him, gardens, especially on a late-summer's evening, were not hectic places. Indeed, just like watching an episode of *The Secret Garden*, having walked along Ivy Cottages paths and across its lawns of an evening, there was a realisation that, whilst you had done that, nothing of note had really happened. But, of course, that was the true beauty of it. A slow walk. Conversation at length. Time passing. Nothing of note happening. No more, no less. Thus, more positively then, the BBC's 1975 version of *The Secret Garden*, 'content to canter along at a slow pace, requires quite a degree of patience and concentration' (McGown and Docherty, 2003: 85).

Although, I would insist that such a disparity of film quality as a result of switching from scene to scene results in *The Secret Garden* – that is, its 1975 incarnation – adopting (admittedly, inadvertently) a heightened 'other worldliness'. Indeed, its media-created 'hyperreal' inner garden (that is, amongst its surroundings of other, real gardens), was something which even the cast found themselves engaging in. In *Remembering the Secret Garden* (2004), a documentary that accompanies the DVD release of the series, Andrew Harrison, who played Dickon, admits that his favourite character was Ben Weatherstaff, the gardener, for the way that he interacted convincingly with such a 'hyperreal' garden, stating that he 'made an art form of standing around and just pretending to cut things off plastic shrubbery in the studios'.

Tom's Midnight Garden, written by Philippa Pearce (1976, first published 1958), and its 1974 BBC adaptation (three episodes, broadcast 7–21 January 1974) was the second of the BBC's three adaptations. Concerned with young Tom Long, who, suffering with measles, is sent to live with 'Aunt Gwen' and 'Uncle Alan' who live in a flat in a converted house owned by an elderly woman, 'Mrs Bartholomew', who 'lives spiderlike at the top' (Townsend, 1987: 245). At night, on hearing the grandfather clock strike thirteen, Tom makes his way along the hall and, through the door at its far end (which he had no reason to ever use before), 'finds his way into the large beautiful garden that belongs to the house – but belongs to it only in the past' (Townsend, 1987: 245). Indeed, quite significantly, feeling that he had been 'lied to' (his aunt, uncle, tenants, and Mrs Bartholomew stated that there was just a 'back-yard' beyond the door), Tom now saw this as his 'secret garden' within which he could climb and hide in the trees, so that '[w]hen they came calling him, he would hide, silent and safe as a bird, among this richness of leaf and bough and treetrunk' (Pearce, 1976: 25).

So, repeatedly visiting the garden night after night, Tom finds himself, again and again, back in time, wandering the house and its gardens during its golden years of the late 1800s. There, he befriends a young girl of the house, Hatty, and although she can actually see him (which Hatty's family and her family's servants fail to do), she perceives him to be a ghost. Indeed, one passage of the book describes Tom's walk across the garden – where, with the garden drenched in dew, and his footsteps softened by the previous year's rotting leaves, 'he slipped along, like a ghost' (Pearce, 1976: 41). Furthermore, whilst Tom visits the garden on a nightly basis, to Hatty his visits are sporadic, often with lengthy gaps in between. Thus, whilst Tom ages gradually, Hatty matures more rapidly, eventually outgrowing him both physically and emotionally. Finally, when Tom prepares to leave his Aunt and Uncles house, in order to return home, he meets the aged Mrs Bartholomew and, in a profound moment of realisation, acknowledges that this is now Hatty in the twilight of her years. There are, of course, two issues of note here: Firstly, with *Tom's Midnight Garden*, is the suggestion that people in the present day have the potential to be ghosts *of* the future and *from* the future (as with the young Peter of the 1970s, as already discussed at length in Chapter 1); and, secondly, that the present day house co-exists with a late Victorian, even Edwardian, version of itself (that is, again, like Ivy Cottage when Peter and his family lived there).

Whilst critics highlight 'that Tom has a ridiculous pudding bowl haircut in this 70s update' (McGown and Docherty, 2003: 215), thus locating this particular BBC adaptation firmly within that decade, it can also be appreciated that, more generally, Tom is not reduced to merely characterisation, for, instead, 'he is any child, any person' (Townsend, 1971: 166). Indeed, fundamentally, '[h]e could be you' (Townsend, 1971: 167). Furthermore, and according to *The Oxford Companion to Children's Literature* (1995), Philippa Pearce's work is often twin-themed, concerned with not only the links between childhood and old age but 'the solitary child's creation of a fantasy world which can be both enriching and destructive' (Carpenter and Prichard, 1995: 398). Moreover, *Tom's Midnight Garden*, suggests – with time travel adding another dimension to reality – a 'four-dimensional wholeness' to life itself, where '[i]n the child the old person is implicit' and 'in the old person the child remains' (Townsend, 1971: 167).

The setting of *Tom's Midnight Garden* is that of the garden that accompanied Pearce's own childhood home, Mill House, East Anglia (all sold shortly after her father's retirement from milling). Indeed, Pearce, in interview, was adamant that, in comparing Mill House to Tom Long's Aunt and Uncle's home, '[i]t's exactly the house of Tom's Midnight Garden, with a storey added for Mrs Bartholomew' and 'its garden is – or was – almost exactly that garden' (Pearce, cited in Townsend, 1971: 170). Thus, in this particular work, Pearce not only explores issues to do with youth and ageing as one, but makes connections between the garden of her own childhood and that of the universality of the garden of childhood that can be appreciated, primarily, through one's senses. *Tom's Midnight Garden*, then, possesses 'the beauty of a theorem but it is not abstract', and, as a result, 'it is sensuously as well as intellectually satisfying' – to the extent that '[t]he garden is so real that you have the scent of it in your nostrils' (Townsend, 1987: 245). Indeed, and as appreciated following a reading of Pearce's seminal work, 'the beauty of any garden is an evanescent sensuousness' (Townsend, 1971: 68). Robin C. Moore (1986), led by two of her child respondents, Jill and Lesley, to places they frequented, commented upon such a 'sensuous' dimension of a child's outdoor play where touch is vital:

> I questioned them closely about where, specifically, they played on the grass. They took me to a small, 'soft and mossy', level spot where they mentioned doing handstands and 'just sitting around'. Down on our hands and knees, we felt the velvety spongy texture of a subtly differentiated patch of dark green compact moss; conditioned, presumably, by the character of the soil or some combination of micro-ecological factors (Moore, 1986: 155).

Peter holds a very similar sensory-based memory of one particular part of his childhood garden.

I'm at the north-east facing side of the house (the side at which the pantry is located). It is mid-afternoon, mid-summer, yet it is (as it always is) dark and damp here. There are no flowers or shrubs here, just a lonely fern. This part of the garden – which consists of a narrow stretch of quite luxurious, deep-green grass – is hemmed in, on one side, by one of Ivy Cottage's tall gable ends, and, on the other, by a dense hedge which is provided with an added density with its morphing into the neighbouring wasteland beyond. Crouching down, I peer through gaps in the hedge that our cats have made, peeking into their dim prowling tunnels, and their flattened, laid-upon nests. Breathing in slowly and deeply, I inhale the moist air: the air smells differently here – it's as if the garden tastes differently on this side of the house. Despite its quietness, none of us ever spend any significant amount of time here. Instead, this is purely a part of the garden that we seem to be forever passing through. Yet, stopping for a moment, and now on my knees, I place my hand into the lawn, and feel the sponginess of the moss that is woven within. This, then, is what stillness and seclusion sound like, smell like, taste like, feels like.

Whilst, by no stretch of the imagination, a true secret garden, it was this most secluded spot of Ivy Cottage's garden that possessed, for Peter, the essence of a 'secret space', for '[s]ecret spaces may be found inside, outdoors, or in the middle of nowhere' (Goodenough, 2003: 2). But, one thing is certain, 'the lure of secret spaces finds its first fulfilment in the local, somewhere within or just outside the safe matrix of home' (Goodenough, 2003: 3). A childhood garden, then, is the perfect matrix within which a child, like Peter, can discover – and claim as theirs – such 'secret spaces' of the senses (smell, taste, touch).

Woodsheds and Rats

Author Christopher Fowler, in his account of growing up as a book-obsessed boy and teenager across the late-1960s and early 1970s, admits the fascination that pulp horror novels held for him at that young age, where he 'discovered a wealth of beautifully written short stories hidden behind tacky covers' (Fowler, 2009: 90).[14] Fowler singles out – from all such horror anthologies – the Pan Books of Horror, the first 25 volumes of which were edited by Herbert Van Thal. Published from 1959 until 1989 (that is, apart from 1961, a volume a year), one of the major attractions of the books were their lurid, gruesome bindings that, by the late-1960s, 'would veer from the absurd 'portrait' shots to beautifully painted covers' (Mains, 2010: xi). Although, come the early 1970s, as 'the covers became more violent and outlandish'

---

14   Such horror anthologies, with these 'tacky covers', provides Peter with one of his earliest, most vivid memories. Prior to living at Ivy Cottage, Peter and his family lived in a council house in Cimla, Neath. And, to this day, Peter has a memory of one edition of one such anthology (left, most probably by his mother) on the sill of the small window that lit the area at the top of the stairs. On this book's cover was a tackily composed photograph, with its centrepiece being a tarantula. Aged three, perhaps four, Peter, attempting to walk down the stairs, was frozen to the spot, unable to pass that book's cover. Peter, as an adult, attributes his arachnophobia to the sight of that cover.

(Mains, 2010: xi), there was also a discernible increase in the graphically visceral content of the stories, where many demonstrated 'an almost cavalier attitude to horrendous violence, tossing aside the supernatural and psychological tales that had gone before in favour of cheap sadistic thrills, rape and extreme body torture' (Mains, 2010: xi). Noting the parallel increased violence of the times they were now being written in (the mid-to-late 1970s), Fowler agrees, noting dismally that 'heavier shocks were clearly required in jaundiced times' (2009: 92).

Significantly, it was the younger consumers of the stories that proved the most avid readers of the Pan Books of Horror, as '[f]or three generations of children, it was a grisly winner' (Kibble-White, 2005a: 140). Indeed, Fowler, quite profoundly (and quite guiltily), explains that '[t]he darkest shadows are found in brightest sunlight, so it's natural to discover them in childhood' (Fowler, 2009: 92). Although, children weren't only to be found (often secretly) reading them, as they, occasionally (and most shockingly) were the focus of the stories' macabre characterisation: 'Many were disturbing indeed ... best of all, lovingly described scenes of methodical dismemberment, preferably carried out by innocent young children' (Kibble-White, 2005a: 140). Thus, with *The Twelfth Pan Book of Horror Stories* (1978, first published 1971), Robert Ashley's 'Pieces of Mary' is a gruesome tale – only lasting a total of three pages – of two highly inquisitive, 'innocent' boys, John and David, who, having been quickly bored with dissecting of their pet mouse, amass a motley collection of household implements and tools, perform an impromptu lobotomy on the little girl that lives next door, Mary. With it being a quiet half-term Monday, this grisly act is carried out at the bottom of the boys' garden, in the seclusion of the wooden shed. Following, then, two whole pages of incessant gore, the horrific events are interrupted by – and the short story ended with – the reaffirming of this taking place entirely within the tranquil setting of a leafy suburban garden:

> Just at that moment, when they were most absorbed with their work, they could hear their mother calling from the other end of the garden. It was time for lunch. They wiped the blood and bits from their hands as best they could and went towards the house. After lunch they could come back and look at the brain again and also at some of the other pieces of the head. They could even take out Mary's heart if there was enough time before tea. Daddy might like to see their work when he came home (Ashley, 1978: 132).

Whilst Ashley's short story – with children as both victim and perpetrators of the horror that unfolds – makes explicit the malevolent aspects of the suburban family's house and garden, it is also worth noting (as its most disturbing passages take place, of course, within the confines of the woodshed), a child's engagement with so-called 'space-mood' in such places, where 'garden sheds are full of mysterious (often tantalizingly forbidden) things to stimulate inventive play' (Day, 2007: 124). But, if the Pan Books of Horror could claim any form of literary achievement, then it is the considerable number of its young readers who, eventually, would become professional writers as a direct consequence of reading these books (and the anthologies' most grisly short stories in particular) as, quite often, 'you can still find authors such as Clive Barker, Shaun Hutson, Mark Morris, Philip Pullman and Muriel Gray talking about the books and the effect that they had on them' (Mains, 2010: xiv). Indeed, the author John Llewellyn Probert, on a Pan Book of Horror appreciation forum, admitted: 'Ah, Volume 12 and more terrific memories. I rewrote 'Pieces of Mary' for an English homework assignment when I was 11, much to the horror of the rather delicate young chap who was teaching us at the time' (Anon., vaultofevil.proboards.com, 9 June 2008). Eventually, though, the Pan Books of Horror suffered a spectacular decrease in both their sales and overall popularity as a result of the readers who had grown up with them now consuming their horror via other media forms: by the late-1980s, 'it was already apparent that readers preferred their visceral horror on the big screen or home video' (Mains, 201: xi).

Whilst Ivy Cottage did not have a woodshed within which sadistic body torture at the hands of children took place, it did have rats, and lots of them. Indeed, despite Mabey, during the mid-1970s, generally encouraging an embrace of the wildlife that exists within the towns and the cities, he admitted the difficulty of extending this degree of tolerance in relation to the brown rat:

> Centuries of association with dirt and disease have made it virtually impossible to look at this creature objectively. Even in bald physical terms, though, he's hardly one of nature's beauties. Working from nose to tail you have a long and pointed face, large pink ears, coarse fur and a hairless rope of a tail (Mabey, 1974: 77).

Meanwhile, Mabey adds, they are very much at home in an urban setting, and devourers of almost anything:

> They hole up in canal banks, rubbish dumps, industrial buildings, sewers, and particularly any store or warehouse where food is kept. They will eat anything, including each other if alternative foods are in short supply (Mabey, 1974: 77–8).

Peter has, in particular, two memories of the garden and its infestation of rats (that is, rats with seemingly extraordinary dimensions and food-harvesting capabilities).

It's a grey, windy, late-Autumn day. The fallen leaves are being whipped up, and blown around the garden in great swirls. We've just put bread out on the path, and the birds, battered by the breeze, struggling to stay on the ground as they peck at the chunks and the crumbs. Looking out of the kitchen window (with the elevated vantage point that it offers), we see it, first, emerging from the undergrowth to the right, at the foot of the trees, then, secondly, brazenly approach the path in a dash-stop-dash manner. Finally, it runs towards the birds, scattering them in all directions. Then, firmly clamping one of the biggest pieces of bread between its oversized incisors, it darts for its cover of foliage once more.

The rats are back in the garden. As a writhing mass on the path and the grass, snatching at the remnants of the birds' bread, they run amok. I grab Sam, our rather bedraggled tom, and, opening the two doors that lead from the hall, through the back porch, and onto the steps that run down onto the rear garden, I let him go. As I do so, I whisper the alarm after him 'Rats! Rats!' I run, excitedly, back to the kitchen window, and, peer out expectantly. There he is: keeping low, and hugging the damp ground, Sam darts for the gathering of rats. At first a blur of black-and-white fur, he, all of a sudden, halts. Realising he is both outnumbered, and outsized, he turns, and runs for the house, terror in his eyes. The rats make chase.

Indeed, Peter's home was overrun with rats (most probably as a result of the warehouse next door, and the close proximity of the 'tip') to the extent that his family, adopting a siege mentality, often made attempts to exterminate them. First, individually.

Getting in from school, throwing down my bag, and taking off my coat. My mother tells me about her afternoon encounter with the rats in the garden: 'I looked out of the window, and I saw it moving under the tarpaulin. So, I went out, grabbed the spade, and gave it a bloody good whack – then I run like hell back in! Oh, it was about and hour later when I was brave enough to go back out, pull up the tarpaulin, and there its was, dead' At this point, fag in hand, my mother – imitating the dead rat – pulls up both hands, drooped together, to her chin, and closes her eyes. She then laughs herself silly in a billowing blue cloud of Benson and Hedges smoke.

Then, secondly, en masse.

Having got home from school, my mother hurriedly tells me of the result of us having put down rat traps in the back garden that morning: Endlessly clapping her hands together, she said they – 'all afternoon' – went off 'Like this! And this! And this! And this!'.

The rat (individually) and a plague of rats (as a writhing, unified mass) became, then, synonymous with a Britain of the 1970s; a nation blighted by economic, social, and cultural downturn, that, taken together, brought about a self-referencing of the nation as nothing but a putrid mound of rubbish teetering upon collapse. Indeed, bearing in mind the Stranglers' debut LP, entitled *Rattus Norvegicus* (1977), and the modest success of the Bob Geldof-led Boomtown Rats, '[t]he rat soon became a common shorthand for social decline, particularly in rock and roll' (Turner, 2008: 45). No surprise, then, that the rat often starred on TV during the 1970s. For example, the second of the six-episode series of plays by Nigel Kneale, *Beasts* (ATV, 1976), entitled 'During Barty's Party', portrayed the degeneration of a middle-class couple's idyllic life in the country, as a result of – and symbolised by – 'the marauding terror of a tribe of super-rats with a taste for human flesh' (Turner, 2008: 45). Cleverly never showing a single rat, the viewer's growing perception of the couple's increasingly terrifying plight was suggested by sound only, with 'the noise of the rats' unceasing scratching growing ever louder as the play continued' (Kibble-White, 2005a: 22).

With the refuse collectors' strikes of autumn 1970 and 1975 (especially with the latter, centred upon Glasgow), rats were the biggest hazard faced by the troops who had been called in to clear the resulting mountains of rubbish. Right in the middle of these two bouts of industrial action, this much maligned rodent made a spectacular appearance on the shelves of Britain's bookshops and newsagents – with the publication of James Herbert's first novel, *The Rats*, in 1974, which was written in 'a proletarian prose style that combined episodic narrative with an unflinching eye for visceral violence' (Turner, 2008: 44). Yet, despite its 'proletarian' style (or, rather, precisely *because* of its adoption of a lumpen vernacular), *The Rats* was a highly popular literary debut, 'particularly among secondary schoolchildren, who passed it on from hand to hand with salivating enthusiasm, so that its readership massively out-numbered even its sales figures' (Turner, 2008: 44).[15]

Significantly, then, James Herbert's follow-up to *The Rats* was *The Lair* (1979), and was no longer a critique of the slums of London, but the suggestion that the vermin horrors would continue, intensify even, amid the British countryside – namely, across Epping Forest's green belt (although, still in close proximity to London – the place of origin of the rats). Indeed, as Herbert himself admitted:

> My idea for the sequel was to have the rats move out from their squalid habitat to the wealthier suburbs, and then into the green belt that adjoins the capital, the idea being that no one was safe ... that privilege was no protection (Herbert, 1993: 85).

---

15   Peter's first exposure to Herbert's *The Rats* was at his secondary school's lunchtime, unofficial 'book club'. One of the few mixed gender activities experienced by Peter, this often involved one of the 'harder' (and not necessarily literate) boys, Mucker (not his real Christian name, obviously), reading in hushed tones passages from the book. This resulted in (certainly for Peter) great embarrassment, in such company, when the pages containing graphic sex were read aloud. This consumption of non-curricula pulp novels in schools during the 1970s is referred to by Leon Hunt, in *British Low Culture* (1998), as '"behind the school desk" fiction' (75–9).

Thus, Herbert, with *Lair*, aimed to demonstrate that no-one, irrespective of where they lived (and what social strata they belonged to), was safe from this scavenging rodent – in effect, then, '[t]he countryside as well as the city was vulnerable' (Herbert, cited in Cabell, 2003: 94). Furthermore, *Lair* makes it explicit 'that the natural splendour of the countryside was no protection from the horror of the rats' (Cabell, 2003: 98). Indeed, whilst the bombsites, wastelands, and terraced squalor of Herbert's own East End childhood neighbourhood provided inspiration for *The Rats*, it was an opportunity (again, as a deprived, inner-city child, with assistance from the charity Country Holiday Fund) to holiday in the countryside around Rayleigh in Essex and Beccles in Norfolk, that, later in life, supplied him with such a quiet, leafy backdrop to *The Lair*. For, on one such childhood holiday, amid such 'lonely places' of inspiration, 'where silence is a precursor to terror' (Herbert, 1993: 101), Herbert observed the inhabitants of an entire village, frenzied in the thrill of the kill, taking part in a rabbit cull, noting chillingly that, 'I've never forgotten that bloodlust, nor the special shine in the eyes of those perpetrators and spectators alike' (Herbert, 1993: 85).

Thus, in a perverse reversal of 'the gaze' of those about to engage in their kill, Herbert, in *The Lair*, places one victim, Reverend Jonathan Matthews (62 pages before he meets his grisly death), under the rats' intense gaze as he surveys his suburban parish (a parish that sits between the urbanity of London and the rurality of Epping Forest):

> The great woodland was surrounded on all sides by suburbia, the forest fringes cut dead by bricks and mortar. Less than ten miles away was the city's centre … (Herbert, 1979: 33).

Indeed, this suburban parish, where the urban and the rural jarred against one another, was now, for Matthews, sensing he is being watched, a site of great unease:

> But he was in a depressed mood and he wondered if it was this that made the forest seem so oppressive. The vicar felt he was being watched. Or was he merely exhausted mentally? Could that be why there seemed to be dozens of eyes watching from the shadows beneath the leafy trees, stripping away his façade, looking deep into his guilt?

> He shook his head, knowing he had to repress this dreadful feeling before it broke him. Yet the forest did have a different atmosphere lately. None of his parishioners mentioned it, but he had caught certain looks in the eyes of the forest keepers. An uneasiness as they studied the undergrowth.

> He searched the distant foliage and tried to penetrate the dark areas. Was that a movement? No, just a fern stirred by the breeze. He had to snap out of this destructive mood, had to get a grip on himself. Epping Forest and its inhabitants

were his life. He loved the forest. Why then did it seem so menacing? (Herbert, 1979: 35).

Lynne Ramsay's *Ratcatcher* (1999), whilst it is a film set in the mid-1970s (and centred upon the exploits of 12-year-old James Gillespie, who belongs to a working-class, slum tenement-dwelling family), all of its 'signifiers of 'pastness' are understated' (Kuhn, 2008: 20). So, somewhat un-expectantly, it lacks all of that 'tasteless' decade's clichéd period details, to the extent that 'there is certainly no overt 1970s retro feel about the décor and furniture' (Kuhn, 2008: 32). Yet, the convincing setting of the film's action at the height of the 1975 Glasgow refuse collectors' strike – that is, its actual capturing of the 'pastness' of the mid-1970s – is achieved through a graphic depiction of not only the piling up of rubbish on the streets of that city, but the local population's encounter with the burgeoning plague of rats as the strike drags on. Indeed, the film's title, *Ratcatcher*, is a direct reference to children of the area and their macabre playing with the rats amid the tenement's back court. For, '[i]t is here that the bags of rubbish pile up most rapidly and profusely ... where children hurl refuse about, beating the bags with sticks to flush out rats' (Kuhn, 2008: 40). Yet, as the back court is awash with rat-infested waste, and is the site of outdoor WCs and washhouses, '[i]f there is enjoyment to be had among the rubbish, the fun is laced with danger and the risk of disease' (Kuhn, 2008: 44).

Conclusion

Peter, as a young boy, watching his mother toil in the garden, and, then, in watching *Gardener's World* with her, was engaging in a process of, together, learning about their 'edible landscape'. This was, in a way, a shared passing on of knowledge from mother to son and media to mother and son. Indeed, it is a form of 'passing on' that is no longer a certainty, as '[t]he parent or grandparent who traditionally passed on essential wisdom about food and survival can no longer be taken as given in many families' (Burke, 2005: 246). But it was more than a passing on; it was a means of escape for all.

Gardens – to the philosopher Yi-Fu Tuan, in *Escapism* (1998) – are a means of near-escape from nature, as '[t]hey show how humans can escape nature's rawness without moving so far from it as to appear to deny roots in the organic world' (Tuan, 1998: 24–5). Thus, to Peter and his family, the garden offered escape on a variety of levels: to his father, a garden around a detached house provided relief, after years of living in council housing, of having no neighbours (with the gardens and roads acting as buffers from all); to his mother, it was escape from the kitchen, the cooking, and the cleaning; to Peter it was escape from the confines of the house (either through the front door, or via the back porch). This notion of childhood escape from the house into the garden – especially the moment of childhood realisation that there is, indeed, a safe 'out there' – was reiterated, many, many years later, at the time of writing this chapter. Peter's 21-month-old daughter, Millie, in an attempt to say the word 'garden' would endlessly repeat her version – 'ga-ga'. This she would do upon getting up, before going to bed, and countless times in between. Pointing to the back garden via the door or the windows, she would softly say 'ga-ga'; a 'dwt' – or toddler (as her father once was) – expressing a desire to be 'out there', in the garden, as opposed to being 'in here', in the house. 'Ga-ga' as sheer escapism.

With a constant to-ing and fro-ing, the garden at Ivy Cottage is to be conceptualised as a 'middle landscape' of 'escapism' that, historically, reclaims itself, then is reclaimed, then reclaims itself once again, and so on and so on. For, 'the middle landscape, whatever the kind, proves unstable' and, thus, '[i]t reverts to nature' (Tuan, 1998: 25). The garden, during the period that Peter and his family lived there – the 1970s into the early 1980s – was a decreasing (as bit by bit it was cultivated) 'unofficial countryside'. A garden, at first completely overgrown, as 'wasteland', eventually cultivated, as a 'polite landscape'. As the garden took countless hours, days, weeks, even months at a time, of hard labour to cultivate fully, many areas of the garden remained untouched for years. It was only a few years before Peter's family had to sell up and move on, that the gardens of Ivy Cottage managed to regain their former glory and reach anywhere near their former extent.

One of the Ladybird series of books for children, Brian Vesey-Fitzgerald's *Garden Flowers* (1960), has, as its first entry, a mention of the cyclical way in which the Forsythia shrub both grows and should be cared for: 'After flowering, the old wood must be cut out to make room for the new, which will flower the following year' (Vesey-Fitzgerald, 1960: 4). Whilst being one of Peter's mother's favourite bushes at Ivy Cottage (a particularly glorious sight, with a blaze of yellow flowers early each year), it is, like most of what was planted and nurtured by Peter and his family, no longer there. But, that is the way with both homes and their gardens. The garden of Ivy Cottage, having once more 'flowered' while Peter and his family lived there, was to eventually have its 'old wood' 'cut out' by those that were to live there afterwards: 'to make room for the new'. And, as gardens tend to do – as the gardens of Ivy Cottage have done – they, we can be sure, 'will flower the following year', with new plants grown by new families. Yet, at some stage in the future, Ivy Cottage's gardens may also find themselves, in turn, abandoned and, as a result, overgrown again. As Paul Farley and Michael Symmons Roberts, in *Edgelands – Journeys Into England's True Wilderness* (2011), place great emphasis upon the fact that '[g]ardens come to the end of their managed lives every day, too', as they reach, what they term, 'a tipping point', which is '[t]he point at which species begin to take full advantage of our unconcern' (Farley and Roberts, 2011: 104). Such 'unconcern', of course, will then usher in the return of the 'uncultivated' once more. And then, Ivy Cottage will await yet another 'dwt' to be placed down, and to feel lost, amid its 'wastelands'.

Chapter 4

The Childhood Spaces of the Street

About 2.30 p.m., accident outside our house. Two cars towed away. Kathleen took little girl, boy, and mother out of car (Millie's diary, Sunday, 23 April 1978).

Gas men digging pathway up when I came home from Neath 9.30 p.m. ... Gas leak outside (Millie's diary, Tuesday, 19 December 1978).

Introduction

Leaving behind his childhood home and garden, Peter now finds himself on the main road running through his neighbourhood – New Road, Skewen. Indeed, (and in keeping with autoethnography's preoccupation with a more creative means of expression), this particular memory of Peter's has much in common with Bill Douglas's trilogy of films from the 1970s, in which a certain 'cinematic poetry' allows a child's memories (that is, those of Jamie) to evoke both emotion and a sense of place. Thus, with the monochrome *My Childhood* (1972), *My Ain Folk* (1973), and *My Way Home* (1978) – and with this book's chapters (and this chapter in particular) – '[w]e are presented largely with an oblique series of autobiographical fragments, organised not by straightforward exposition but the vividness of each distinct evocation of memory' (Flanagan, 2008: 10). In particular, Peter's memory of leaving behind his home and garden, and, via the gate, entering the bright sunlight, is highly reminiscent of the way in which Douglas concludes the last of the trilogy:

> [A]t the close of *My Way Home*, Douglas's camera explores the barren living room of his subject's childhood, moving across fireplace, door and roof before lurching toward a flood of light from the open window. The effect is thrillingly enigmatic, transforming Jamie's space of memory into what the screenplay describes as 'a gradual opening out to something all-embracing' (Flanagan, 2008: 11).

Hence, leaving behind his home and garden, Peter too senses 'a gradual opening out to something all-embracing' – the neighbourhood of his youth.

Opening the garden gate, and stepping out onto the sun-soaked pavement, I find myself on New Road, Skewen. To my right (that is, 'down the road') is the village of Neath Abbey. Left (or 'up the hill'), is the village of Skewen proper. So, here, the very start of New Road (and St. John's Terrace in particular), due to its 'not-

> quite-here' and 'not-quite-there', is neither wholly part of Skewen nor Neath
> Abbey. Yet, it (St. John's Terrace) possesses – certainly to me, a young boy with
> quite limited horizons – the quality of a hazy, but self-contained neighbourhood
> caught in between two quite distinct neighbourhoods.

Furthermore, this 'opening out' – from Peter's home and garden, into the neighbourhood of his youth – is his engagement with one of the central aspects of cultural geography: the crossing over, or breaking through, the borders and boundaries to be found between the private and public spheres. Although, David Sibley (2005), whilst highlighting the permeable nature of such borders and boundaries (in Peter's case, between that of the childhood home and its immediate neighbourhood), insists that, quite often, an encountering of such binary-derived tensions, that exist between the private and the public, is common place. Therefore, for Peter especially, such tensions are experienced following his leaving behind (no matter how momentarily) of the comfort and security that is to be found amid the private of his childhood home, Ivy Cottage, and his engagement with (again, no matter how briefly) the palpable discomfort and insecurities that are to be found out in the public of adulthood that is St. John's Terrace.

Neighbourhood

This chapter, then, aims to examine the childhood spaces of Peter's neighbourhood amid the context of 1970s media-informed notions of the high street and its surrounding neighbourhood – for example, *Sesame Street* (1969–present). Firstly, as it is directly opposite the Ivy Cottage's garden gate, the bus stop will be examined; then, secondly, as it was a little further along New Road (and on the same side as the bus stop), the phone box; thirdly, and lastly, just further along the road (but back to the same side as Ivy Cottage), Miriam's, the Newsagent. Indeed, what will be touched upon with regards these (often confined, claustrophobic) spaces of childhood are issues to do with light (such as the sparkle of sweets, the vibrant packaging of toys), and the dark (the shadowy interiors of shops, late winter afternoons and early evenings, and so on). Furthermore, and as with previous chapters, not only will children's texts of the 1970s be re-examined (for example, such children's television programmes as *Mr Benn*) in order to provide the cultural context of these aspects of the 'light' and 'dark' to be found amid children's spaces of the high street and neighbourhood, but adult texts as well – that is, adult texts that would be consumed (often illicitly) by the children of the decade. And, finally, to reiterate: The 'Peter' referred to here – in particular, his memories of his childhood home, Ivy Cottage, and his remembering of the spaces of his childhood (the bus stop, phone box, and Miriam's the newsagents) – is not to be confused with the author of this book. For they are of a different time, and a different place.

Created by Joan Ganz Cooney, *Sesame Street* (PBS/Children's Television Workshop, 1969–present) was an educational television programme aimed at preschool children. Filmed on a set that was meant to replicate a typical American, low income, inner-city ghetto it specifically targeted (and often bringing on to the set as 'everyday people') children representative of America's 'melting pot' of peoples – Afro-American, Latino, Asian, and so on. Yet, despite its American-centric setting, it proved an immensely popular export – with children in the United Kingdom especially, due to the fact that, as made explicit in Chapter 2, children in the UK during the 1970s were immersed in, and totally familiar with, American culture as a result of a televisual diet of endless cartoons and 'cop shows' from the US. As a result of this familiarity with America – its culture, its geographical make-up, and even its urban criminality – *Sesame Street*, for many a British child, was 'your favourite Harlem back alley, where a policeman was a person in your neighbourhood' (Lewis, 2006: 271).

Adopting a bright, engaging mix of education, humour (often of the slapstick variety), and music, *Sesame Street* promoted open displays of humanist behaviour – tolerance of difference especially – through 'songs about co-operation, community spirit and mutual respect' (Lewis, 2006: 272). Such a 'community spirit' was at the heart of Sesame Street's 'neighbourhood'. Indeed, the 'neighbourhood' that was *Sesame Street* was, of course, very much a utopian one, 'where all races get along, where people sit on their porches and co-operate with their neighbours, where people take a genuine interest in the lives of the others around them in their urban community' (Lewis, 2006: 272–3). Its utopian values were often glazed in a sickly-sweet sense of unobtainable community, where '[t]he weather was always clement, the children were always happy, it was always late summer, where the echoes of some distant ball game and barking dog mixed with glowing feelings of safety, security and nostalgia' (Lewis, 2006: 273). Its unobtainable utopia could, arguably, be blamed (in part) for the failure of true racial harmony (and social integration more generally) amid the American inner-cities, as 'by the mid-1970s, the show had become a major symbol of racial, ethnic, and gender tolerance – of multiculturalism' – yet, by the same measure, '[o]ne can only wonder how much of the rosy, illusory quality many Americans perceive in multiculturalism can be traced to *Sesame Street*'s intentionally sweet and innocent vision of community' (Morrow, 2006: 159).

Yet, in its defence, *Sesame Street*'s utopian falseness was borne out of realist source material. In a deliberate move to eschew accepted children's television conventions of fantasy-based locations, Jon Stone (who was, originally, responsible for the show's writing, casting, and format) drew from the limited – yet ultimately rewarding – play options open to children of the American inner-cities: 'For a preschool child in Harlem, the street is where the action is' as 'from the vantage point of her apartment, the sidewalk outside must look like Utopia' (cited in Davis, 2008: 155). Thus, the show's set designer, Charles Rosen, in an effort to replicate something that was gritty and urban set about 'scouting locations in and around Harlem, drawing and photographing details of neighbourhoods'

(Davis, 2008: 155). This scouting eventually resulted in the show's set revolving around the comings and goings of 123 Sesame Street, the Fix-It Shop, the carriage house, and a diner/corner store, Hooper's Store – as the latter especially 'were common in cities at a time when no one thought twice about sending kids out to the corner store on their own for candy and groceries' (Gikow, 2009: 66). Fundamentally, of course, *Sesame Street*'s solidification as a media-derived vision of utopian neighbourhood had as much to do with its choice of locals as it did with its faithful reproduction of sidewalks and blocks. As well as being populated by Muppets such as Big Bird, the trashcan-bound Oscar, and the like, the show's human characters – Mr Harold Hopper (the owner of Hopper's Store, played by Will Lee), Bob Johnson (a music teacher, played by Bob McGrath, who lived above Hooper's Store) et al. – very much helped to instil in the minds of their young viewers a true sense of on-screen society in solidarity.

Although, despite an acknowledgement that, in reality, *Sesame Street* offered an unobtainable utopian ideal – and, in particular, a televised neighbourhood as nothing more than a construct – the very fact that it was watched, and highly popular with, the first generation of children to grow up with it meant that their measure of what neighbourhood was and what it meant to be part of a neighbourhood was defined by *Sesame Street*. Fundamentally then, many a child of the 1970s – Peter especially – could not fail to engage with their own neighbourhoods (cognitively, spatially, or otherwise) without some form of reference to *Sesame Street*'s version of neighbourhood. In effect, all children of the 1970s knew their way to *Sesame Street* – that is, the *Sesame Street* of their own neighbourhoods.

New Road

Emyr Gough, in John Bailey and Emyr Gough's *Skewen & District – A History* (1998), explains that:

> [t]he New Road, which until 1950 was the main artery from London to Fishguard, was always a hive of activity, and, although the traffic was nowhere near the density of the present day, it was nevertheless very heavy (1998: 38).

New Road, Skewen, was, for Peter, a childhood space upon which its adult usage encroached increasingly upon – in particular, as Gough makes explicit, through the year-upon-year increasing 'density' of traffic. This, of course, is evident of the erosion of street life which, historically, has been the preserve of children since the early years of urbanisation. Colin Ward, in *The Child in the City* (1978), insists that the priority given to motorists – at the expense of pedestrians, and 'street life' more generally – has meant that the urban environment, 'which used to be transparent to its young citizens who could follow the routes across it unerringly, is now opaque and impenetrable' (Ward, 1978: 118–21). Far more sombrely, Ward notes that such increased levels of traffic also, of course, equated increased levels of pedestrians being injured and killed when attempting to cross such busy roads. Indeed, what is often fondly remembered as culturally part-and-parcel of mediated life during the 1970s – the Green Cross Code (introduced in 1971) – was, in part, ineffectual, as 'very serious doubts arise about the capacity of many children to learn and understand the concepts of the code' (Ward, 1978: 123). As if to underline all of Ward's fears, he goes on to refer to one report by the European Ministers of Transport which stated 'that Britain has the worst child pedestrian casualty rate for all of Europe' (Ward, 1978: 124). New Road, as it leaves Skewen, heading towards Neath Abbey, becomes the B4290 proper. Peter has one memory of walking along that road that underlines both its busyness and its posing of hazards to child pedestrians in particular.

It is late afternoon. My friend and I are walking home from our comprehensive school, idly talking about our day, we spot another pupil from our school (a boy, in the same year as ourselves) also on his way home. Attempting to cross the B4290 at the Cwrt Herbert roundabout, and running in vain to get to the curb on the other side of the road, he is hit by a car at speed. Making impact with the bonnet, square in the middle, he flies, cart-wheeling into the air. My friend and I look at each other in absolute disbelief. The boy lay in a grey, crumpled heap on the road. Thankfully, though badly-injured, he was still alive.

Streets, of course, are far more than hazardous, traffic-prioritising stretches of tarmac. Streets are lined by both houses and shops. This chapter is, first and foremost, concerned with Peter's remembering of his childhood places – shops especially (and, as we'll appreciate a little later on, 'Miriam's' the newsagent in particular) – that were within close proximity of his childhood home, Ivy Cottage. Many shops in the immediate area invoke vivid memories such as 'Thomas the Ironmongers'. David Graham George, in his autobiographical account of life in Skewen during the mid-twentieth century, *A Skewen Boy Looks Back* (n.d.), offers a sensory-loaded recollection of Thomas's early years of business:

> [W]ith its old magnificent shop front, David Thomas behind the counter, perhaps weighing nails, or putty and then wrapping it up in newspaper. Everything seemed to be weighed then, or poured into your bottle or tin, but what I miss today are those old magnificent smells, linseed oil, turpentine, paraffin, I think even the nails had a smell (George, n.d.: 129).

Despite George's nostalgic suggestion that the shop's heyday has long past, Emyr Gough, in *Skewen and District – A History* (1998), insist that, since it opened in 1920, the business has continued to flourish, and that – following the retirement of David Thomas – 'his sons Trevor and Martin have run the business celebrating in 1995 their 75 anniversary' (Gough, cited in Bailey and Gough, 1998: 42). Indeed, during the 1970s, Thomas's was a bustling emporium that, on occasions, Peter found himself within, mesmerised by his imposing surroundings.

Walking hesitantly through the door, and into the shop, the sheer volume of manly tradesmen's tools and materials are overpowering: wood, metal, paint, and so on, is all around me. Tall, narrow, and warehouse-like, I stand in the middle of Thomas's and look up at the ceiling high above me. I feel giddy. Such a disconcerting space is exacerbated by both the shop's interior lighting and the natural daylight that dares to enter via the plate glass windows barely registering upon the shop's dark shelving and nooks and crannies. Full of things that would give you splinters or scratch and cut you, and heavy tools beyond lifting by a mere boy, this is most certainly not a child's space. But, on occasions such as this, it is an adult space that I, as a child, had to enter. Today I am here with my brother Jeremy to fetch paraffin – as a paraffin heater provides the only source of heat in our shared bedroom (in a house without central heating). On times such as these – when I accompany a member of my family to Thomas's the Ironmongers (or when I am even sent on my own, with money and a note to remind me of what I am meant to be getting) – it is always on an errand. I would never, ever, call otherwise. Here, jostled by the burly decorators and DIY enthusiasts, this is most definitely a space for adults. Yes, standing here, as a small boy, I think to myself: 'This is a man's place'.

Peter's memory of visiting Thomas's in order to purchase paraffin is in keeping with the three studies carried out of children and their neighbourhoods in Robin C. Moore's *Childhood's Domain – Play and Place in Child Development* (1986), whereby the children interviewed made little mention of visiting local shops, for '[o]ne reason for the low score was that children associated local shops with running domestic errands – with chores, rather than play' (Moore, 1986: 45–6). Although, that stated, it was also clear that 'local shops were a source of important childhood items and some of the children were highly discriminating about the quality of shops they patronised' (Moore, 1986: 46).

To stress, then, the shops discussed in this chapter, that were frequented by Peter, were not places of play as such: Instead, they were places of both family-orientated errands carried out by Peter and Peter's discriminatory purchasing fuelled by a vivid imagination.

Bus Shelters

Right opposite Peter's childhood home, Ivy Cottage, stood a concrete bus shelter.

The bus shelter is made out of prefabricated slabs of raw, reinforced concrete. Like some modern-day cave dwelling, it seems to be carved out of a lump of concrete. It is obviously reinforced, as, at points, chunks have come away to expose the rusting steel cables. With no windows whatsoever, and the only light entering from the hole that is the entrance-come-exit, it is dark in here. It is always dark in here. Even at midday, in the height of summer. The shelter is a space that we only ever enter in the heaviest of downpours, on the bleakest of winter's days (like today) – for there is no need, of course, to be in such a dark, dank space, but to shelter from the wind and the rain, the sleet and the snow. From where I'm standing, I can see that drips of rain (from cracks in the concrete roof, soaked coats, umbrellas, etc.), along with the muddied water that has been carried into the shelter from shoes and boots, have turned the floor of the shelter into a multi-puddled expanse of muddied mirrors. Also, ahead of the always-late bus arriving, the shelter – as a space that very much lacks space – is cramped, with steaming bodies huddled together. My head womb-height next to my Mammy, I reel as I breathe in the urine-drenched odours that are to be found at such a low level in this most prefabricated of concrete constructs.

This bus shelter was, of course, a communal space in many other respects. As well as providing a rendezvous for late-night, fumbled sexual encounters, it was a communal canvas for the marginalised of Skewen to inscribe their identities – through that most proletariat of means, graffiti. The bus-shelter's walls – both inside and outside – were awash with not only the miss-spelt aggressiveness of youthful frustrations and subcultural allegiance, but the desperate outpouring of young love. What was to be found all over this bus stop's grey surface was the ubiquitous scrawl that was 'Taryn and Tyrone Forever' (and other variants of this declaration of undying love). A teenage couple, angst-ridden and desperately searching for a shared identity (they became Skewen's token 'Punks' come the summer of 1976), they – and the graffiti announcing their relationship – became integral ingredients in the mythologizing of Skewen's youth.

Arguably, of course, the 1970s proved to be *the* decade where an increasing level of urban decay coincided with excessive levels of vandalism in its most aesthetically displeasing form – that of graffiti-daubed brick walls. Many cultural texts of this time – especially those aimed at, or concerned with, children and 'youth issues' – collectively positioned Britain's young as both the cause and victims of such decay and vandalism by incorporating graffiti-daubed walls, fences, etc., as central motifs: motifs, that, in turn, placed emphasis upon the 'street-wise' convictions of those cultural texts.

The Children's Film Foundation's *Hide and Seek* (1972, starring a young Gary Kemp), an adaptation of Roy Brown's novel *The Day of the Pigeons* (1968), is concerned with Keith the 'Deptford Dodger' who, having absconded from an approved school, is in search of his petty-criminal father. Deptford is depicted, in the opening frenetic moments of the film, as typical of London's 'urban jungle' through the credits appearing as paint-daubed graffiti upon corrugated sheeting-enclosed wasteland. Likewise, the title sequence of *4 Idle Hands* (ATV, 1976),[1] after a sepia montage of manual labour and factory work,[1] shows a young black male in front of an intimidating, high brick wall, with the upper floors of a housing estate just about visible, through a low mist, beyond. Significantly, the credits themselves appear as paint-brush graffiti upon the wall. No surprise, then, that this series, aimed at teenage viewers:

> charts the unsteady progress of Mike and Pete, two 16-year-old school-leavers who are suddenly forced to ponder the bewildering but urgent question: what are they going to do for a living? As Mike and Pete's efforts to avoid the dole queue land them a succession of disastrous jobs, 4 Idle Hands humorously details the unremitting difficulties of adolescence (DVD, rear cover).

It was a series that 'took a light-hearted though still realistic look at what was a serious subject in the mid-1970s as unemployment and inflation began to rise' (McGown and Docherty, 2003: 97).

Far from 'light-hearted' was a strip to be found in a violent comic that was very much a product of an increasingly violent decade: 'Kids Rule OK!' in *Action* (1976). With an editorial team determined to produce a 'realistic' children's comic, that 'had to be up-to-date, a comic of its time' (Barker, 1989: 19), provisional, alternative titles for the comic – which resonated with the contemporary theme of 'aggro Britain'[2] – 'ranged from *Boots* to *Dr Martens*' (Barker, 1989: 19). With *Action* being ultimately chosen and launched on 14 February 1976, it very much remained a 'street-wise' weekly comic that contained ultra-violent strips to do with football ('Look Out for Lefty!' which controversially include a seeming endorsement of football hooliganism) and roaming, lawless gangs of youth – the aforementioned 'Kid Rule OK!'. Eventually provoking a media furore and a Commons' debate, all resulting in the comic being withdrawn in December 1976, it is to 'Kids Rule OK!' – and its incorporation of graffiti within its pages – that we now turn.

Set in a near-future where, a virus wipes out almost the entire adult population, the initial instalment – showing two youths, one holding down a sole, remaining 'oldie', whilst the other one boots him in the face – menacingly warned:

---

1   It is important to note that the opening credits of *4 Idle Hands* is redolent of both the cover and content of Paul Willis' classic study of 'the lads', *Learning to Labour – How Working Class Kids Get Working Class Jobs* (1977). A sociological working class boys-to-men tale, that followed Willis' sampled cohort from school-to-work, it was, of course, pre-dated by ATV's series by a year.

2   For an in-depth consideration of how 'aggro Britain' was reflected in children's comics of the 1970s, see Jachimiak (2008).

But the kids remained – roaming freely in gangs in a world where there were suddenly no more rules or petty restrictions. Kids like the Malvern Road Mob of North London (Cited in Barker, 1990: 237).

Across the brick wall, which forms an urban backdrop to this act of random violence, is the strip's title in the form of dripped-paint graffiti. Thus, at the start of each week's strip thereafter, its title was in the form of such paint-tin graffiti upon a dense stretch of brick wall. And with the previous weeks' synopsis appearing as a peeling fly poster upon that wall, there also stood, just in front, at the base of the wall, a drip-festooned paint pot, with the handle of a discarded brush protruding from its open top. No wonder, then, as Barker highlights (1990: 7), that *Action* was termed by the tabloid press as 'The Sevenpenny Nightmare' (*The Sun*, 30 April 1976) and 'Comic Strip Hooligans' (*The Daily Mail*, 17 September 1976).

Graffiti – as both a social and cultural signifier of troublesome (and troubled) youth and urban decay – remained (in fact, intensified) as the 1970s progressed, to the point where so-called 'children's television' proved harder-hitting than their adult counterparts. Southern's *Noah's Castle* (broadcast across April and May, 1980), despite being set in a near future where law-and-order was at breaking point, was a series that 'was within close enough proximity to reality for the audience to take it seriously, especially as inflation rates had been high for four or five years at that point in time' (McGown and Docherty, 2003: 142). Adapted from John Rowe Townsend's 1975 novel for children, the series' credits open dramatically with, the camera at street level, armed youths running in slow-motion towards the viewer, as 'Noah's Castle' appears as gaudy, spray-can on-screen graffiti. Followed by scenes (again, in slow-motion, with the camera virtually on the tarmac) of rioting, with the army barely keeping control) this was a stark equating of urban vandalism with societal disintegration. The sociologist Stanley Cohen highlights such technological advances as the aerosol spray:

Aerosol sprays are much quicker and easier to apply than paint, and fairly long slogans can be sprayed on posters in a matter of seconds. This decreases the chances of detection even in busy public settings and allows a number of offences to be committed in a short time (Cohen, 1973: 221).

On the other hand, according to Colin Ward:

any open-minded student of graffiti will agree that this particular medium has improved the form, if not yet the content, of graffiti, since it raises the standard of lettering simply because it imposes a bold, free-flowing line on the user, by the comparison with the effect of dripping paint or hesitant chalk (Ward, 1973: 305).

Vandalism – of which, of course, graffiti was a major, and highly visible, proportion – was an environmental phenomenon which, by the start of the decade, was not only widespread but under considerable academic debate and media scrutiny. Citing

Stanley Cohen's ground-breaking work on the topic, Colin Ward, in *Vandalism* (1970), notes that with regards vandalism (fundamentally an aggressive act), '[t]he people concerned are likely to have a dead-end education or a dead-end job' (1970: 18) and 'while ordinary people's lives are boring and frustrating, we are bound to get outbursts of meaningless destructiveness' (1970: 18). Furthermore, with regards vandalism carried out by children, Ward adds: 'With children it is different. Life in towns is so fenced-in and buttoned-up, so lacking in what architects call "unmake"' (1970: 18), that is 'why vandalism gives them the thrills they can't get any other way' (1970: 19).

Vandalism – and graffiti in particular – came to equate the urban decay and social decline of the 1970s to such an extent that one of the first retrospectives, Phillip Whitehead's *The Writing On The Wall – Britain in the Seventies* (1985), utilised an expanse of the graffiti-strewn urban brick wall as its cover. In doing so, it also inadvertently paid homage to the cover of Colin Ward's key texts on the subject matter. Ward's book, the afore-mentioned *Vandalism*, published at the very start of that dreary decade, was accompanied by a faeces-coloured cover that was a brick wall covered in both black and white paint lettering that, simultaneously, provided both the book's title and – with 'Up Yours!', 'Bovver', and the like – typical examples of period graffiti.

Red Phone Booths

In order both to commemorate the 25th anniversary of the establishment of the Samaritans and provide young people with a collection of short stories that, it was hoped, would inspire those experiencing the 'loneliness' of childhood to engage in communication, Monica Dickens and Rosemary Sutcliff, in 1978, published *Is Anyone There?* Including contributions from a range of respected children's authors such as Roald Dahl and Alan Garner, what now places this edited text very much in its time is its cover; a stark, mainly black-and-white photo of a dark, run-down end of town, with two daunting tower blocks dominating the backdrop. What dominates the cover, both front and back, in its Post Office Red livery (which, along with the matching red lettering of the title and editors names, is the only colour to be found on the cover) is a phone booth.[3] With a blurred image of a person inside (their back to the reader, as they use the phone), this, quite clearly, is the only haven amid this barren, alienating urban landscape. Furthermore, upon opening the book, the first short story is – at a single page in length – Brian Patten's 'Making a Call' (first published 1969):

> Alone in a red phone booth ... All over cities people standing alone in red phone booths ... relating back to their own reflections in misted-up windows ... I dreamt one night the whole world slept together in a red phone booth (Patten, 1978: 9).

---

3   The full, and official, designation of 'Post Office Red' is 'BS381C – red 538' (Johannessen, 2010: 17).

Patten's short story (which borders on poetry), particularly the evocation of the phone box's 'misted-up windows', reminds Peter of his own childhood memories tied up with such a 'red phone booth'.

It's Friday, mid-morning, and it's raining. Being giving the signal by Mammy, I reach up and (with considerable effort) push the already-positioned 2p coin through the slot. A split second later, and with a deep sense of gratification, I hear it crash, joining all the other change, deep in the belly of the black, dented box. A collection of other coins are warming up in my hand, ready for use. With a gossip-rife conversation going on way above my head (my Mammy engaging in her weekly telephone conversation with Mam – her mother, my only grandmother), I occupy myself silently at the level of her hips. There is the well-thumbed yellow directory, but that is of only momentary, limited interest. What are far more capable of occupying fully the mind of a bored, yet imaginative, young boy such as myself are the windows. Steamed up due to the combined heat of two bodies, my miniature digits make dots (with finger tips), draw lines (by joining-up those dots), and, in vain, attempt to demist entire panes of the kiosk's many rectangular windows (with a flurry of wipes with the side of my hand). Of course, visibility is not improved – the rain lashing against the outside puts paid to that. Still bored, I look down, around and about my plimsolled feet: discarded, squashed fag ends, their yellow nicotine draining away into the myriad of muddy puddles on the floor. And, yes, just like the bus shelter, it stinks of urine. The leather straps, which help support the heavy door, are frayed and blackened by pollution. Thus, after half-an-hour or so of this, it is a relief to, with all of my might, push open the door, and to be, once again, outside, drenched by the incessant downpour.[4]

Peter's memory of being inside the phone booth (and, for that matter, the bus stop), and conscious of his spatial relationship to both his mother (that is, being at 'womb-height' and 'the level of her hips') and proximity to the floor, is in keeping with Christopher Day's *Environment and Children – Passive Lessons from the Everyday Environment* (2007). Day not only insists that children, in comparison with adults, experience spaces and places in often opposing ways, but that children's 'spatial consciousness is also different' (Day, 2007: 5). Whilst children and adults may (often simultaneously) occupy spaces, those space are interpreted differently by a child '[a]s lower eye-level shrinks spatial boundaries' (Day, 2007: 5), and those differences vary according to the age of the child. For,

---

4 Peter is absolutely convinced that he and his mother also used the Phone Box on sunny summers' days (with him usually being used to prop open the door, allowing in fresh air, in order to stop the insides becoming as hot as a greenhouse), but, in keeping with popular collective memory, and as with his memory of waiting inside the bus shelter, it always seemed to be raining when they were in there.

'[s]mall children interact with space more through life-energy than prethought-out rational intention', yet, '[i]n mid-childhood, their actions are mostly led by emotions' (Day, 2007: 5). Crucially, Day also makes a further distinction – even relating it to a child's sensitivity to meteorological considerations: 'Although *people* are more important for children, it is *places* that they tend to remember better. They intimately know every inch of their play territory: how every bit feels in different weathers' (Day, 2007: 8). That is why, then, Peter still associates those spaces of his childhood, such as the bus stop and the phone booth, with being in them accompanied by his mother; but Peter also vividly remembers – still *feels* even – those same childhood spaces as places within which he experienced the elements (rain causing drips and forming puddles, etc.).

The Post Office Red phone booth (actually the 'K6', 'Jubilee Kiosk' – otherwise colloquially referred to as a 'kiosk' or 'phone box') was, certainly by the 1970s, a common site across Britain. Having been launched in 1936 (replacing 'K1s' and 'K3s'), it became Britain's standard kiosk for over three decades, whereby '[i]n that time around 60,000 were erected' (Johannessen, 2010: 12). Yet, as with the bus shelter, the out-of-order and defaced phone booth – especially by the late 1970s – came to epitomise a decaying social order. Indeed, as well as being synonymous with theft and vandalism, they (both broken and working), proved an eyesore, as '[a] bright red telephone box stood out rather too well for some people' (Johannessen, 2010: 12). In a number of Peter's family photographs, taken in the garden, facing New Road as it rises, there, in the background, is to be found that very same red phone booth. It stands there, vibrant in its redness, a sentinel of communication amid the neighbourhood.

Eventually, as these ageing K series booths found themselves being superseded by the more state-of-the-art KX versions, 'there was a surge of nostalgia for what was about to disappear' (Johannessen, 2010: 24). A BBC Wales News online article, noting the decline in usage of phone booths, suggested that any emotionally charged reminiscing of the red versions arose 'as people recall their youth, possibly making calls to girlfriends or boyfriends' (Leonard, 24 March 2011). Taken out of service, the K series booths were either scrapped or sold. Following public auctioning of them en masse, these iconic red phone booths – once again – started to appear in back yards, gardens, etc., to the extent that even entire fields full of them could be found as complete, recycled and restored units were bought by dealers to then be exported world-wide. Meanwhile, and rather bizarrely, many of these now-redundant red phone booths found themselves refurbished and put to use as, amongst other things, cocktail bars, book shelves, fish tanks, and the like. Indeed, '[s]ome have found use in nightclubs and restaurants as housings for payphones!' (Johannessen, 2010: 24).

Sweets, Toys, and Newsagents

In his sympathetic examination of mid-twentith century working-class life, *The Uses of Literacy* (1957), Richard Hoggart notes, with regards notions of the neighbourhood, that '[t]his is an extremely local life, in which everything is remarkably near', whereby 'day-to-day services are just over the road or round the corner, and practically every street has its corner-shop, usually a general grocer's or paper shop' (Hoggart, 2010: 47). Meanwhile, and far more recently, 'celebrity chef' Nigel Slater warmly notes that '[t]o those who like the security and sense of belonging that is part and parcel of living in a small community, the village shop will become the epicentre of their world' (Slater, 2007: 68).

In *Skewen & District – A History* (1998) Emyr Gough takes the reader on a – quite literally – up-hill tour of New Road, shop by shop. His inventory of Skewen's small businesses begins at the very foot of this hilly thoroughfare (just 'up the hill' from Ivy Cottage) with Phillips' the Newsagents: 'Harry Phillips' Newspaper shop ... most recently managed by daughter Miriam and her husband, has been in business from the early 1930s. Tradition says that the shop was the original vicarage' (Gough, cited in Bailey and Gough, 1998: 39–40). Significantly, and despite Gough's regarding of this newsagents as 'Philips', Peter and his family referred to 'Phillips' as 'Miriam's' – in doing so, not only ignoring the work carried out by her husband, Dillwyn, but acknowledging, perhaps, the centrality of the 'Mam' (that is, the generic motherly figure) in Welsh society and culture.

Yet, despite the centrality – and longevity – of such small businesses (and such shopkeepers) as Miriam's, they were, certainly by the mid-1990s, in very real danger of extinction. For villages, like Skewen, that had, over the decades, expanded as a result of new housing developments, their many, localised village shops – since the late 1970s especially – have been in decline. Whilst being out-priced by the multiple stores being the primary factor here, '[s]ome villagers are reluctant to use the local store because they no longer perceive it as fashionable or suitable for their needs' (Bensley, 2009: 42). Out of fashion, and no longer satisfying the needs of the increasingly more discerning customer, the rate that these small businesses are folding is both rapid and heart-rending, for '[t]he tragedy is that we are losing about 300 village shops a year' (Slater, 2007: 69). Of course, with the closure of so many 'corner shops' comes the 'closure' of the interwoven essences of both shopping locally and feeling part of a neighbourhood, to the extent that 'our freedom of choice is jeopardised and the character of our towns is impoverished with every small shop that is destroyed' (Evans and Lawson, 1986: 8).

Children's texts have, historically, placed the 'sweet shop' at the heart of the child's perception of their neighbourhood. In *Mary, Mungo and Midge* (BBC, 1969), for instance, at the start of all 13 episodes, the narrator (Richard Baker) sets the scene, for the young viewers (as the screen with an animated, urban panorama), of both a collective childhood and a shared neighbourhood:

> A town is full of buildings. Some tall. Some short. Some wide. Some narrow. The buildings are flats, and houses, and factories, and shops. They're built in streets. The streets have cars, and lorries, and buses, driving along them ... The cars, and the buses, and the streets, are full of people. In fact, there are a lot of people in the town.

Then, asking the young audience 'Do you live in a town?', the scene shows a bustling, multi-coloured street, with – centre-screen – an outlet bearing the sign 'The Sweet Shop'. Thus, come the very start of the 1970s, the children watching would not only have had a clear understanding of 'town' (indeed, *their* town, *their* neighbourhood), but the centrality of those shops that catered just for them – especially the sweet shop – within their neighbourhood.

According to Dominic Sandbrook (2010), children in the 1970s found themselves not only to be part of a generation entitled to free state education and national health care, 'but they were also lucky to be growing up at a time when, thanks to the boom in living standards since the 1950s, affluence had gently trickled down the generations' (Sandbrook, 2010: 348). With pocket money now the preserve of working class children, a 'shared experience' (that is, despite the continuing existence of class-based inequalities) characterised the 1970s child and their financial ability to engage in consumerist-based play:

> British children in the 1970s arguably had more of a common culture than any generation before them. Rich or poor, all but a tiny minority has a stake in the world of Action Man, Star Wars and Scalextrix, yo-yos, roller-skates an Sindy dolls, Uno, Mastermind and the Magna Doodle (Sandbrook, 2010: 348).

This 'common culture' (as, of course, alluded to in *Mary, Mungo and Midge*, and other children's television) meant that, for children, 'the political and economic shocks of the seventies hardly registered even as a distant rumbling on the horizon', whereby 'most children were barely affected by the major news stories of the day' (Sandbrook, 2010: 347).[5] Even if the decade's hardships did register with children, they were almost always overshadowed by the more mundane – but, for them, far more exciting – everyday. For instance, Sandbrook highlights that, in her diary (New Year's Day 1974, to be exact), a 12-year-old Essex girl inscribed details to do with on-going energy crisis and the resultant power cuts, but, equally importantly, 'her other diary entries during the national crisis were taken up with camping expeditions, trips to sweet shops and Chinese takeaways' (Sandbrook, 2010: 347). With those dark, candle-lit, winter evenings of the mid-1970s in mind, let us allow Nigel Slater to wax-lyrical over such a trip to the sweet shop that many a child would have typically had made at this time:

> On the wall behind the counter were row upon row of sweetie jars ... There were sweets of vermilion and rose, saffron and lemon, and twists of amber and green. Pear shapes, lozenges and elegant little comfits, wine gums with 'port' and 'brandy' embossed upon them, and black-and-white humbugs as shiny as

---

5   Sandbrook (2010) also suggest that this 'common culture', and the resulting children's ignorance of the political and economic hardships of the decade, has resulted in the 1970s generation – now 'forty-something' adults – looking back on that decade with such a rose-tinted nostalgia.

a Venetian marble floor. Some shone emerald and deepest ruby like precious gems, others pale and delicate in old-lady shades of violet and lavender. Fairy drops and barley sugars, chocolate toffees and midget gems, fruit jellies, glacier fruits and sugared almonds, all imprisoned in glass jars so large it took two hands to upend their contents into the weighing scales (Slater, 2007: 188–9).

Although, by the 1970s, not all the enticing sweets on offer were so poetic in their appeal. Gary Robertson, in *Skeem Life – Growing Up in the Seventies* (2010), makes explicit that – certainly experiencing that decade as a child in the 'harder', inner-city estates (as he did in Dundee) – many sweets, both traditional and 'trendy', of the era were consumed solely because of their 'hard' characteristics. Thus, 'Victory V and Fisherman's lozenges were fairly popular and sometimes we'd stuff a whole packet of them into our mouths … If you were really mental you'd drink a big glass of ice-cold water after you'd swallowed them which was disturbingly uncomfortable' (2010: 145). Meanwhile, 'Space Dust had an altogether different effect and the little lumps of candy exploded like dynamite in your mouth, so naturally you stuffed the whole packet in!' (2010: 148). Needless to say, but Peter holds similarly vivid memories of visiting the sweetshop (and eating Space Dust by the packet!) – the 'sweetshop' being, of course, Miriam's the newsagents.

I'm slowly walking the short distance home from Miriam's. Miriam's is so close to home that, there and back, I'm still in the comfort of carpet slippers and not proper shoes. Further comfort is provided by a hastily-placed sweet already melting away in my impatient mouth. Laden with paper bags full of 'a quarter' of this and 'a quarter' of that, they are all going to be, in a few moments time, be shared with Mammy. All afternoon and all evening, they will rattle around in her mouth, clashing noisily every now and again with her false teeth. All of the sweets, of course, have just been paid for with that shiny, new, fifty pence piece (decimalisation had only been a few years earlier) given to me by Daddy who – having coming home a little sozzled from a visit to one of the local pubs on the way home from work – is 'flush' following a win at the 'bookies'.[6]

Tom Sweetman, in his article 'The Devil in the Shop' (2007b), acknowledges the intoxicating – and, thus, ever-tempting – contents of the 'corner shop' that he frequently visited as a child, known locally as 'Barnes Papershop', 'Mr Barnes', or 'Barnsies'. For, to clarify, the 'devil' alluded to in title of his article was the

---

6　Despite Sandbrook (2010) insisting that economic hardships of the 1970s barely registered with the children of that decade, Peter was more than aware of his families struggle to make ends meet financially. Peter remembers that, on one occasion, he and his father joked about that week's 'take home pay' was insufficient – that, let alone to feed a family, it was not enough to 'feed the cats'.

combined, highly-addictive lure of not only the aforementioned sweets, but the equally colourful weekly comics and plastic toys. Sweetman places emphasis upon the fact that the term 'newsagent was a totally inadequate description of what was on offer at Barnsies (likewise, at Miriam's), as:

> [t]his was your *Waterstones*, *Thorntons*, *Hamleys* and *Woolworths* rolled into one tobacco scented, newsprint stained convenience store dedicated to the joys of visual and oral recreation. Along the shelves was the chocolate and beyond the chocolate were the books, the annuals and the toys (Sweetman, 2007b: 42).

Furthermore, Sweetman has a particular memory of his visits to Barnsies which resonates with Peter's own memories of being in Miriam's (not to mention Peter's other spatially-orientated recollections of being at the bus stop and in the phone box):

> In my memory I always seem to be standing behind women with rain dripping from coats and umbrellas on to the linoleum floors that glistened and reflected the lights (Sweetman, 2007b: 42).

So, it is to the toys sold at Barnsies, Miriam's, and at all the other newsagents during the 1970s, that we now turn. Newsagents, to those children that lived near them, often served as their respective neighbourhoods' only toyshop, and, as Anthony Burton, in *Children's Pleasures* (1996), makes clear, '[t]o visit a toyshop is one of childhood's most exquisite experiences'. In particular, then, it is one type of toy – one specific brand even – that we are concerned with here, that, come the 1970s, was being marketed in increasingly bold and dramatic packaging: Airfix model kits.

Come the beginning of the 1970s, Airfix dominated both the toy market and a model-making craze at the height of its popularity. This was demonstrated by the fact that '[t]he company was releasing newer and better kits at a prodigious rate every month' (Ward, 2009: 91), and that, by the middle of the decade, it was at its financial zenith, as '[i]n the 1974/75 financial year Airfix Industries turnover was up 38 per cent and profits had leapt a staggering 30 per cent' (Ward, 2004: 45). Indeed, key to their unchallenged success had been the realisation, at the start of the previous decade, that the illustrations utilised upon the packaging – or, rather, the 'boxtop' – 'had to convey colour and excitement to attract customers' (Cross and Ward, 2002: 20). In an emerging consumer society, it was no longer sufficient for a product to merely sit on a shelf, hoping to be picked up. Instead, the packaging needed to catch the eye, in order to raise itself – as a desirable product – above its competitors. Thus, 'Airfix decided to promote their kits via a style of dramatic, full-colour artwork' (Pask, 2011: 47). To this end, several regular artists were commissioned to carry out the illustration of these boxtops, with the two most renowned being Brian Knight and Roy Cross, for whilst '[t]heir paintings were almost photographically accurate representations, … the aircraft, tanks, cars and figures were placed in idealised situations that no photographer could ever have captured' (Pask, 2011: 47). For example, during the 1970s, the so-called 'Dog Fight Doubles' were not only an excellent marketing ploy, where Airfix managed to combine two related (and already existing) kits in one box, but, '[a]ided by Roy Cross's stirring artwork designed to trigger the imaginations of young purchasers, this series was an enormous success' (Ward, 2009: 95). Indeed, with regards the inspirational boxtop artwork of Roy Cross in particular, Arthur Ward – author of a number of books to do with Airfix and its artists – admits:

> They certainly inspired me. I would rush home from the toyshop eager to try to recreate the events suggested by Roy's box-top painting (Ward, 2009: 107).

Like Ward, Peter, too, would – seconds after purchasing such a 'Dog Fight Double' from Miriam's – run off home, and hurriedly assemble the two warplanes, in order to re-enact Cross's boxtop conflict.

———————————

I have now been gazing at the glorious array of dramatically illustrated Airfix boxtops – all to be found in a row along one of Miriam's windows – for what seems hours (though it's probably only been a few minutes). It's 1973 and, with the lure of Airfix at its prime, I am captivated by these wondrously bright depictions of battles being won on land, sea and in the air. One in particular has caught my eye: the '72nd Scale', World War One 'Camel & Albatross'. Fronted by a typically exhilarating Roy Cross boxtop it shows the unfortunate German bi-plane, the Albatross, plummeting to the ground; a streak of red, yellow, and black flames, with smoke billowing from its bullet-holed engine. This, of course, leaves the vivid red, white, and blue livery of the triumphant British Camel at the centre of the box's rousing illustration of aerial battle. Following Dillwyn's straining reach into the window (from behind the counter, through a sliding access hatch), it is, along with glue, swiftly bought and bagged, as I then dash home. Within half and hour they are both assembled. Seconds later, the Albatross is in my hand, hurtling to its doom on the carpeted floor of our living room. In my mind, the flames lick the fuselage, black smoke chokes the already fatally injured pilot. Finally, my voice gleefully mimics the screams of the engine in its downward spiral, the eventual splintering crash, and the resultant all-engulfing explosion.

———————————

The 1970s was a particularly violent decade, and a constant manifest aggression (it was hoped) would be, in part, tempered through the sanitising of warplaying toys – Airfix boxtops in particular. Thus, '1977 saw the start of a complete repackaging programme, removing all depictions of violence from box artwork' (Ward, 2009: 111). The Third Reich emblem of the swastika was no longer to be seen upon the boxtops – indeed, it had been already illegal to do so, 'a blind eye had been turned for many years' (Peter Allen, Airfix Designer, cited in Ward, 2009: 111). Yet, with the merest suggestion of bombing raids, blazing machine guns, and the like, now – by the late 1970s – gone, many at Airfix felt that this 'sanitisation of the boxtops' had gone too far, as:

> everything became a bit bland … These things were fighters. They were bombers. They shot at each other or dropped bombs. This is what you expected to see (Trevor Snowden, Airfix's Product Development Manager, cited in Ward, 2009: 174).

Every well-made Airfix kit involved not only the painstaking placing of decals and careful brushing on of Humbrol paint, it required, of course, assembly via the meticulous dropping and spreading of glue. The use of this glue (referred to in the trade as 'cement') by children is something well-and-truly a 1970s memory, as purchasing such 'cement' by a child is now illegal. That is not to say that during the heyday of Airfix such a product was not abused by children. As Richard Lewis, in *The Bumper Book of Fads and Crazes* (2005), jokingly alludes that those children that were not so adept – or even remotely interested in – modelling Airfix kits 'found other uses for leftover solvents' (2005: 9). No surprise, then, that one of the most notorious 'do-it-yourself' fanzines of late-1970s Punk named itself obstinately *Sniffin' Glue*. Running for 12 issues across 1976 and 1977 (and most unlike a pristine, proudly finished Airfix kit), and put together 'by just one disaffected youth … Deptford punk fan Mark Perry' (Spencer, 2005: 191), it 'was a mess of hand printing and mis-typed interviews – representing in print the values of punk' (Spencer, 2005: 192).

With the Airfix generation ageing at a time of Punk and its aftermath, growing recession, increasing unemployment, and poor pre-Christmas toy spending across December 1980, Airfix were now in dire straits. With wholesalers letting their stock of kits dwindle, pre-tax losses, a decline in turnover, and a losing battle to reduce its bank borrowings, it began to sell off many of its companies. Eventually suspending it shares, it called in the receivers:

> Airfix products ceased trading in January 1981. Cruel irony dictated that the announcement of this sudden misfortune was made at the 1981 Earls Court Toy Fair (Ward, 2004: 45).[7]

Thus, with the passing of time, for the children – boys in particular, of course – who grew up in the 1970s, Airfix was far more than a model you put together – as John Wells, Secretary of the Airfix Collectors Club, nostalgically-muses: 'Airfix? It's about childhood. It's the summer holidays when the sun always shone. I suppose those are remembered as the happiest times' (cited in, Ward, 1999: 98).

But, if only he had looked more carefully. Many of those colourful boxes, often those at the top of windows, the ones that were always difficult for Dillwyn to

---

7   All was not lost, for in 1981 Airfix underwent a transfer of ownership to Palitoy.

reach, were often dusty and faded by sunlight – in fact, just like neighbourhood's collective memories of the two World Wars themselves. Peter, one of the few children that lived in this aged neighbourhood, was usually the only child who purchased these staples of a 1970s childhood.

Magical Shops

As already discussed in Chapter 2, the television within the home – right from its inception – can be regarded as a form of 'haunted media'. With the introduction of coloured television into British homes (from 1967 onwards), the television and its programming now took on an even more *heimlich*-yet-*unheimlich* edge. Children's television of this time, the early 1970s, embraced fully the increased opportunities to enchant their young audience through the new medium of colour. For many of the programmes aimed at children, from the first half of the decade especially, brought the bright, garish colours and patterns of late-1960s psychedelia, and incorporate them within the child's everyday experience of watching television. Furthermore, the child's everyday that was the visit to the sweetshop, the toy shop, the newsagents, etc., now became something akin to a mysterious adventure as a result of a number of children's television programmes from this era – with the local or corner shop, and shopkeepers as their focus – not only embracing the possibilities of full-colour broadcasting but the incorporation of elements of magic within their storylines.

Each episode of *The Magic Ball* (Granada, 1971) begins, along with music box accompaniment, with the narrator (Eric Thompson) introducing us to a small boy, Sam, who lives in a busy seaside town, Haythornethwaite, and a shop in a side street ('away from the main busyness') run by his Aunt Mill that 'sells interesting things' (such as birdcages, grandfather clocks, Buddhas, rocking horses, etc.). Brian Cosgrove's stylised animation, with its lurid pinks, acidic greens, and proliferation of flowery motifs, was 'like a late 1960s cartoon book or a piece of psychedelic artwork, with all the colour you'd expect from the era. And at times, the animation gets more than a little quirky, with the odd bit of inspiration taken from the Beatles' Yellow Submarine and in some episodes (like The Story Of The Chimney Sweep), mixing in some live footage of the day' (23 November 2006).[8] Crucially, the narrator is at pains to explain the ordinariness of this extraordinary television series for children: 'Now, Sam was just like other boys, except for one thing – he had a magic ball which could take him to all sorts of different places and bring him back again'. Yet, despite Sam's (and the programme's young audiences') ordinariness, Aunt Mill's shop, as the site where the magical qualities of *The Magic Ball* begin (that is, both the programme itself, and Sam's own magic ball), meant that such shops – and the shops that the young audience visited in their everyday ordinariness – now took on other-worldly dimensions.

---

8   See www.retrotog.com

Likewise, *Mr Benn* (BBC, 1971–1972), an equally colourful representation of shops, shopkeepers, and the British high street, showed – in each and every one of the series' 13 instalments – the bowler-hatted, pinstriped-suited protagonist visiting a 'special costume shop', within which the shopkeeper would appear 'as if by magic'. Indeed, to the young viewers, there was no doubt that 'the shopkeeper is magical', as '[h]e sends Mr Benn on adventures in different worlds then he leads him back home' (Read, 2001: 174). Mr Benn's entry and exit, in and out of these 'adventures' relied upon a portal, to be found deep within this costume shop's interior. When Mr Benn 'walked back out of the changing room door, he would find himself transported into some strange land where we would experience a colourful and elaborately-constructed scenario based upon his costume' (Lewis, 2006: 205–6). The closure of each episode (thus, each 'adventure'):

> would always be signalled by the sudden appearance of the shopkeeper who would guide him back to normality, through a door which mysteriously appeared and led back to the changing room (Lewis, 2006: 206).

Significantly, the shopkeeper's magical attributes – and the costume shop's blend of *heimlich* and *unheimlich* – were denoted by not only his general demeanour but his quirky dress sense as well:

> His cheery wave and smiling greeting make his exotic magical shop a homely place to be, but his purple Fez and uncanny knack of knowing which costume would best suit Mr Benn's day show that he is not an ordinary man (Read, 2001: 174).

Whilst not wearing Fezzes, or having any obvious magical qualities, to Peter, the family of shopkeepers that ran Thomas's the Ironmongers (already considered in detail, of course, earlier in this chapter), nevertheless, displayed a rather 'uncanny' collective persona.

The men who work in Thomas's the Ironmongers scare me. They all look alike. And they all wear those tight brown overalls, every button done up, like shopworkers' straightjackets. I never like being served by them. It is an eerie, unsettling experience precisely because of what they wear, how they appear to me, and how they look at me with their bespectacled suspicion. They all remind me of the Fez-wearing assistant in Mr Benn; these doppelganger men, all in their matching shop overalls (amid these otherworldly premises), are of another time, another place – even another world.

Not all children's television of the early to mid-1970s, of course, uniformly represented shops and shopkeepers in such a manner that aligned itself to a post-psychedelic Britain. Programmes such as *Bagpuss* (BBC, 1974) drew upon the previous decade's preoccupation with Edwardiana, and – eschewing a lurid colour scheme and a frenetic pursuit of adventure – embraced, in order to present another facet of 'otherness', turn-of-the-century, faded photography, slow-motion awakenings, and puzzlement-come-inventions. Oliver Postgate (one of the two series' creators), when developing ideas as to what type of shop should be the series' focus (and how, in turn, both the shop and each week's episode should be introduced), tentatively pondered that:

> The shop itself was probably antique. In fact the whole scene would be set at the turn of the century, using some early sepia vignetted photographs as an introduction (Postgate, 2000: 296–7).

Each episode, following its sepia-tinged start, would, rather reluctantly, transform into a colour transmission (albeit, in a noticeably washed-out palette of colours), only at the command of the series' sole human character – a child named Emily. So, ostensibly, '[t]hey were all alive, the toys: all it took was the sound of Emily's voice and they would all wake up' (Lewis, 2006: 28). Although, the transformation from sepia to colour, and the gradual, reluctant manner within which the shop's inanimate content would now come to life, suggested that they were indeed real – but, more than likely, in Emily's (and, of course, the viewers') minds only.

Postgate was adamant that such a series should distance itself as much as possible from contemporary notions of shops and shopping: 'Ordinary shops sold things. That was a bit too ordinary ... So this shop didn't sell anything' (Postgate, 2000: 296). Thus, the shop in *Bagpuss* fell considerably short of being a 'small business' in that it seemingly failed to do any business at all, as the objects on display in the shop were not for sale. Instead, lost, broken objects – upon being found, and brought to the shop, by Emily – would be placed in sight of Bagpuss (a rather overweight, pink and cream striped cat), where, after a recital of a poem by Emily, all of the shop's characters would wake up to examine, and then mend, the object.[9] Finally, 'they would put it in the shop window so that whoever it belonged to could come in and collect it' (Postgate, 2000: 296).

In a final analysis, *Bagpuss* was a mid-1970s series for children that, in many respects, merged the eerie and the unsettling of the past (through Edwardian stills of the cast, human and inanimate) with the predictability of the present (the everyday that is the shop). Come the end of each and every episode, all of the shop's inhabitants 'would eventually lapse back into a kind of gloomy torpor' (Lewis, 2006: 29). Although, the young viewers would witness this return to normality knowing full well that, come the next episode of *Bagpuss*, all would, once again, spring to life – and that was, in its uncannyness, expectably comforting:

---

9   In keeping with *Bagpuss*' otherworldly feel, the folk-tinged music which, each week, helped tell the tale attached to each and every found, broken object (prior to its mending) was recoded in 'a fairly silent room in a remote house' (Postgate, 2000: 297).

> Today was just like yesterday and tomorrow would be the same. It was
> predictable and homely. There is a kind of reassurance in that (Lewis, 2006: 29).

With all of these programmes in mind, no wonder Tom Sweetman – with
his memories of buying sweets, comics and toys at Barnsies – pleads: 'You
might find this difficult to believe but papershops were once magical places'
(Sweetman, 2007: 41). For like Aunt Mill's shop in *The Magic Ball*, the costume
shop in *Mr Benn*, and the antique shop of *Bagpuss*, Barnsies, to a young Sweetman,
was a magical place.

Dark Shops and the Otherness of the High Street

Miriam's was not magical in any literal, obvious way – but, through its combined
lure of jar after jar of glitteringly mouth-watering sweets, row after row of bright-
bannered comics, and box after box of exhilaratingly illustrated model kits,
it did exude an enchanting public façade. That is not to say that Miriam's also
did not languish in its own shadows as Peter remembers of his visits there of a
winter's morning.

> *Getting ready for school, and in need of breakfast, I quickly nip to Miriam's to*
> *purchase a Jacob's Club biscuit (to be munched over a steaming hot mug of tea*
> *as I sat in front of the kitchen gas fire). Only just after 7am, and it is still pitch*
> *black outside – with the inside of Miriam's not much lighter. I can only just about*
> *(and fleetingly at that), catch a glimpse of Dillwyn, deep within shadows of the*
> *shop's rear, as he prepares the papers for delivery, his newsprint-blackened*
> *fingers as even deeper smudges of black within the blackness. To me, the*
> *whole interior of Miriam's exists in a perpetual semi-darkness throughout the*
> *entirety of its opening hours in wintertime. Furthermore, Dillwyn – more so*
> *than Miriam – always seems to be constantly behind the scenes; a shadow*
> *within shadows.*

Peter's memory of a shadowy Miriam's is no different to Sweetman's memory of
Barnsies, where there was to be found 'a musty old room and a chap who always
had a cigarette in his mouth' (Sweetman, 2007b: 41). So, with Miriam's shadow-
infested interior in mind, we turn to Junichirō Tanizaki's *In Praise of Shadows*
(2001), where it is noted that in relation to non-Western, 'Oriental' cultures (in
particular, in traditional Japanese life), 'darkness causes us no discontent, [as] we
resign ourselves to it as inevitable', for '[i]f light is scarce then light is scarce;
we will immerse ourselves in the darkness and there discover its own beauty'

(Tanizaki, 2001: 48). In an empowering, literary sweep, Tanizaki implores an aesthetic welcoming of shadows and shadowy spaces:

> I would call back at least for literature this world of shadows we are losing. In the mansion called literature I would have eaves deep and the walls dark, I would push back into the shadows the things that come forward too clearly (Tanizaki, 2001: 63).

This clarion call, especially from the perspective of this age where our towns and cities are over-illuminated, and suffering from the ills of light pollution, begs for an appreciation of a time and place – Miriam's, the 1970s (the decade, of course, of power cuts without warning) – where and when shadows were both inevitable and, in a manner of resignation, welcome.

Although, the darkness of Miriam's – indeed, of all of these small businesses from that gloomy era – is not something to be only remembered in an aesthetically affectionate manner. It is no coincidence that, in Peter's continuing obsession with James Herbert's work (as he grew from a child to a teenager), his eagerly awaited purchasing of *The Dark* (1980) was from this dingy, ill-lit newsagents. As this pulp horror's truncated title suggests, darkness is not only something inherently evil, but, in its ability to envelope, has the tendency to be all-pervading:

> The Dark drifted on, an evil, creeping blackness that had no substance, yet was full of invisible energy, and expanding shadow that existed only in other shadows, an incorporeal thing that sucked at human minds, invading and searching for the hidden repressed impulses that were of itself. There were solid, dark shapes within it and these were the forms of men and women whose will it did not just govern, but who embodied the material part of it, those who physically enacted the evil that it was, its earthly force … It was a dark stain on the night (Herbert, 1980: 199).

Yet, crucially, come the 1970s, it was not only such dark, small businesses that seemed to harbour a dark side, as even the bright, neon-lit (yet, still, grubby) high-street supermarkets were often the site of the supernatural. Indeed, Nigel Kneale's highly acclaimed six televised plays, *Beasts* (ATV, 1976), included one episode, 'Special Offer', whereby a poltergeist that is amok amid a supermarket is initiated by the workplace harassment and rejection of 'Noreen' (played by a 17 year-old Pauline Quirke). Typical of Kneale's work, this is a tale of a haunting in a setting of absolute mundaneness. Broadcast in the form of a claustrophobic, low-budget television drama, 'it's the characters – their beliefs, their latent desires, their frustrations, their fears – that are really pivotal in driving the drama' (DVD booklet: 14). Significantly, Noreen's knowing awareness of the poltergeist's playfully paranormal, in-store activities are jokingly explained away by her insistence that this haunting is to be blamed upon 'Briteway Billy' – the supermarket chain's promotional chipmunk-like mascot.

This 'otherness' of the British highstreet (and, in particular, the interior and content of its shops) was made more than explicit – right at the very start of the decade – with 'Spearhead From Space' (1970), Jon Pertwee's first role as *Doctor Who*. The first *Doctor* ... series to be broadcast in colour – adding, arguably, to its living-room 'otherness' – it was also (due to industrial strife at the BBC) shot entirely on location and on film (as opposed to video), which serves to suggest that, with the introduction of this new 'Time Lord' at the start of a new decade, a far more believable direction was being pursued by the series. 'Spearhead From Space' (actually filmed on Ealing High Street), contained the highly memorable sequence where the Autons, masquerading as in-store mannequins, burst through the pane glass, and, stepping on to the pavement, begin to massacre people as they shop, wait for buses, etc.: 'All over the country, shop dummies come alive and burst from department store windows, killing anyone in their way' (Howe and Walker, 1996: 51). Indeed, despite *Doctor Who* being, essentially, 'merely' children's television, its content – during the early to mid-1970s – bordering upon being adult-only fare, was outright terrifying at times:

> Everything about the story is adult, from the gritty realism given to the production by the enforced use of location filming, ... to the impressive and memorable scenes of Auton dummies smashing their way out of shop windows – all the more effective as no glass is ever seen being broken' (Howe, cited in Howe and Walker, 1996: 52), as 'the faceless Auton dummies, with their guns memorably hidden within their hands, are particularly frightening (Walker, cited in Howe and Walker, 1996: 53).

It was, of course, *Doctor Who*'s elements of horror which particularly appealed to the upper-end of their young audience, as '[f]or slightly older children' the series was perceived to be 'at its peak in the 1970s' (Sandbrook, 2010: 348), as 'viewing figures regularly topped 10 million' (Sandbrook, 2010: 349). Yet, the various 'clean up TV' campaigners that were prevalent during that decade decreed that *Doctor Who* had become far too frightening for children – to the extent that, eventually, 'Terror of the Autons' (1971) was debated within Parliament, and a report conducted by the BBC itself declared 'that *Doctor Who* was the single most violent programme on television' (Sandbrook, 2010: 349). Ultimately, the concerned adults had their way, with the series, in 1977, curbing the programme's high levels of horror.

So much, then, for the 'otherness' of the British high street. What about its familiarity – especially the familiarity of its shops and its shopkeepers in the eyes of a child?

The Familiar Shopkeeper

Set in a northern – what Richard Hoggart would term – 'general grocer', the BBC's *Open All Hours* (first aired in 1976),[10] was a gentle, Sunday evening sitcom written by Roy Clarke, with each and every episode bookended by a dark morning's sleepy opening and an equally dark evening's pensive closing (hence the series' title) by Arkwright the shopkeeper (played by Ronnie Barker). Amid Arkwright's shop are the old-fashioned (yet still, even as late as the mid-1970s, familiar) tools of the trade: meat slicer, weighing scales, and an antiquated, temperamental till. It is, in effect, an Aladdin's Cave of 'tat' (as all of these shops tended to be), with a mouse-infested rear stockroom (and shop more generally), that Arkwright's nephew Granville refers to as 'the land of the midnight, 40-watt bulb'.[11] Yet, such an archaic shop (with its aged shopkeeper) would still be, certainly at the time of the first series' broadcast a recognisable feature of the British high street. Furthermore, Granville would appeal to the sitcom's younger audience – children in particular – as he was endlessly portrayed (by David Jason) as mischievously young-at-heart. Indeed, often referred to as merely an 'errand boy', Granville was – throughout the entire series – depicted, in his Fair Isle tank top, as a perpetual middle-aged child. So, like Miriam's, darkness and dinginess characterised Arkwright's, and, perhaps more importantly, children of the era – such as Peter – would associate with, in Granville, the childlike aspects of shopkeeping. Prophetically, Arkwright expresses his fears – and those of many a shopkeeper at the time the series was broadcast – by exclaiming 'Oh, dear! You know? Sometimes I lie in bed, awake at nights, and on a clear night I swear I can hear the sound of small businesses collapsing. Oh, dear!'.[12]

Shutting Up Shop – The Decline of the Traditional Small Shop (2007) is John Londei's fifteen-year photographic cataloguing, from the 1970s onwards, of sixty shops. Finishing the project in 1987, and returning twenty years later in order to ascertain what change had taken place in the interim, Londei insists that '[j]ust as important as the shops were the shopkeepers' (2007: 5). As, to Londei, the shopkeepers – after a lifetime of service – had managed to transform their small businesses 'into living entities' (2007: 5), with the shopkeepers themselves recognised and valued as 'long serving members of the community' (2007: 5). It was the passing of time itself which added such architectural gravitas to these traditional shops, and it was the same passing of time which placed so much emphasis upon the age of the shopkeepers – with many still serving well into retirement. Quite simply, then, '[i]n the end, for so many of the traditional small shopkeepers represented here, it would be ill health, or death, that brought down the shutters on their cherished shops forever' (2007: 5). On 7 December 1982, Will

---

10   With a pilot broadcast in 1973 (as part of the *Seven Of One* series), *Open All Hours* was screened in 1976, 1981–1982, and 1985 (that is, four series in total). I mention, above, that it was a 'Sunday evening sitcom', but the first series was broadcast on Fridays.

11   Series 1, Episode 4, 'Beware of the Dog'.

12   Series 1, Episode 3, 'A Nice Cosy Little Disease'.

Lee, who, of course, played Mr Hooper the storekeeper in *Sesame Street*, died, leaving the production staff with a true dilemma: 'how to tell the show's millions of preschool viewers why Mr Hooper was not behind the counter at his corner store anymore' (Gikow, 2009: 182). In the end, after deliberating over the use of such explanatory terms such as 'old' and 'sick' in the episodes that followed, they simply decided upon the far more poignant Big Bird-spoken reason as to why Mr Hooper had died and would be no longer seen on screen: 'Just because'. Thus, in such familiar shops run by elderly shopkeepers, death was an ever-present aspect of daily life.

With regards British cultural texts' varied representations of shopkeepers (where, above, we have already noted that children's television often presented them, along with their shops, as 'magical'), horror films often depicted them as the Devil incarnate or the like. For example, *From Beyond the Grave* (Kevin Connor, 1973), via a portmanteau structure favoured by its production house Amicus (that weaves its story segments together via a narrative link), the films many main characters fail to cross each others paths, as they are successive customers calling by a creepy antiques shop. The owner of this antiques shop (a role filled by horror stalwart Peter Cushing), as well as bringing about the various tales that comprise the portmanteau, sells a diverse range of bric-a-brac to these customers which, eventually, lead them to their fate. In his flat cap and duffel coat, Cushing's shopkeeper is placed amongst all of his oddities for sale 'like just another part of the antiquated décor' (Rigby, 2002: 218). Indeed, most significantly of all, the shopkeeper 'is ultimately revealed as a supernatural entity ... [when] we are lead to believe that the shopkeeper is not entirely human' (Hutchings, 2002: 138). Yet, his inhuman qualities are still of the stiff-upper-lip variety, as Amicus' portmanteau horrors (of which *From Beyond the Grave* is only one), are produced in such a way that they all exude a particular Britishness – with regards their lists of casts, their distinctive locations, and, in particular, 'their attention to and familiarity with the minutiae of British life' (Hutchings, 2002: 142).

Uncannily familiar, and peculiarly British, Peter Cushing – as this supernatural shopkeeper – enters into a particularly intimate relationship with both the camera and the audience, displaying an acknowledgement of both that is not to be had by the film's multiple lead characters. Thus, Cushing, as the owner of the shop, engages us (the audience) at the closing of the film (indeed, the shop) with an aside, whereby he addresses us directly via the camera, suggesting that – should we enter such a shop (and attempt such swindles as those unfortunate customers that have just met their doom) we would, in all probability, suffer a similar outcome. Yet, this chilling warning is carried out in a rather warm, familiar manner:

> At the end of *From Beyond the Grave* the shopkeeper looks up at the camera as it enters, addressing it (and us) as a new customer. 'Come in', he says, 'I'm sure I have the very thing to tempt you. Lots of bargains. All tastes catered for. Oh – and a big novelty surprise goes with every purchase. Do come in. Anytime. I'm always open' (Hutchings, 2002: 138).

With these ominous words of enticement, the owner of this sinister antiques shop 'retreats, ambiguity personified, into the gloom of his lumber-ridden shop' (Rigby, 2002: 218). Thus, for Peter, having watched Peter Cushing's chillingly convincing performance as this elderly shopkeeper-come-supernatural entity, watching Arkwright in *Open All Hours* and popping to Miriam's to buy a quarter of sherbet lemons (with Dillwyn still lurking deep within the gloomy shadows), was, thereafter, a rather sinister experience.

The Rotting Corner Shop

Returning, for a moment, to Arkwright's insomnia, induced by an imagined 'sound of small businesses collapsing', we should note that Emyr Gough, in *Skewen and District – A History* (1998), whilst recognising the defiant, continued trading of Miriam's, solemnly acknowledged that 'Mrs Merryfield's shop next door closed after many decades of trading' (Gough, cited in Bailey and Gough, 1998: 40). It should come as no surprise, then, that by the time I had the opportunity, in 2006, to revisit the neighbourhood of Peter's childhood, Miriam's had shut up shop for good. Looking at the accompanying photographs (Figure 4.1 and Figure 4.2, taken by me that gloomy, drizzly day), Miriam's is now far from being the bustling emporium it once was. Along the top, just above head height, the fascia is open (as the shop's sign, once proudly displaying 'H. PHILLIPS', having fallen to the

Figure 4.1   Miriam's, 2006 – The corner shop now closed forever
Source: Author's own collection.

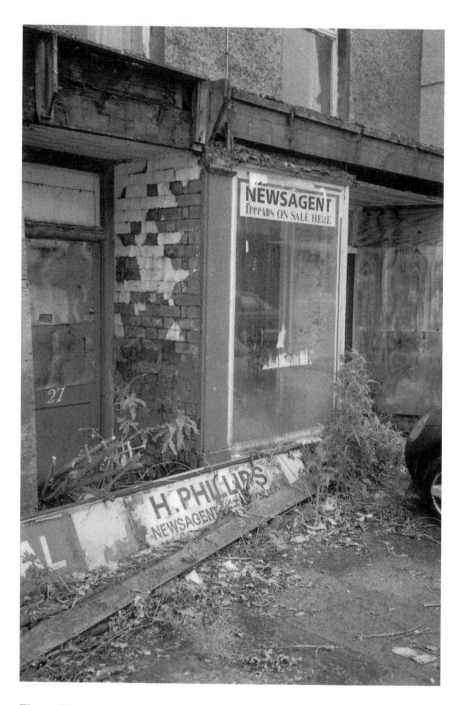

Figure 4.2   Miriam's, 2006 – The fallen sign
Source: Author's own collection.

floor) and, now exposed to the elements, is visibly rotting away. The paintwork of the 'supporting' pilasters – that is, the left and right columns – is faded, chipped, and peeling. Stall-boards (window sills) decayed to the extent that they are now, virtually, non-existent. With the stallriser (the walls just above the pavement, that go the entire lengths of both windows) now naked, weather-worn brickwork. Meanwhile, the Lobby (the recessed entrance in front of the door) is overgrown with weeds. Indeed, the only remnant of the former glory of Miriam's is the barely visible – but, nevertheless, still there – small sections of cornice above each dilapidated pilaster.[13]

It is the apparent lack of architectural merit (which plagues many a local shop) that is of significance here, as Bill Evans and Andrew Lawson, in *A Nation of Shopkeepers* (1986), stress that whilst '[t]he architect likes to build for posterity', a shopkeeper is primarily concerned with ensuring that their 'public face [is] constantly up-to-date' (Evans and Lawson, 1986: 117). Additionally, the shopkeeper strives to utilise the largest expanse of available window space in order to maximise their display of merchandise, this means that, for them, the perfect shopfront 'is a massive expanse of glass with the minimum visible means of support' (Evans and Lawson, 1986: 117). This, of course, goes against an architect's instincts, as it is a fundamental principal of architecture (indeed, of common sense) that any building should be its most secure, and, thus, sturdy at floor level, with its most flimsy and airy aspects further up. So, the architect aims to provide those that occupy a building with the confidence that the structure that surrounds them is capable of providing them with continued safe shelter. Like Miriam's (and other corner shops – both still trading and derelict), '[a] building that consists effectively of a gaping hole beneath a solid façade seems both visually unbalanced and structurally insecure' (Evans and Lawson, 1986: 117). With, then, these pictures of Miriam's in such a dilapidated state, the whole structure not only seems 'visually unbalanced' and 'structurally insecure' in its extreme, but the boarded-up and mildewed condition of what was once an 'expanse of glass', add even further frailty to this former shop – for it now seems that even the windows are no longer able to support themselves from either the elements or the vandals. An additional issue which preoccupies the shop architect is the construction of a shopfront that is attuned with the building within which it is seemingly grounded within. Quite often, though – and, perhaps, just like Miriam's – the shopfront appears as if it has been 'superimposed on a building of an earlier period and [thus] it is difficult to achieve harmony' (Evans and Lawson, 1986: 120).

Focusing upon the forlorn, fallen sign's tobacco advertising – 'Embassy REGAL' – which, with its light blue background, shares equal (if not greater) prominence with the proprietor's surname, brings back, for Peter, clear memories of being sent on illicit errands to purchase cigarettes for his mother and tobacco for his father. This sign that once adorned the entrance to Miriam's begs us to draw

---

13   This structural dissection of Miriam's is indebted to Kathryn A. Morrison's 'guide to shopfront design', *English Shops and Shopping* (2003: 41).

parallels here with the relationship between the decaying shopfront sign and the decline of small businesses on the British high street. Entitled 'The Writing on the Walls', Stephen Bayley's article for *The Independent on Sunday* (17 June 2001) draws our attention to urban, wall-mounted signage that advertise goods and services that, very often, are no longer with us in any shape or form. The survival of these signs is even more emotionally charged, as signwriting, as well as these long-gone goods and services – and like many high street small businesses – are 'in memoriam' (Bayley, 17 June 2001: 26). Bayley maintains that the convincingly stout mercantile language used by those signwriters that created such advertising was based upon the steadfast beliefs and morals of the Victorian era that had yet to be 'tested by global competition or supermarket price wars', and are now, as such, 'a charming testament to a slower, less frenetic world' (Bayley, 17 June 2001: 28). The article continues with an insistence that both the art and age of signwriting was to do with the promotion of 'products' and most certainly not 'brands', at a time when the business world appeared to be far more stable and not (as it seemingly is now) built upon shifting sands. More significantly, for Bayley, when we absentmindedly stroll down Britain's high streets, '[w]e walk past these chimeras of long-lost products and think of things we will never now be able to have', and, worse still, '[v]ery soon these signs will ... exist only in memory' (Bayley, 17 June 2001: 28).

Concerned, then, with the very real 'fading' (both historically and visibly) of signwriting as an advertising technique that once characterised the British inner-city high street, Bayley's article confides that '[i]f you know where to look, our cities are full of these faint, but visible, ghosts: we are haunted by memories of the commercial flagships of the Imperial economy, now slowly dissolving in exhausted and peeling paint' (Bayley, 17 June 2001: 25). That is why, as this chapter draws to a close, I would also reiterate that it is essential that we look around our neighbourhoods (present and past) in a far more perceptive manner, in order that we make ourselves fully aware of these 'faint, but visible, ghosts' that are 'slowly dissolving in exhausted and peeling paint'. Of course, Bayley refers to the loss of the art of the high street signwriter specifically, but I am, more generally, attempting to raise an awareness of the, quite literal, rotting away of the 'corner shop', its signage (both traditional and more contemporary), and the high street. Whilst aesthetically nowhere near as pleasing to the eye as the signage discussed within Bayley's article (indeed, far from it!), the fallen, decaying sign captured in my photographs – 'H. Phillips', on the floor, rotting, and covered in leaves and litter – is, in its own way, a 'faint, but visible, ghost', that is testimony to an age of both the high street and 'corner shops' that are increasingly to be found in the past.

In these photographs, the fact that the modern-day signage has fallen from the shop's aged structure would suggest that this 'building of an earlier period' is striving to regain its harmonious equilibrium by rejecting what was 'superimposed' ahead of its eventual closure. The windows, both boarded up and obscured by mildew, remnants of torn-away posters, and reflections of New Road itself, seem to, with their nullifying depth of blackness, deny the entry of light to the shop's interior – interiors that, during Peter's childhood on dark winters' early mornings and late afternoons, seemed alive with a myriad of lights. Now, all that is left is the dark. A darkness that has swallowed up the shop's insides. Swallowing up its histories. Swallowing up its memories. Even, as we will now appreciate, swallowing up its ghosts.

Conclusion

This chapter has offered an understanding of childhood spaces in which – if not play as such, but childhood imagination – is entered into by children. Certain childhood spaces within which Peter allowed his imagination to run riot, such as the bus stop and the phone box, were, during the day, childhood spaces which, at night, became adolescent and adult spaces – and spaces of adolescent and adult activities, such as graffiti, urination, sexual activity, etc. Furthermore, in Peter's case in particular, other spaces of childhood – perhaps Miriam's the newsagents especially – were childhood spaces that were shared with the very old. Indeed, St. John's Terrace (as part of the wider New Road area), which was Peter's immediate neighbourhood, was, predominantly, an elderly neighbourhood. For both Miriam and Dillwyn, even when Peter was a child, back in the 1970s, were old. And it was obvious, even then, that retirement beckoned. It should have come as no surprise to Peter that, when he returned to Skewen in 2006, they were long gone, with the shop having been closed for many a year. Thus, we turn to John Londei, and, in *Shutting Up Shop – The Decline of the Traditional Small Shop* (2007), his explanation as to why – having documented with his camera, over a 15 year period, 60 traditional British shops – he waited another 20 years to then publish them:

> As far as the shop pictures were concerned, although I was eager to publish them, the time just wasn't right; I felt these photographs needed the passage of time to mature. It seemed their poignancy would only be realised when most of the shops had ceased trading (Londei, 2007: 128).

Thus, the significance of Miriam's – that is, as a newsagent that, now, no longer trades – carries more and more emotional weight with each and every passing year. Indeed, my return to Miriam's after, what must be, a quarter of a century since Peter walked across its lobbied entrance, and into the dimly-lit interior, is strikingly similar to Londei's nigh-on eerie return to the shops that he catalogued with his camera all those years ago:

> In 2004 I began the task of updating what had become of the shops and the shopkeepers that I'd photographed so long ago. With 60 shops around the country it wasn't always easy to retrace my footsteps back in time. More often than not I seemed to be chasing ghosts (Londei, 2007: 128).

Thus, to me, walking Peter's childhood neighbourhood of New Road, and photographing Miriam's as it lay there 'visually unbalanced' and seemingly 'structurally insecure', was a difficult experience akin to 'chasing ghosts'. For, these 'ghosts' were not just those of Miriam, Dillwyn, and the shop itself. Indeed, Tom Sweetman's childhood recollections of shopping at Barnsies, also recalls the night when, being babysat by Mr and Mrs Barnes, they allowed him to go, from their accommodation above the shop, down into the darkened interior of the shop: 'Colours swirling and images that leapt out of the darkness. I didn't know where the lights were and surveyed the wonders by the moonlight that shone through the toy-strewn window' (Sweetman, 2007b: 43). Wistfully thinking back to that night, Sweetman catches a glimpse of his younger self as a separate spirit; a child spirit that, all those years ago, never really left Barnsies: 'He's still there somewhere in the ghosts that drift around that room and that time' (Sweetman, 2007b: 43). For, as with Sweetman's young 'ghost' forever haunting Barnsies', Peter, the young boy, is most probably still there, at Miriam's: On the outside, in the dark, excitedly pointing at an exhilaratingly illustrated Airfix boxtop that has caught his eager eyes, as Dillwyn, straining, reaches from behind the counter, through the sliding access hatch, into the brightly lit window.

It is time to leave Hooper's Store, Barnsies, Miriam's, and all those other, now derelict, stores and newsagents behind, and their ghosts in peace. Best to leave the window lights on, though, as '[t]he paper-shop window is a litter of odds-and-bobs; if the light is kept on at nights the children make it a meeting-place' (Hoggart, 2010: 47).

Chapter 5

The Childhood Spaces of Suburbia

Rain. Peter still not well. Unable to go to school. Marjorie gone up the village shopping. I am hoping to go into Neath to fetch my pension (Millie's diary, Monday, 26 January 1981).

Lovely day again … Marjorie and Peter and me going over to the bring and buy sale over at the school. Bought quite a few things there. I stayed in the rest of the day (Millie's diary, Saturday, 14 February 1981).

Introduction

With this chapter we move, as Peter grows up, far and wide, considering his – and his family's – world beyond Ivy Cottage, its garden, the surrounding streets and immediate neighbourhood. We consider the infrastructure of suburbia: schools, borstals, libraries, public houses, working men's clubs, cemeteries, the railway, and so on. Thus, the chapter will be an exploration of the social institutions of suburbia that Peter, his family, and his neighbours, engage with on a daily basis. This chapter is not only concerned with such suburban social institutions that were integral to Peter's – and his family's and his neighbours' – notions of 'suburban community', but it makes explicit the *physicality* of those institutions: that is, not just the size and scale of those institutions, but the tactile nature of the raw materials out of which they were constructed. For, in *Environment and Children – Passive Lessons from the Everyday Environment* (2007), Christopher Day, in considering children living with the 'elements', makes explicit their engagement with 'stone' and, to them, the centrality, and solidity, of stone in the construction of buildings, whereby '[s]tone endures' and, as a result, '[s]tone buildings more easily feel ageless than brick, stucco or wooden ones' (Day, 2007: 223). Furthermore, considering that, for example, '[m]asonry arches are held together by gravity', and '[h]eavy, flared bases root buildings into ground', such 'solidity and reliability are characteristics of earth-element buildings' (Day, 2007: 223–4). For, '[t]hese qualities are all about *security*', and '[t]his is a major need for small children' (Day, 2007: 224). As such, this chapter considers metals, minerals, stone, concrete, and so on, and how those substances were made reference to in the children's texts of the 1970s.

Schools as Sites of History

Screened amongst the first series of ITV's *Shadows*, a children's TV show with a supernatural fixation, was the particularly memorable 'After School'. Broadcast on 17 September 1975, the story is set in an 'ordinary' comprehensive school, Bryn Haffes, that serves a small Welsh community. With a period charm enhanced by its school-play-like shaky set, it 'cleverly deploys a minimum of establishing shots of a run-down Welsh mining village before using only two sets and two schoolboy actors for the remainder of the piece' (McGown and Docherty, 2003: 92). Reprimanded, and forced to stay behind after school's hours as a result, the two main protagonists – Poodle and Seth – are detained within this gloomy Victorian-era institution only to be eventually scared witless by a psychic phenomenon. With the traumatic experience involving the spirit of a boy miner who had died in a mid-nineteenth-century pit accident (and, for Poodle and Seth, a 'reliving' of the moment of that boy's death), this was not only a genuinely terrifying piece of late-afternoon children's television, but it was educational as well, for '[a]s with many ghost stories for children, several episodes functioned as exciting ways of teaching history', where '[t]he ghost who haunted the present gave us vivid glimpses of the past' (McGown and Docherty, 2003: 91). With 'After School', the childhood audience are enlightened collectively by 'the miserable existence of a boy working in the Welsh coalmines 150 years earlier' (McGown and Dcoherty, 2003: 91). Although, 'After School' provides far more than both a vivid retelling of history and a 'reliving' of that history; as, by having Poodle and Seth 'experience' the young miner's death, the episode (and, thus, the series itself) educates its audience in matters of both life and death – which, arguably, are the two fundamental elements of history. Such an approach – that is, attempting to educate children and young adults in issues to do with death and dying – is a relatively recent phenomenon within schools, colleges, and universities, that is fundamentally linked with those that have experienced life in the post-war period:

> The death education movement has been a relative newcomer to academia, but is one that is seeing a general increase in interest and attention as the wave of the baby-boomer generation crests and an increasingly large percentage of the population collectively nears that unavoidable end (Moreman, 2008: 2).

Following the 1870 Education Act, and the resultant introduction of school boards (with the related switch from church- to state-sponsored education), an intense programme of school building resulted in the establishment of educational institutions, right across the country, that were of a highly recognisable nature due to them sharing many common characteristics of construction. Those being, 'simple buildings in brick or occasionally stone, with large windows and – usually – rows of gables' (Harwood, 2010: 35). Such 'board schools', with their design defined by both financial constraints and a preoccupation with adequate lighting (hence these buildings' signature high roofs and large gables), an encouragement of a localised honouring of these institutions was 'reflected in the buildings' emblematic signage and many plaques' (Harwood, 2010: 36). Following on from an initial 'schoolroom plan' design – that is, separate rooms for boys, girls, and infants, with further peripheral classrooms (where trainee teachers or teaching assistants would operate under close supervision) – the 1880s witnessed the introduction of the 'Queen Anne style'. Also known as the 'Prussian model' (as it was adopted from German school design), it reversed the internal planning of schools by having classrooms (which could accommodate up to 80 pupils) that branched off from 'a central schoolroom or hall' (Harwood, 2010: 39). Mynachlog Nedd, or Skewen Lower, was Peter's junior school from 1973 until 1977. A classic example of the 'board school' of the late nineteenth century, it stood, across New Road, right opposite Ivy Cottage itself. Built in 1868, it consisted of (as per the County Series' OS map for Glamorgan, 1876) a single block – titled 'Boys, Girls & Infants'. And that was the way it remained until a separate, rear block was built which the 1940 variant of the County Series' map shows for the first time.

Come the early 1970s, Peter's experience of the school built environment was virtually the same as that of countless generations of local children: in effect, then, Peter – during the majority of the 1970s – prayed and went to class in surroundings which, fundamentally, had not changed for a century. And it was a form of institutional environment, common to many schoolchildren of that decade, that still existed due to the very harsh sturdiness of the school buildings themselves: For the schools of the late-nineteenth century 'were solidly constructed, yet spartan', with '[g]lazed brick and tiled surfaces made for easy cleaning and fumigation' (Harwood, 2010: 43). For Peter and many of his generation, physical contact with these hard, easily sanitised surfaces proved exceptionally memorable – especially that of walking or running across a wooden block floor or tarmac playground whilst wearing 'Blakeys'. Robert Elms, in *The Way We Wore – A Life In Threads* (2005), recounts the way in which he, during his first year at the Orange Hill Grammar School, Burnt Oak, north-west London (1971–1972), subverted the wearing of his school's uniform, item by item. With the cap gone, and official trousers replaced by a far more 'trendy' pair (although still in grey), footwear was modified accordingly:

> Sensible shoes were replaced by whatever was that week's loafer in regulation black of course, but with Blakeys added. These were small crescent-shaped metal plates with protruding nails, designed to protect the heel of your shoe. They were popular among noisy oiks because they made a wondrous ringing sound as you stalked the corridor, and even produced sparks if you caught them just right in the playground (Elms, 2005: 75).

With Elms' sense of subversion when wearing Blakeys in mind, here is Peter's recollection of them on his shoes.

I'd spent Sunday afternoon down in the cellar, my clumpy lace-up shoes balanced on the heavy, rusty, tri-limbed iron last, trying desperately not to catch my fingers on the sharp metal spikes of the Blakeys, or with the weight of the claw hammer, clumsily whacking them into place; off-centre, on the outside edge of both heels. Now, Monday morning, ten-to-eight, I walk with pride (and some hesitancy) through the school gate, and across the tarmac, towards the door to the main hall. In time with my little steps the Blakeys call out. 'Click! Clack! Click! Clack! Click! Clack!'. I smirk to myself. I am – just like the well-dressed, suited Yank cops on TV – a man. I am certain about this over-night/next-morning coming of age, as my echoing footsteps tell me, and others within earshot, so.

Images of Youth – Growing up in Birmingham in the 1970s (published by City of Birmingham Education Committee in February, 1974) is a unique book, as it not only captures that city at a time of immense transformation, but it articulates the experience of that change through the words and pictures of children from the city. As Marjorie Brown, Lord Mayor of the City of Birmingham 1973–1974, states in the foreword:

> [O]ver 180,000 school children are growing up in the city, and this publication is an attempt to give them the opportunity of saying what it is like to be young in Birmingham at this time (n.p.).

Furthermore, she continues, the latter half of the book 'concerns itself with what the children do at (and through) their schools' (n. p.), where, 'it is hoped that the children's contributions, often presented in the original handwriting, will tell their own stories, simply, sensitively, and directly' (n.p.).[1] So, here is Lona Mcloughlin's entry (at the time, aged 11), and her own account of her last few months at her junior school, Lozells, a school soon to be demolished – an account that is tinged throughout with a realisation of impending loss – the loss of her school, and her own loss of past:

> Our school will soon be
> knocked down and all will be
> forgotten. But me I wont ever for
> get Miss Clarcke or the school or
> my friends I cant say more
> Because tears are coming in my
> eyes (Mcloughlin, 1974: 123).

As with Lona, come 1978 – his last year at his already antiquated junior school – Peter had not only amassed fond memories of his four years there, but he had become acutely aware that in September, and his starting at the local 'Comp', change, transition, and consequential personal loss were, inevitably, going to be

1   Rather insightfully, the Mayor's one-page foreword ends with the hope that '[i]t could be that in another 25 years time the social historian will find these offerings of interest as original material' (n.p.). Hence, with no further justification, I include extracts of the book here.

foisted upon him. Such a sense of loss made the last few weeks of junior school, and the summer holidays that followed, a particularly poignant moment in Peter's childhood.

So, a few days ago, we left Mynachlog Nedd for the last time. Smiling and waving as we walked through the gates, we cheerily said to one another 'See you over the summer!' Thus, today, I'm seeing Jonesy – my best friend – this afternoon. Although, as I speak to him over the phone, to firm up on exactly what time he would call 'round, I now find myself whispering, half-embarrassed, my request that he should bring Action Man along with him. Whilst this was something that I had done many a time over the past few summers, this time it feels awkward to do so. Thus, it comes as no surprise that he simply, and quietly, says 'No'. I now know that such 'childish things' should be put aside, and never mentioned again. Anyhow, it's two o'clock and he's here, and we – straightaway, in our usual boisterous manner – enter into rough play, wrestling each other on the armchairs, sofa, and floor of the parlour. Eventually, hot and flushed, we laugh ourselves into dizzy hysterics. But, I'm also very sad, as I realise that I will never mention to him ever again our Action Men.

In addition to this experience of the many ways in which childhood is 'lost', following Peter's first day at Rhyd Hir, Longford (the location of his first year at Comprehensive School that began as that summer ended), he and 'Jonesy' were never to be in the same class together again. Indeed, upon leaving school in 1982, he was never to see him again.

Yet, not all children of that era felt such a sense of disjuncture or loss. Instead, many welcomed change and its ushering in of the new. Following on from a December 1967 edition of the *Observer*, whereby secondary schoolchildren were invited to enter a competition themed 'The School that I'd Like', many of the entries were, a few years later, compiled into a Penguin Education Special, of the same name, edited by Edward Blishen (himself a teacher-come-author). Published in 1969, *The School That I'd Like* included a number of entries which criticised school buildings (mostly past, but some present). One in particular, hinting that, after all, this was the post-Wilson 'white heat of technology' era, provides us with an insight into, not only the educational hopes and aspirations of certain children as they entered the new decade that was the 1970s, but it highlights their rejection of history and an antiquated past within which they still found themselves:

Children live in synthetic fibre houses and then have to spend half their lives in dark relics that our age is afraid to demolish because of the loss of a grasp with the past. Children have changed, the schools should! A school should be filled with the amenities and inventions of our century. It should teach children more about the future and less about the past ('Lynda, 16', 1969: 48).

Junior Schools

Peter attended his junior school, Mynachlog Nedd, at a time when *Survivors* was being screened on British television. Televised in 38 episodes over three series (1975–1977), *Survivors* offers a bleak depiction of a near-future in which a worldwide plague decimates the majority of the world's population, and, in doing so, provides a valuable insight into the period's 'representation of survivalist anxieties' (Sawyer, 2006: 132). Against this doomsday backdrop, where small, isolated groups of people struggle to survive in a post-apocalyptic Britain, we should briefly consider the dark tone of boy's comics at this time, where 'coping' and, ultimately, 'survival' were key themes amid both the strips contained within and the harsh lives led by a significant number of their young readers.

D.C. Thomson of Dundee, in an attempt to capitalise upon the success of their Second-World-War fixated weekly comic *Warlord*, which heralded the emergence of the British 'new wave' that came to characterise the boys' comics of the mid- to late-1970s, attempted to capture a younger, more trend-conscious readership with both *Bullet* and *The Crunch*.[2] Indeed, such 'new wave' comics – of which *Action* (1976–1977) of IPC London was the most notorious – were radical in that they provided their readers with highly identifiable heroes (or, more typically, 'anti-heroes'): As James Chapman, in *British Comics – A Cultural History* (2011), asserts, '"real" people facing up to their own problems and anxieties rather than fantasy supermen or unbelievably flawless heroic archetypes' (2011: 138).

With *The Crunch*, the notion that a comic should portray – and, thus, encourage its readers to acknowledge that they were – 'real people' tackling their 'own problems and anxieties' was, according to Kibble-White (2005b), the comic's 'high concept', to be found in the title itself, that made reference to that life-affirming – no, life-changing – moment where 'men had to be men and take the tough line' (Kibble-White, 2005b: 93). Accordingly, and rather incredulously, *The Crunch* even had a similarly-themed 'problem page':

> A problem page? In a boys' comic? You'd better believe it, and one that offered up a two quid postal order for every one printed, and a snazzy Sinclair calculator for the letter Andy liked best (Kibble-White, 2005b: 94).

Such disbelief that a boys' comic could offer – in such violent times – a 'problem page' (which, of course, had come to typify girls' comics and magazines aimed at women), was countered by the fact that *The Crunch* was, after all, part of the 'new wave'. Indeed, it was precisely because that comic came into being during

---

2   These three boys' comics are very much of their time (the 1970s), with regards both themes addressed by their respective strips and their collective periods of publication: *Warlord*, every Thursday, 1974–1986; *Bullet*, every Tuesday, 1976–1978; *The Crunch*, every Monday, 1979–1980.

such 'violent times', that a 'problem page' was both needed and justified. For the 'problem page' was, each week, headed with a variation of the following:

THE CRUNCH QUESTION.

Are YOU facing the CRUNCH in your life? Got a problem you need help in solving ... at home ... at school ... with your friends? Write to me – Andy – at Crunch ... (No. 2, 27 January 1979: 10).

No surprise, then, those readers wrote in and shared their angst with regards, for instance, school and bullying:

Letter of the Week

VICTIM of a BULLY.

Dear Andy,
I'm having trouble with a bigger boy at my school. For some reason, he has decided to make my life a misery (No. 2, 27 January 1979: 10).

MONEY ... OR A BEATING.

Dear Andy,
I have trouble with bigger boys at my school. One night, when I was going to my Youth Club one of them met me and said that if I didn't give him my money, he would beat me up. So I gave him some money.
The next night, I went to the club and he came over with some of his pals and said to give him more money. I said I had no more.
They took me outside and gave me a beating. Can you help? (No. 11, 31 March 1979: 22).

Although, considering that the 1970s seemingly became increasingly violent as the decade progressed, the readers' letters reflected an increasingly violent society, more generally, with both the public and private spheres merging within their (often bleak) content:

Letter of the Week

BABY BATTERING!

Dear Andy,
A few months ago, a family from London moved into the house next to ours and I'm convinced that the three children in the house are victims of baby battering. Both parents drink very heavily, and when they go out, they leave their 13-year-

old daughter in charge of the two younger children. Sometimes we even hear the children screaming when their parents return from the pub, and next day, they are covered in bruises (No. 5, 17 February 1979: 22).

For if, by the 1970s, 'baby battering' was a growing problem of the private sphere that had now entered the very public sphere of boys' comics, *The Crunch*'s 'problem page' also began to include readers' letters that were very much of their moment Moral Panic-wise:

Letter of the Week

GLUE SNIFFER.

Dear Andy,
I am very worried about a friend of mine who persists in glue sniffing. Although he has tried to kick the habit many times, he cannot. As I have recently read that glue sniffing can be very dangerous, I have started to get very concerned (No. 19, 26 May 1979: 15).

Not content with laying bare societal ills of the era, such 'new wave' British boys' comics also offered, through their radical scripts and equally radical editorial content, a range of coping strategies in order to deal with such 'crunch' moments – as *Bullet* did so with its 'survival'-orientated themes.

Launched on 14 February 1976 (the same day as London's IPC's far more violent and far more controversial *Action*), *Bullet* starred – across one of it strips – the rather dashing-yet-camp karate-kicking exploits of Fireball (the fictitious nephew of his debonair, yet equally fictitious, uncle, Lord Peter Flint of *Warlord*). Nevertheless, Fireball clicked with the young boys of the mid-1970s, such as Peter, due to his physical blending of martial arts with King's Road fashions of the day. As Graham Kibble-White, in *The Ultimate Book of British Comics – 70 Years of Mischief, Mayhem and Cow Pies* (2005b) attests, whilst Flint was the DC Thomson's increasingly-outdated 'John Steed' of boys' comics, Fireball was the far more swinging 'Jason King': For, '[r]esplendent in his luxury-issue moustache, wavy hair and medallion, he wore his shirt open to the navel and travelled the world on the back of his steely business card' (Kibble-White, 2005: 55–6). Thus, ousted was the post-war spy that was Flint, for here, instead, was the far more mercenary Fireball of the urban guerrilla decade.

Come issue two of *Bullet*, readers were encouraged to sign up as members of the Fireball Club for the price of a 25p Postal Order (which Peter duly did). Thus, clutching wallets which contained an identity card, two calling cards, and other Fireball-related paraphernalia, and resplendent with plastic replicas of Fireball's medallion swinging upon their hairless chests, such club members – in their droves as gangs – hung suavely around on street corners and playgrounds amid Britain's towns and inner cities in search of exploits fitting for such diminutive 1970s playboys.[3] Although, in keeping with the decade's economic and social hardship, these wannabe Fireballs were, each week, encouraged to 'cut out and keep' tips on survival in their respective harsh, urban jungles. So, instalments of *Bullet* provided its young, male readers with explicit instructions on how to 'survive' life in the 1970s: No. 5, what to do '[w]hen someone is drowning'; when 'lost', signalling with a can lid (utilising the Sun's rays), using 'body semaphore', using 'whistles', using 'signal fires (including smoke); No. 7, 'breaking your fall – without breaking your neck' (upon being attacked, or in a house fire); No. 8, 'capsized boat'; No. 10, 'super fitness', etc. The comic even had its own strip – entitled 'Survivor' – whereby teenage 'Dick Arnold', having survived a light-aircraft crash, struggles to survive in the mountains and rainforests of South America. All things considered, then, it is of little surprise that a young Peter – caught up in this wave of flare-wearing survival – attempted, one schoolday afternoon, to 'survive'. Indeed, Peter's gazing upon Mynachlog Nedd, and its adjacent field (used during breaks and sports days), during a blazing hot afternoon in 2005, brings back a memory of that 'survival afternoon' – just there, just behind the fence.

It is an overcast, grey afternoon. With water from the cold water tap in the boys' toilet, and a fire made out of dried twigs and trouser pocket fluff (lit with a damp match), there is a solitary tea bag boiling away in an old, empty tobacco tin (which, up until a few days ago, stored Daddy's 'Old Holborn'). There is blue smoke wafting everywhere, as me and Gareth Mallon nonchalantly suck on glucose sweets, and shelter under a black bin bag which is, in lean-to fashion against the wire-mesh perimeter fence, being held down by a small number of pebbles. I can see my house – my bedroom window even – from where we are in our school field. The tea, now stewed – and with no milk – tastes bitterly of smoke and tobacco. But, we are both smugly happy: we are 'survivors'. Eventually, a couple of hours later – having 'survived' the afternoon – we go back to class.

Tim Gill, in *No Fear – Growing Up in a Risk Averse Society* (2007), makes explicit that, over at least three decades (at least), pre-adolescent children have been subjected to ever-greater parental monitoring and, as a result, have found their 'freedom of action' subjected to significant restraint, with the disparities between childhood during the early 1970s and childhood come the early 1990s all too alarmingly obvious:

---

3 Wallets and, in particular, medallions – as symbols of ultra-masculinity – were seemingly everywhere during the 1970s. But, they were especially so upon the pages of boys' comics. As *The Crunch*'s strip 'Mantracker', with the American 'Bearpaw Jay' (as a present-day 'Indian Warrior-come-Bounty Hunter'), has its protagonist wearing a typically oversized variant that has a heraldic eagle embossed upon its surface.

In 1971 eight out of ten children aged seven or eight years went to school on their own. By 1990 this figure had dropped to less than one in ten. Again, in 1971 the average seven-year-old was making trips to their friends or the shops on their own. By 1990 that freedom was being withheld until the age of ten, meaning that in just 19 years children had 'lost' up to three years of freedom of movement (Gill, 2007: 12).

This loss of freedom of both action and movement (which has led to a shrinking, over recent years, of the so-called 'children's domain') has occurred, of course, amid the context of an emergence of a 'culture of fear' whereby parents and other adults are fixated – often to the extent of collective paranoia – with the notion of 'stranger danger'. Resultantly, there is an increasing tendency within society, especially in relation to child-rearing, to engage obsessively with 'risk aversion' – itself a consequence of other, more broader, lifestyle changes, whereby:

[t]he growth of road traffic and of car-dependent lifestyles, parents' longer working hours, a decline in the quantity and quality of public space, and the growth of indoor leisure activities have all reinforced the logic of containment (Gill, 2007: 14).[4]

Peter's 'survival afternoon' – in reality, a couple of hours in the school's adjacent field (with both school and field, of course, just across the road from his home, Ivy Cottage), brewing tea in an old tobacco tin – can be understood as the type of activity that is of absolute necessity to today's children who are now, arguably, suffering from what Richard Louv (2009) terms 'nature-deficit disorder'. This 'disorder', a technology-dependent malaise of interior-bound children, can, according to Louv, be easily 'treated' by reintroducing (or, in some extreme instances, introducing) those children 'infected' to nature. Of course, Louv insists, this need not necessarily be lakes, woodland, mountain ranges, and the like, as the 'nature' to be found in a suburban garden or a patch of urban greenery – indeed, the 'nature' to be found adjoining the childhood home will suffice, as 'the first physical entry point into nature is the backyard' (Louv, 2009: 170).

---

4   The irony is that Peter's 'survival afternoon' was, of course, conducted within the safe confines of his primary school's enclosed field, following adult/teacher permission being granted. Whilst, at the same time, Peter's mother insisted that, during play, he was not allowed to leave the confines of his home and its garden. However, as detailed within Chapter 3, the gardens were extensive (especially when Peter was allowed to play, out of sight, on the 'wastelands' that surrounded the warehouse that was next to Ivy Cottage). And, furthermore, Peter was also free to wander to the shops on both errands and to spend his own pocket money (see previously, Chapter 4). In effect, then, despite certain restrictions, Peter did operate within his own, quite far-reaching, 'childhood domain'.

Secondary Schools

As a result of inner-city bomb damage during the Second World War, the Ministry of Education, in 1943, insisted upon authorities adopting a rebuilding programme that was highly dependent upon standardised, prefabricated components. Despite the 1949 cuts, such ready-made construction was stepped-up thereafter, yet it was 'only suited to single-storey buildings', as it was 'inappropriate for large secondary schools' (Harwood, 2010: 74). Thus, across the late-1940s and 1950s, aluminium, steel, and concrete were all incorporated into such ready-made structures so that larger, multi-storey prefabricated schools could be erected. A significant advancement in such prefabrication was the introduction of CLASP: '[A] pin-jointed and spring-loaded light steel frame at first clad with timber and tiles giving it a vernacular quality, lost in later versions that used concrete panels' (Harwood, 2010: 75). As this was often the preferred method of prefabrication in mining areas (such as South Wales) due to subsidence, such a programme of construction – that was, again, dependent upon spring-loaded foundations – resulted in many of these buildings being termed 'rock and roll schools'. But, if it was the inclusion of sturdy, modern components (such as concrete) which appealed to the children of the late 1960s and 1970s, to others it was the lighter, more airy construction materials which appealed. As another entry in Edward Blishen's *The School That I'd Like* (1969), by 'Janet, 13', makes mention of the child's desire for newer construction materials being used, in conjunction with aspects of nature, when planning and building new schools:

> I like plenty of space to play in at breaks, with a variation of grass, concrete, trees and bushes ('Janet, 13', 1969: 52).

Additionally, for others, such as 'Janet, 16', a certain inherent obsolescence was an essential of these prefabricated structures:

> The building in which my school is housed will be light and modern, surrounded by large, unprohibited lawns and tarmac areas and not built to last for ever ('Janet, 13', 1969: 52).

Of course, such 'ready-made' structures from the 1940s and 1950s, with a supposed self-limiting shelf-life, did last far longer than intended – that is, the 1970s and beyond. Indeed, this unpredicted longevity typified the entire post-war rebuilding programme for both schools and houses, as Colin Ward, in *British School Buildings – Design and Appraisals, 1964–1974*, attests (bearing in mind that this book was published in 1976):

> [J]ust as the post-war prefabricated houses built for a ten-year life-span are still with us, so there is no suggestion that the earliest system-built schools are at the end of their useful life (Ward, 1976: x).

Figure 5.1   Rhydhir School, Longford – Time, frozen in time
Source: Author's own collection.

Yet, there were, throughout the 1970s in particular, significant concerns over the on-going instability of, and associated health and safety issues with, prefabricated schools that had been built during the immediate, post-war period. For, in extreme instances – following the actual collapse of some buildings – enforced school closures were resorted to whilst investigations were carried out on aspects of other structurally suspect sites. Such investigations focused upon the anticipated weaknesses in, or suspected shortcomings of, prefabricated components, such as:

> the stability of the seating of precast, prestressed wide-span beams; the loadbearing capacity of high-alumina cement; the stability of laminated timber roofs under conditions of humidity; the fire risks associated with compressed straw or wood-wool or some plastic materials (Ward, 1976: x).

That is why Peter's secondary school – at Rhydhir, Longford, very much still characterised locally by its ready-made-ness – does not deserve to continue to stand; but it, resolutely, still does. Built in 1953, published photos exist of it from the mid-to-late 1950s onwards that proudly display the school's pre-fabricated newness;[5] however, it is the photo that we have here (Figure 5.1) – again, taken in 2005 – that is more illustrative of it as a building not built to last still managing to stand. It is indicative that, in this photograph, the clock's hands are still (taken

---

5   See, for example, the photograph entitled 'Staff of Rhydhir secondary modern, 1959', in Robert King and Bryan King's *Images of Wales – Around Neath, the Second Selection* (2005: 83).

early afternoon, the clock, on one side is frozen at '7:55', whilst, on the other, at just coming up to '7:30'). For, as well as Peter never, ever recalling the clock working during his days as a pupil there, with the multiple hands stuck as they are, they reinforce the reality that – as far as this ready-made secondary school is concerned – time is standing still. This, in turn, underpins the seemingly ever-lasting nature of such pre-fabricated structures as we have entered the twenty-first century.[6]

Included in *Images of Youth – Growing up in Birmingham in the 1970s* (1974) is an entry from Lesley Duce (then aged 14) that makes evident her awe when, while still at junior school, visiting what was to be her secondary school: 'I was amazed at the size of the school, and the big hall we could get three of our halls in there … I remember thinking it was massive' (1970: 160). This was similar to the impression that Peter had on his first day, of his first year, at secondary school.

It's just before 9 o'clock in the morning, and I'm standing on one of the many tarmac paths that criss-cross the grounds of this school, Rhydhir. I'm in my brand-new uniform: white shirt, striped tie, blazer (with the school sew-on patch on its breast pocket), trousers, socks, and shoes (and gym kit in my duffel bag), all as per the specified regulations. I am surrounded by hundreds that look just like me; milling around, and looking awkward, we all eye strange faces with suspicion. But it is the sheer size of this 'big-huge' school that over-awes me; the seemingly countless number of pre-fabricated buildings that make up its sprawl that overwhelms me. The vast number of schoolchildren around me – and the noisy chatter we nervously generate – threatens to wash over like a flood. Most unsettling, though, is the awareness of being – amid this uniformed mass – anonymous.

Such a fast-paced, chaotic first day at secondary school is captured in the first ever episode of *Grange Hill* (BBC, 1978–2008). The title of the programme being the name of the institutional-like secondary school within which this 'gritty', late-afternoon children's drama series is mainly set. The writer, Phil Redmond, pays particular attention – across the opening scene – to the, at times, sheer bewilderment of the 'first formers' arrival at Grange Hill, whereby he 'constructed almost the first full ten minutes of episode one to sketch in the backgrounds of the pupils making their way to Grange Hill for the first time' (McGown and Docherty, 2003: 113). Indeed, it is the 'first formers' 'with whom this season is almost exclusively concerned' (McGown and Docherty, 2003: 113). So, realistically portraying the collective experiences' of 1st-year pupils as they start secondary school, and being

---

6   As this book was being prepared for publication, Rhydhir School was demolished. However, this does not detract from the reality that such a non-permanent, pre-fabricated school stood for 60 years.

first screened in 1978 – the year that Peter himself went to his 'Comp' – it is no wonder that this series resonated so much with Peter and his generation.

The comprehensive school system – certainly as graphically portrayed in *Grange Hill* – was a controversial institution. A select number of authorities in England tenaciously hung on to a system of educational selection. Indeed, '[f]or them, and their defenders in the media, the comprehensive school was an institution which threatened academic standards and destroyed the established 'high culture' of state secondary education, embodied in the grammar school' (Jones and Davies, 2002: 145). Yet, come the mid-1970s, the majority of the local authorities in England, and all of them in Scotland and Wales, had 'gone comprehensive'. In *1970s Britain* (2012), Janet and John Shepherd note that, by the middle of the decade, the majority of LEAs (Local Education Authorities) had embraced non-selective comprehensive education, whereby grammar schools merged with secondary moderns, to such an extent that 'the national move towards comprehensive education had progressed too far to be halted' (Shepherd and Shepherd, 2012: 64). In relation to this 'unstoppable tide' of educational progress, and its consequential creation of mega-schools (that is, with regards both size of school and catchment areas), '[b]etween 1970 and 1974, the percentage of children attending comprehensives almost doubled, to 62 per cent' (Shepherd and Shepherd, 2012: 64–5). It was the sheer number of children attending such immense institutions that many critics blamed for the unruliness that was perceived to take place at every new 'Comp' during the 1970s. A *Panorama* programme of 1977 screened so-called 'fly on the wall' material, filmed at Ealing's Faraday High School, 'revealing scenes of chaotic indiscipline' (Shepherd and Shepherd, 2012: 65). For it was the vastness of the 'Comps', as oversized institutions, which resulted in the comprehensive systems' inherent problems – problems which were particularly apparent come the mid-1970s – being reflected in cultural texts of the time. As the state system underwent change – that is, from secondary moderns to comprehensives – children's media (comics and television in particular) was eventually to adopt, certainly by the late 1970s, a nastier, more explicit edge in their representation of, what was for many, the 'no future' of education and schooling. Thus, in 1978, *Grange Hill* was very much a prime example of that cultural trend.

For some the comprehensives represented radical educational institutions that were hell-bent on eroding established and proven modes of discipline and learning. Non-attendance, lack of discipline, politicized teachers and their regular tampering with the curriculum were all acknowledged as:

> different faces of an assault on traditional educational order through which the tried-and-tested curriculum of the grammar school was being ousted by one which depended on negotiation with interests and experiences of students (Jones and Davies, 2002: 146).

The general public and right-wing politicians interpreted this debasing of education, that they perceived was taking place within each and every comprehensive school, as being part-and-parcel of what was happening on a wider scale: deprived inner-cities populated by a increasingly lawless youth. The rise of Punk, 'race riots' where the National Front battled it out with the Anti-Nazi League, and pupils' involvement in teacher-led dissent were all interpreted as evidence that – not only was both the social order crumbling and comprehensive education not working – but that education itself was inciting social unrest. So, for *Grange Hill* to appear on television screens in 1978, whereby unruly school-kids were openly encouraged to swear on national television (well, they said 'Flippin' 'eck!' a lot), was antagonistic in itself, but for it all to be located 'in a modern mixed-background, mixed-ability comprehensive school' (McGown and Docherty, 2003: 113) was perceived to be tantamount to an incitement to riot. So, '[t]o make a programme based in a largely working-class London comprehensive school was thus from the beginning to court controversy' (Jones and Davies, 2002: 146).

Grange Hill was seen as a children's programme that 'bullied' public service television (for it was made by, and shown on, the BBC), into the worrying realm of 'realism', whereby the representation of the everyday would, it was feared, detrimentally effect the minds and attitudes of its young viewers. To the more conservatively-inclined viewers then, *Grange Hill* 'presented evidence not just of overall cultural decline, but of a betrayal by public service professionals of their original mandate and responsbilities' (Jones and Davies, 2002: 146). Although, that stated, the initial series of 16 episodes included little subversive material; but, come the second and third series, the upholders of moral decency were up in arms about the programme's content; no wonder, for each and every episode seemed to be 'all about student militancy and behind the bike shed and horrendous things like periods and first bras' (Jones and Davies, 2002: 147). Initiated by Benny Green being name-called because he is black, *Grange Hill*'s first 'issue' addressed was racism – only to be followed by bullying, teenage pregnancy, drug-taking, date rape, asylum seekers, the commercialisation of schooling, etc. In doing so, *Grange Hill* quite often made explicit – or, at the very least, alluded to – aspects of school life which had been, historically, ignored by texts aimed at children, 'namely, the lives lived by *children* in the margins or interstices of institutions designed by adults' (Jones and Davies, 2002: 150). That is why, in *Grange Hill*, pupils are often seen prowling around – or being accosted amid – such secret or barely visited places within the school as boiler rooms and toilets. In effect:

> [c]hildren's spaces such as the cloakroom, the walk to and from school, or the local shopping centre provided the site of the drama alongside the more familiar teacher-dominated school spaces such as the classroom (Jones and Davies, 2002: 150).

Despite *Grange Hill*'s claim to present an 'honest' and 'gritty' portrayal of life in an inner-city comprehensive school, we have to remember that – as with the majority of televisual representations – its version of 'reality' was, often for purely dramatic purposes, an exaggerated one. Whilst the drab and dreary sets provided it with a veneer of the ordinary and the everyday, even the banal incidents shown on screen 'were always slightly larger than life' (McGown and Docherty, 2003: 113). Furthermore, despite all the claims that *Grange Hill* was radically different to all of the other previous representations of schools and schooling, as the series was, more often than not, merely a re-representation of what had already gone before. Borrowing from previous tales of school and schooling (that is, those to be found in literature, comics, TV and film) *Grange Hill* often:

> used and re-used characters and story-lines that owed a lot to these forbears and featured such recognizable character types as the school swot, the cheeky rebel and the 'good girl' tempted by romance (Jones and Davies, 2002: 147).

Rather than a weekly radical overthrow of accepted educational/parenting norms and values, it – conversely – consistently proved to be a programme which regimentally adhered to the status quo: as even the most controversial plots were settled, more often than not, as a result of the involvement of a well-meaning teacher or parent, to the extent that, quite clearly, *Grange Hill* 'relied much more heavily than its critics recognized on resolutions and closures that affirmed conventional values' (Jones and Davies, 2002: 147). Furthermore, as a children's television drama *Grange Hill* has 'been the most watched and the most consistently controversial within the genre bar none' (McGown and Docherty, 2003: 113). Thus, '[u]nlikely as it would have seemed in 1978 ... [it became] an institution in both senses of the word' (McGown and Docherty, 2003: 115).

Tony Parson's first novel, a piece of 'youthploitation' pulp fiction of the highest (or, rather, lowest) order was *The Kids* (1976). This sordid tale of delinquents 'Blondie', 'Dogend', 'Rod', and 'Chiv', revolves around underage drinking in pubs and discothèques, where their nightly bouts of aggressiveness are fuelled by copious amounts of 'Mandies' (or Mandrax tablets). But it is their absolute detestation – and vastness – of the institution that is secondary school which is made obvious early on:

> The comprehensive school they went to was, and still is, with 3,000 pupils, ridiculously overcrowded. In most classes there were over 40 students, if you can call them that. Truancy was rampant and many of them rarely bothered to go in ... No one cared if they didn't show up for school, least of all the overworked teachers. The less they had in their classes the better (Parsons, 1976: 20).

And, furthermore, the crowded immensity of the secondary school of the kids bred, and perpetuated, a gang culture:

> Many of them moved in gangs. They were getting nothing out of the education that society had provided for them and they saw it all as a battle of wits between them and the teachers (Parsons, 1976: 20).

For, ultimately, such vast, anonymous institutions proved superfluous in their lives that were fundamentally solely based upon the pursuit of 'urban survival':

> They could teach the kids nothing about life they had not already learned on the streets (Parsons, 1976: 21).[7]

The notion that – by the mid-1970s – Britain's schools were teething with a mass of increasingly wayward youths was, then, a fear that did not come alone. There was a wider, cultural perception of the onset of a country in crisis: increasingly ungovernable, this was, according to Leon Hunt, in *British Low Culture* (1998), an 'Aggro Britain', whereby, exchanged in school classrooms and playgrounds, there was, what Hunt terms, a whole swathe of subversive, and certainly non-curriculum '"behind the school desk" fiction' (Hunt, 1998: 75) – such as Parsons' *The Kids* (1976) and, even more infamously, Richard Allen's *Skinhead* (1970). Published by New English Library, these mass-market pulps, primarily aimed at youths who saw no benefit in the reading of school set texts, were commonly consumed in a secretive manner – as Hunt's term makes explicit – behind the school desk: an illicit consumption that, as Hunt notes, 'summons up images of counter-education, of subcultural capital smuggled into the classroom' (Hunt, 1998: 75). As one reader puts it:

> [f]or any kid attending a comprehensive school between 1971 and 1977, Richard Allen's books were required reading … it was New English Library's Skinhead wot provided your sex'n'violence education (cited in Hunt, 1998: 75).

Yet, by the late-1970s – at the height of the all-too-tangible crisis that was 'Aggro Britain' – there were some (mainly Marxists sociologists) that were beginning to listen to, and sympathise with, working-class kids, and what they had to say about education and schooling in relation to the lack of opportunities in their lives. Paul Willis, in his classic text *Learning to Labour – How Working Class Kids Get Working Class Jobs* (1977), conducted a study of the Hammertown Boys, whom he termed the Lads. In constant conflict with the stifling authority in their lives that was education and schooling, they defined themselves through their opposition to teachers and, what they termed, the 'Ear 'Oles' – these 'Ear 'Oles' (according to the Lads) were unmasculine weaklings who had allowed themselves to become pawns in the hierarchy that was the classroom. Unlike the Ear 'Oles, the Lads spent their time 'dossing, blagging, wagging' and 'having a laff', and yearning for the day that they could leave school, get a job and earn money.

Meanwhile, Paul Corrigan's *Schooling the Smash Street Kids* (1979) made more than explicit that – for the pupils that he spoke to (of both Municipal Comprehensive School and Cunningham Secondary School) – education and schooling was nothing more than an imposition that should be, at worse, endured

---

7   As such, Fireball's tips on how to survive in such an urban jungle (as outlined earlier in this chapter), all of a sudden, lose completely their comic edge.

and, at best, avoided. Rather amusingly, from our Millennial perspective, Corrigan (as a true Marxist) describes the schoolchildren, in relation to the imposition that was their nominal engagement with education and schooling, as in a 'guerilla struggle' (Corrigan, 1979: 70), insisting that '[t]eachers and pupils in secondary schools at the moment will recognize this analogy as a day-to-day reality' (1979: 71). Well, if that was the case, a favourite guerilla tactic of these schoolchildren – in their endeavour to avoid the imposition of education and schooling – was truancy. For the pupils that Corrigan spoke to, truancy – or dolling off – was a consequence of schooling being compulsory. As Corrigan makes clear:

> [i]t may seem farcical but it did appear that school might not be so bad if you did not HAVE to go. Therefore *having* to go to school – in effect the reverse of truancy, but also its major cause – was where the boys started off their everyday school experiences (Corrigan, 1979: 18).

Borstals

To such schoolboys, who got nothing about life from school, and who had learnt all they needed to learn on the streets, such institutionalism as the comprehensive school system proved unbearable. So much so that their attendance would become increasingly erratic-to-non-existent, and petty crime and violence would become their absolute priorities in life – and, thus, not teachers, lessons, books, etc. Inevitably, other forms of institutionalism would take over their lives and, during the 1970s in particular, one infamous, and controversial, institution for such wayward boys was Borstal. Two of the kids of Parsons' novel, Rod and Chiv, end up 'doing time' in Borstal. Sentenced for two years for the violent robbing of a pawnbroker, their very first glimpse of this notorious institution ensured that Borstal, all of a sudden, made the formerly stifling institution of school seem suddenly more akin to that of a holiday camp:

> The first thing that Rod and Chiv saw of Borstal was a massive gate set in a high brick wall. On top of the wall, broken glass and jagged stones were cemented. Over that there were two strands of barbed wire running along the wall, suspended on angle irons. It was a cold and forbidding sight and both felt the palms of their hands to be clammy with sweat (Parsons, 1976: 71).

Named after the first young offenders institution at Borstal Prison in Kent, and a means of imprisonment for 15 to 21-year-olds (with the minimum age raised to 17 in 1969), they were abolished in 1982.[8] Highly representative of what Erving Goffman (1961) termed 'total institutions', they imposed a strict, timetabled day

---

8   Borstals, being abolished in 1982, was a significant part of that decade's – the 1980s – 'closure' of the decade before, the 1970s.

upon their young inmates. For as Roger Whiting, in *Crime and Punishment – A Study Across Time* (1986), notes – taking Huntercombe Borstal, Oxfordshire, as a prime example – the day begins early with '06.45 cells unlocked', and ends, prematurely, with '21.00 roll call; lock up' (Whiting, 1986: 188).

As such, Borstal was an institution for delinquent youths which manifested itself across a multitude of media texts of the time. With regards film, it ranged from, just prior to the start of the decade, the lesser known – such as *Bronco Bullfrog* (1969), with the title character being 'a free agent fresh out of Borstal' (Leggott, 2010: 236) – to the far more notorious towards the end of the decade such as *Scum* (1979). In the latter, director Alan Clarke, with the young inmate Ben Archer (played by Mick Ford), offers a highly contentious assertion that the adult governors and wardens of the borstals were just as institutionalised (and, thus, damaged) as those youths that were sent there for rehabilitation. In the scene where Archer enters into a sympathetic dialogue, over a hot drink and biscuits, with one of the more accessible wardens, Officer Duke (Bill Dean), the youth does nothing but articulately undermine authority and institutionalisation from the off:

> But it's when he suggests that the lot of the officers is no better than that of the inmates that Archer really touches a nerve. As Duke yelps: 'I give you my fucking coffee and you think you can take the piss out of me?' we know the answer is yes, he just has (Newkey-Burden, 2004: 89).

A key sociological study of 'Milltown' (a rough suburb of a Welsh city), by Howard and Pip Williamson, carried out as the 1970s were in full swing, examined 67 working-class males, 'the Boys', from school through to work.[9] Entitled *Five Years* (1981), the title referred to the length of the study (carried out from 1973, when they were just 13, to 1978, when they legally became men at 18), and it is a sympathetic, yet honest, account of their lives and lifestyles during that period. The study is particularly illuminating with regards their criminal selves and their encounters with, and attitudes towards, the penal system. For instance, when they were 16 – significantly still classed as juveniles in the eyes of the law – they balked at the Magistrates' mention of Borstal even though their sentences, for the more and more serious crimes that they were committing, were becoming worthy of longer spells of probation or actual confinement in detention centres. Indeed, by 16, whilst '[n]one had been 'upstairs' to Crown Court for Borstal', some of them 'had been threatened with it (and would continue to be threatened with it)' (Williamson, 1981: 38). No surprise, then, that come the age of 17, a number were eventually to be sent to Borstal for their crimes, and, as a result, one key

---

9   Howard Williamson's doctoral thesis, out of which *Five Years* (1981) emerged, actually, on its acknowledgements' page, pays special thanks to a 'core' of 12, and mentions a further 41. The remaining 14 of the total sample of 67, were, admittedly, peripheral – at best – to the study.

characteristic of 'going away' to Borstal they found particularly difficult to cope with – the 'indeterminate sentence'.

For whilst detention centres and prison meant sentences of explicit length, to the 'Milltown Boys' 'Borstal constituted an indeterminate sentence and ... anything indeterminate was frightening' (Williamson, 1981: 61). Yet, their fear of Borstal was not only founded upon the 'indeterminate' nature of its sentencing, but how the notion of 'remand' failed to impact upon that 'indeterminate sentence'. For, 'at least in prison, the time that you had spent on remand counted towards your sentence', but, quite significantly, '[i]t did not with Borstal' (Williamson, 1981: 61). Perhaps even more illuminating is Howard Williamson's follow-up study, *The Milltown Boys* (2004), which makes connections between their eventual sending to Borstal and life-long consecutive prison sentences. Out of four of those studied that encountered 'Borstal training' – again, involving them serving indeterminate sentences of between six months and two years – three 'subsequently did time in prison' (Williamson, 2004: 69).

Such serious studies of Borstal were occasionally, amid children's texts in particular, offset by tinges of fantasy impinging upon such bleak reality. *Raven* (ATV, 1977) had, as its unlikely modern-day Arthurian hero, a young ex-Borstal boy. Raven, played by Phil Daniels, as part of his on-going rehabilitation, is sent to take part in an archaeological exploration of a cave system. With Professor Young in charge of proceedings, the series' fantasy elements merge with an ecologically aware plot, whereby a government-sponsored nuclear waste processing plant plans to store toxic waste in the caves. Set against a backdrop of dark, dank caves, and ancient standing stones, *Raven* is seemingly of the mould of 'many psychedelic eco-fantasies of the 70s' (McGown and Docherty, 2003: 111); but still the writers, Jeremy Burnham and Trevor Ray, then go against all expectations and 'present a surprising piece of social realism through the character of Raven' (McGown and Docherty, 2003: 111).

Instead of some delinquent stereotype, Raven is bent on conforming, as he willingly sets off on a voyage of self-discovery. Furthermore, the TV tie-in novelisation, from its opening pages, makes explicit that Raven was deserving of his Borstal sentence (that is, for taking part in a riot-scale incident of football hooliganism), and has the hero, upon being confronted by a railway ticket-collector for occupying first-class seating when being in possession of second-class documentation, blatantly lying about his criminal background in an act of anti-institutional bravado:

> He was frowning at the warrants. 'Ferndown ... that where you come from? I've heard of that. That's a Borstal, isn't it?'
>
> 'Borstal?' Raven exploded. 'You got to be joking, squire'. He could hardly prevent the laughter. 'One of the oldest public schools in the country, Ferndown'. That barrack. That grey misery of wire and tarmac that converted the imposed silence into a noise inside your head ... how could a man as old as this one,

willing to wear his life away inside a uniform, pockets full of authority, a cap braided with self-importance, hope to understand the joke (Burnham and Ray, 1977b: 12).

Like *Scum* – whilst, of course, still operating at the level of a children's text – *Raven* makes explicit the lineage between school (in this case public), Borstal, and other, more adult, institutions and institutional conformity, such as the Army (with the mention of 'barrack') and a man's willingness to don a uniform. And it is the uniform – whether a school one, or as worn by an institutionalised adult – that signifies to Parson's 'Kids', Williamsons' 'Boys' the stifling nature of the institutions of adults and adulthood. Yet, at many points in the storyline, it is obvious that Raven is seemingly beyond deinstitutionalising, as, in the very first episode, when Professor Young's wife enters Raven's room at night, the ex-Borstal boy leaps out of bed, and, standing to attention, shouts 'Sir!'. Seconds later, when being accused of stealing cutlery, Raven openly reveals he has pocketed a knife and fork, explaining that, in Borstal, it was regulation to use, clean, and keep hold of your own set of cutlery between meals.

Yet, with regards the media's depiction of Borstal life within popular culture more generally, it was very much a case of grim reality over any suggestion of fantasy. As, Jim Melly, in *'Last Orders, Please' – Rod Stewart, The Faces, and the Britain We Forgot* (2003), making reference to the song 'Borstal Boys' on The Faces' LP *Ooh La La* (1973), states that – with its opening fanfare of a wailing siren that signals a riot or even a breakout is taking place – this is a straight forward tune 'about the inmates of one of the country's penal institutions for young offenders' (Melly, 2003: 219). Providing detail of a Borstal's daily routine, and the stories behind its inmates' crimes and sentencing, it was the very fact that The Faces felt the need to compose such a track that reflects the state of Britain during the 1970s. As, '[t]o write and record a song on this subject was simply to reflect the general feeling in Britain that young people were increasingly out of control' (Melly, 2003: 219).

With the above in mind, it is perhaps unsurprising that one of Peter's most vivid memories is of how, quite often, the Borstal cast a long, dark shadow over even the most tranquil of suburban schools. As a primary school pupil who thoroughly enjoyed those years of education in particular, Peter recalls an occasion, with absolute clarity, when ex-Borstal boys (that is, ex-pupils of his primary school who, having been expelled from secondary school, were institutionalised through such incarceration) were to be found outside the gates, intent in forcing their way in past the teachers, and causing mayhem.

All of a sudden, our teachers hurriedly start to usher us back inside: but, we plea, 'It's still our break, can't we stay outside?'. Yet, staying outside is no longer an option. As we're herded up the stone steps, and in through the entrance into our block, I catch a glimpse of them: Just beyond the school gates there are five boys.

Two are astride bicycles, whilst the others stand with their thumbs in the pockets of their flared jeans. All are grimacing menacingly. They, without a doubt, are 'trouble'. Reluctantly, I go back to class early. And, as I do so, I glance back at Mr Emmanuel, our teacher; he looks worried. He fought in Korea. So, why-oh-why does he look so worried about these boys?

Even when such 'Borstal boys' were not actually hanging around the gates of Peter's primary school, they were 'used' by other 'harder' boys as local 'folk devils'-come-'bogey men' as a form of bullying in themselves.

I'm playing by myself in the school yard; totally lost in my imaginative play. Then, all of a sudden, one of my classmates, Bailey, comes running up to me, and begins to taunt me: 'Woah! You'd better watch out, as so-and-so (their name doesn't mean anything to me – but even his name sounds frightening!), is out, and he's coming here, to school, to get you! Watch out! Watch out!!!'. Terrified, I run inside, and hide in the toilets. I'm crying now, and I want my Mammy.

Libraries

A *BBC News* online article, highlighting the potential consequences of planned Government Public Sector cuts upon library provision, made reference to Nicky Wire – of the Welsh rock band, The Manic Street Preachers – and his support of the protection of such local services ('Manics star joins libraries fight', 8 February 2011). In particular, the report noted that Wire, and other members of the band, were not only champions of public libraries, but that – in the song 'A Design For Life' (where they included the line 'libraries gave us power') – they acknowledged how such libraries had historically educated – and, thus, politicised – the working class in south Wales. Indeed, that song's line is taken from 'Knowledge is Power', originally 'an inscription above the entrance to a former library in Newport' ('Manics star joins libraries fight', *BBC News* online, 8 February 2011). Wire, in conversation with the *Guardian*'s Robin Turner (7 February 2011), insisted that such ideologically imbued phrasing (that is, both the band's lyric, and the original carved words upon which it is based), and the stately, bookish institutions, to be found within such blue-collar communities, 'become intertwined with an idea about what the miners had given back to society when they built municipal halls and centres across the country' (Monday, 7 February 2011). Furthermore, Wire makes connections with such libraries' everydayness, and the opportunities that their literary content affords: 'So often absolutely ordinary in appearance, a good library should offer escape routes down the most extraordinary avenues, pathways into different worlds from the one you've left outside' (Monday, 7 February 2011).

Whilst Skewen Library, admittedly, did not originate as one, it is worth noting that '[b]y 1934 there were more than a hundred miners' libraries in the Welsh coalfields, with an average stock of about three thousand volumes', where, 'in smaller villages the collection might consist of only a few hundred books, and the librarian was usually a miner who volunteered to mind the shop one evening a week' (Rose, 2010: 237). Fundamentally, then, Skewen Library – no matter how small, and modest – can only be understood proper amid the historical context of the particularly Welsh tradition of Miners' Libraries.

Liz Greenhalgh et al., in *Libraries in a World of Cultural Change* (1995), assert why libraries, and what they term their '"libraryness" factor', possess such social, cultural, and emotional weight within communities. Reminding us that libraries were once the preserve of monastic institutions, that they are places of semi-holy contemplation, whereby '"[l]ibraryness" partly derives from the large-scale presence of books, which themselves historically evince a quasi-religious or spiritual aura' to the extent that '[l]ibraries are in some senses seen as quasi-sacred places' (Greenhalgh et al., 1995: 51). Likewise, in an effort to understand fully what makes libraries so special, they outline the ways in which they can be understood as social objects in their own right, for '[a]s public places, library buildings in some ways represent values of the public realm – the world of social exchange' (Greenhalgh et al., 1995: 53). Furthermore, and despite their austere, dark, yet hallowed origins, even the prefab libraries of the postwar era – such as Skewen's – managed, and still manage, to instil notions of the public: 'Modern buildings and bright interiors continue to reflect ideals of intellectual rights, the centrality of education in our system and the role of public libraries in helping to sustain a public realm' (Greenhalgh et al., 1995: 53). Of course, this sense of a public realm is reinforced by one simple fact: whilst libraries (especially in the age of rampant consumption) do not sell anything, they continue to lend a great deal; and, in doing so, 'they recycle artefacts and other cultural goods ... within the local culture' (Greenhalgh et al., 1995: 53).

It is raining, and me and Mammy – having done the shopping, and now heading home – call into the library. The blast of the electric fan heater above the entrance warms us instantly, and, having left the grey, dark day outside, the fluorescent lights of its interior leave us blinking. But, before we go into its carpeted inside proper (and before we get a chance to sit, squeakily, on the plastic armchairs at its heart), we stop at the returns trolley. Here we find the relatively new but already highly popular books that have recently been brought back, and are about to be put back upon the shelves into their allocated slot. There is something very special about this trolley and its selection of books: pristine in both appearance and feel, this is where all returned books (irrespective of their classifications and themes, whether they be 'adult' or for 'children') come together. Having just been placed there temporarily, they are in sudden danger of being lost once back in their true place on the shelves. It is on this returns trolley that the true treasures of the library can be found.

To Greenhalgh et al., the returns trolley had a particular place in the social that was the library, as it 'is the part of the library where users get a direct sense of what others are reading', where '[t]he books just brought back have an immediate recommendation attached that distinguishes them from other books anonymously arranged on the shelves' (Greenhalgh et al., 1995: 62). Thus, quite simply, '[t]he fascination for the returns trolley is more than the eccentric behaviour of library users' as 'it demonstrates the latent interest in what others are reading' (Greenhalgh et al., 1995: 62).

Furthermore, and taking into account the importance Greenhalgh et al. place upon the increasing need for libraries (again, bearing in mind their dim interiors of old) to embrace glass and light in an age of increasing transparency, Skewen Library – especially to a young Peter during the 1970s – was to be forever caught in its semi-solid, prefabricated-ness.

Standing in the middle of the library, I look around. Flimsy in its construction, with the books the sturdiest things to be found within this prefabricated box, it's as if the books are side-by-side, and on top of one another, to form the very walls of the library. Staring at these walls of books, and then gazing up to the fluorescent strip lighting, I imagine that they – the row after row of books, that are to be found upon shelf after shelf – are holding up the ceiling and the flat roof that is above. Yet, standing on synthetic, carpeted square floor tiles, and looking at a huddle of cream-coloured, faux-leather, plastic armchairs, fan heaters, and the building's emergency exit; this flimsy box – one of the centres of my little world – is both sturdy yet fragile. Permanent yet temporary. It is a home from home.

Despite its prefabricated-ness (especially in relation to Ivy Cottage's late-nineteenth-century solidity), this was an alternative home for Peter: a home, perhaps, due to its homely interior – that is, on rainy days, a warm refuge from the elements outside, and so on. Greenhalgh et al. claim that the trend for smaller libraries to adopt a décor akin to that of the domestic sphere of the house is in alignment with 'the predominance of women amongst library staff and the way in which female staff have helped create a sense of hospitality' (Greenhalgh et al., 1995: 64).

Such hospitality, to Peter, his mother, and others who frequented Skewen library, often extended further than merely the lending of books.

Getting back home after our shopping trip up Skewen, Mammy – shouting out a frustrated 'Bloody Hell!' – realises that a large share of our groceries are missing, and that we probably left them in the library when we briefly called in there to return her books. I am swiftly sent back 'up the hill' to retrieve it. Upon seeing me approach the desk, a huddle of buxom women with child-bearing hips, momentarily leaving behind their 'cuppas' and Rich Tea biscuits in the 'staff-only', back room, whoosh out, not even saying a word, and hand me the left-behind bag. Both they and I are used to this, of course, as it was an umbrella last week, library books the week before ... Smiling, with both thanks and embarrassment, I turn, and start my trek back down Skewen hill.

To Peter, the female staff at Skewen Library were not only recognisable female faces (and feminine physiques), but, in many respects, they were – both individually and collectively – his 'surrogate mothers' of the neighbourhood. They, after all, through their inspecting of his library tickets several times a week (as well as the repeated handing to him of his mother's lost property), knew who he was, his age, where he lived, and so on. Thus, the job that Skewen library's female staff did – based upon their recognition of their patrons, all founded upon intimate knowledge – underlined the fact that 'women in public librarianship support the library's role as a nurturing institution of the state' (Greenhalgh, et al. 1995: 64).

Libraries, of course, are not only gender-based providers of employment, but class-imbued institutions, as – despite their attempts otherwise – they are (along with reading itself) largely a middle-class pursuit, whereby '[t]he public library has always found difficulty in attracting users from the very lowest social group' (Black, 2000: 145). That is not to say that the working-classes are not users of libraries, but they 'have generally done so in lower numbers than one would expect if the proportion they represent in the population as a whole is taken into consideration' (Black, 2000: 145). As with other welfare-state bolstered post-war institutions (such as the NHS) it was middle-class users that seemed to embrace (exploit even) such increased 'access for all'. No surprise, then, that by the mid-1970s, a number of reports warned of libraries becoming middle-class-only -enclaves, that 'had assumed an unmistakably middle-class identity, in keeping with its historic image as an institution of highbrow culture and social refinement' (Black, 2000: 147). Although it has to be acknowledged that many patrons of libraries – especially smaller libraries such as that to be found in Skewen – were resolutely working-class. Peter's mother, and even Peter himself, through the very act of regularly visiting Skewen library and repeatedly borrowing its books, were classics examples of members of a working-class family attempting to better themselves through the ritual of reading.

With the above in mind, a counter-trend – led by a number of class-aware librarians and library educators – was also detectable come the end of the decade, that, in reversing such discrimination of the lower classes (that, quite significantly, included members of ethnic minorities of course), initiated a new approach, 'community librarianship', which 'entailed a focusing of resources on the vulnerable and the needy, not least the rising army of the unemployed' (Black, 2000: 148).

However, such reform was, by the mid-1980s, being challenged by cuts in public services and the ushering in of a competitive, 'entrepreneurial' ethos, whereby '[m]any librarians, armed with the latest management jargon, became managers first and librarians second' (Black, 2000: 151).

Returning to the notion of the library as a local institution that offered – children and young adults especially – 'avenues of escape', we consider, once again, the words of Nicky Wire (7 February 2011):

> Libraries have always reassuringly been there when I needed them. Blackwood library in Wales helped me through my O- and A-Levels. They have given my parents decades of pleasure, satiating their desire to read and learn ... My wife Rachel worked as a librarian across the branches in Newport. My brother Patrick worked in Blackwood library ... For these and countless other reasons, the public library was a key factor in shaping who I am today (Wire, cited in Turner, Monday, 7 February 2011).

Perhaps, then, for Wire, for a young Peter, and countless other working-class people who have – through the years – borrowed books from their local libraries, they are not just avenues of escape, but gateways of opportunity.

Public Houses and Social Clubs

John Bailey and Emyr Gough, in *Skewen & District – A History* (1998), remind us of the variety of social institutions that such Welsh villages as Skewen and Neath Abbey were founded upon:

> The growth of any centre of population will include naturally the development of services to meet the needs of that population. Along with the spiritual needs, the chapels and churches, come the materialistic needs, and Skewen was not left behind in the development of beer houses and inns (Bailey and Gough, 1998: 117).

With regards Skewen's social institutions, the versions which Peter had a clear cognitive and geographical mapping of where those frequented solely by his father after work and of an evening: public houses, or the local 'pubs'. It seemed quite fitting to Peter that his father should inhabit such places following a particularly hard day's graft, for they were often named after burly, blue-collar workers – The Farmer's Arms and The Miner's Arms for example (the former to be found 'at the top' of Old Road, the latter 'at the top' of New Road). Quite interestingly, Jacqueline Simpson's *Green Men & White Swans – The Folklore of British Pub Names* (2010), notes that the naming of such pubs in seemingly noble recognition of manual labourers is, in reality, a Bacchus-leaning, beer-fuelled subverting of age-old heraldic acknowledgment of the ruling classes. In a subsection entitled 'Puns & Old Jokes' (Simpson, 2010: 138–9), it is explained that – as an elaborate form of satire – one of the most common puns entered into when naming a pub was to draw comparison between 'heraldic arms' of the upper classes and the 'physical arms' of lowly labourers. Thus, whilst many ale houses are reverent to local aristocracy or national royalty by taking on a recognisable name and combining it with some form of heraldic iconography, other pubs and taverns mockingly (this is, at the expense of those that ruled the working class), honoured the 'arms' of those men that carried out manual work – 'Blacksmith's Arms, Bricklayer's Arms, Butcher's Arms, Forester's Arms, Gardener's Arms, Miner's Arms, and so forth, the craft chosen often being historically linked to that locality' (Simpson, 2010: 139). As expected, then, David Graham George's *A Skewen Boy Looks Back* (n.d.), when detailing the history of Skewen's collieries, the inclusion of the author's own photographs of the signboards for The Miner's Arms and The Collier's is accompanied by the note that these are '[t]wo reminders of Skewen's mining past' (George, n.d.: 203). Of course, the very fact that neither of these pubs now no longer exist (as per the death of the pub as part of the death of the high street), solemnly reminds us of the loss of such banal societal reminders of local history.

When walking through Skewen or Neath Abbey, Peter would, when passing such drinking dens, gaze up at the realistically painted signboards.

Gently swinging in the breeze, the creak of the signboard makes me look up. We – me and Mammy – are walking past The Miner's. It's closed (as the solid-wood door is firmly closed and locked), and Mammy mutters under her breath 'Oh, and this is one of your father's second homes'. As we pass, I look up at the signboard and, now, twisting my neck and turning my head backwards – whilst still walking forwards – to examine the other side. Looking at the miner's well-defined arms, I think of my father both in work and at work, and I see his arms, straining and sweating.

Such sweat, of course, would often be replenished, late in the afternoon, or throughout the evening, by Peter's father – and other blue-collar workers of the locale – consuming many a post-shift pint of beer in Skewen's pubs. Yet, a signboard's realisation of the straining, sweating arms of the working man, is very much in keeping with the visual styles adopted by such public house artwork, as '[s]ometimes the signboard displays the appropriate tools in a heraldic style, but more often it shows a muscular workman with his sleeves rolled up' (Simpson, 2010: 139).

Furthermore, many of these pubs within which Peter's father could be found seemed, by their very titling, to merge the locale's muscled workforce with its local geology – thus, whilst The Smith's Arms was to be found in Neath Abbey, further up Skewen Hill, Old Road, was The Rock and Fountain. Even though these establishments were strictly 'adult only' (for when Peter was a child, there were no such thing as family friendly pubs), they still provided children such as Peter a method of, when walking past them, mapping their surroundings – or, perhaps more importantly, a means by which they could map the leisure activities of (in the main) the male members of their family, such as fathers, brothers, uncles, and the like. In Peter's mind, there existed a mental map of his father's staggered walks home of an evening from pubs such as The Miner's and The Collier's, which, in the end – and no matter what route was taken – all led back to Ivy Cottage.

The sleevenotes to the compilation CD *Working Man's Soul – Rare Funk, Rock, Soul & Jazz from the UK Cabaret Scene* (Anon., 2006), as well as providing an overview of the interconnected genres of music played by the many semi-professional British bands and musicians of the late-1960s and 1970s, offers an illuminating insight into a form of leisure activity – indeed, a whole nightlife – that has, since that decade, all but disappeared. That is the (now often underestimated) popularity of the cabaret scene that ran in parallel with the widespread working-class experience of the toil of hard labour. As well as there being, in reality, little or no alternative to an evening at a local cabaret, various other cultural aspects had an impact as well: With public transport often ending by early evening, and taxis (that is, if you could afford one), far and few between, when you – as a working-class man or woman – were in search of an evening's entertainment, 'you walked to the local Miners Welfare, Working Man's or Factory Social Club, just like everyone else' (Anon., 2006, sleevenotes to the CD *Working Man's Soul*). So popular were the 'Workies' and 'Socials' during the 1970s especially, that a particular television variety show, broadcast by Granada Television, attempted to replicate the experience of such in-club cabaret for the small screen, with *The Wheeltappers and Shunters Social Club*.

With its title derived from particular forms of railway-based employment (and the social life associated with railway work from the late-1800s onwards), and televised from 1974 until 1977, *The Wheeltappers and Shunters Social Club* – with its smoke-filled and ale-stained studio space – replicated, down to its last fag-filled ashtray and soaked beer mat, a typical 'Workies' or 'Social' for TV consumption. It was, without doubt, a form of working-class evening's entertainment for viewers that, if they weren't in front of the television at the moment of broadcast, were actually to be found at their local cabaret club:

> Indeed can a television programme have ever been aimed at a less aspirant section of the general public? We don't think so, and in this age of demographics and ABC1s we're certain we will never see its like again (Kibble-White, 2005: 210–11).

Thus, *The Wheeltappers and Shunters Social Club* was of its time, as working-class life – back in the 1970s – was also of its time:

> It is worth remembering that society was structured very differently back in those days. Huge sections of the population of a given town or city would be employed at a single factory, steelworks or pit. Here, the workers and the unions operated

their own social calendar to boost the spirits and turn a profit for union coffers at the same time. These social clubs were the hub of the community – a concept alien to current times (Anon., 2006, sleevenotes to the CD *Working Man's Soul*).

No surprise, then, that as well as being a patron of Skewen's public houses, Peter's father – as a blue-collar worker – was a member of the local 'Workies', 'Socials', and the like. The 1970s was still an era (perhaps the last decade) when formal evening wear – that is, often a dinner jacket and bow tie – was the working-class uniform for a blue-collar worker attending an evening's cabaret. Peter's father would often, on a weekend, early evening, leave Ivy Cottage intent on visiting a number of Skewen's pubs and clubs, dressed in such sober attire. One of the most popular comedy series of the time, which mirrored such debonair forms of pub- and club-frequenting working-class masculinity was *Dave Allen at Large*. Even though Allen achieved stardom as early as the middle of the 'Swinging Sixties', 'the 1970s was the decade in which he arrived at his prime' (McCann, 2005: 19). *Dave Allen at Large* was shown on the BBC across not only five series, but three specials, from 1971–1979. Thus, if there was one television series, where one man – that is, one form of suave masculinity during the post-Hippie era – was the programme's entire focus, it was *Dave Allen at Large*. Where, for other entertainers, a form of adherence to a scruffy, flamboyant, or even decadent manner of dressing was to be their on-stage trademarks, Dave Allen was a smooth, calm, and dignified sit-down stand-up comedian. Casually astride his trademark black leather, on-stage chair-come-barstool – its (from his perspective) right-hand Formica rest for his ever-present cut-glass whiskey tumbler (which actually was brimming with champagne), cigarettes, matches, and ashtray – here was the most elegantly amusing and charming man, in the pub, in your living room. In short, he was both the Workingman's Club compere and comedian – only even more immaculately dressed. When shifted effortlessly from 1960s pre-fame to his height of popularity in the 1970s, this was seemingly achieved by Allen donning 'an even better class of bespoke three-piece suit, as he charmed and challenged and entertained much of the nation' (McCann, 2005: 15).

Not only was Allen's on-stage dress-code immaculate, so was his comedic timing based upon his ability to anticipate both his audience's laughter, and perhaps more importantly, their silence. In doing this, he often revelled in pausing as he was telling a joke or a story; then, whilst taking a long sip of his whiskey, or lengthy drag on his cigarette, he would make seemingly endless eye contact with both the audience and the viewers, as all shared a momentary thought that needed little or no further comment. Indeed, '[i]t was an intimate, urbane, sophisticated style that was ideal for a medium as inquisitive as television' (McCann, 2005: 15). According to McCann (2005), with *Dave Allen at Large*, Allen 'proceeded to give a master-class in expert narrative technique and elegant comic timing' (2005: 23), where the comedian 'always controlled the shape and sound and syntax, choreographing every last little stroke of the hair, sip of the drink, puff of the cigarette and brush of the clothes as he delivered the material' (2005: 24). No wonder that, with his father already out, frequenting the pubs, 'Workies', and 'Socials' of Skewen, *Dave Allen at Large* aided and abetted Peter's imagining of his father: Nonchalantly propped up against a bar in Skewen, here was – alongside many other dinner-suited blue-collar workers – a rather more serious, and far more tipsy, Allen for the locals. For, equally dapper as his on-stage variant, here was an urbane *Dave Allen at Large* writ suburban small.

Standing Stones

Neath poet Chris Torrance, living in a remote cottage situated between Pontneddfechan and Ystradfellta, has written many books and compiled many a poetry anthology that, as a body of work, 'reflect life in the valley' (Absalom and King, 2005: 127). What follows is an extract from 'Mirages' (from *Citrinas – The Magic Door Book II*, 1977, n.p.):

> CARREG BICA. Massive. Myriad
> initials
> carved on the sandstone forefinger
> threatening the sky
> drawing from the earth source.

Carreg Bica – or Careg Bica – is a standing stone of imposing dimensions: Ten feet tall, it is to be found atop of Y Mynydd Drummau (Drummau Mountain, which overlooks the lower Neath valley), and, as with all such monoliths, there is uncertainty with regards its origins and meaning. With a photograph of this standing stone just ahead of the contents page of Stephen Absalom and Robert King's *Around Neath* (2005), the authors speculate that '[o]ne legend has it that Careg Bica goes down to the River Neath on Easter morning for a drink of water' (n.p.). Having just read the extract from Torrance's 'Mirages', Absalom and King cite a strange fact associated with the stone, that the poet himself perpetuates. That is, 'if you strip to your waist on a very cold day, and lay against the stone with the wind biting into you, you will feel a heat travel through your body' (n.p.).

Stone, and geology more generally, are common motifs within children's literature – and, more specifically, absolutely central to the narrative of science fiction and fantasy aimed at children and adolescents. Indeed, they are absolutely fundamental to the works of Alan Garner, where his native Cheshire – not merely a north-western county – is an empirical framework from which all his works emerge. For, '[g]eology is to Garner what economics was to Marx: the base on which the superstructure of human life and culture ultimately rests, and that determines its possibilities', whereby '[r]ather than being a backdrop to the action, the land forms his characters, both physically and spiritually' (Butler, 2006: 46). No surprise, then, that 'generally his working methods are characterized by the kind of research-driven, iterative hypothesis-building more usually associated with scientific and historical disciplines' (Butler, 2006: 47). Moreover, for Garner, geology is the site of a life source often bordering on the magical; that is, a magic that 'is not simply foisted onto the passive land by the writer's imagination', but, instead, where 'the writer perceives and communicates what is already latent (and sometimes not so latent) in the land itself' (Butler, 2006: 46).

In Garner's work, standing stones often make unsettling appearances as not only central characters themselves but, occasionally, they provide the very title of a book. For example, *The Old Man of Mow* (1967) is quite an unconventional picture book, whereby Garner's words are inter-spread throughout with photographs by Roger Hill, and is concerned with two boys that scour the Cheshire landscape in order to locate the Old Man of the picture book's title, 'unaware till the end that he is a curiously-shaped rock' (Carpenter and Prichard, 1995: 200). Meanwhile, with *The Stone Book Quartet* (with *The Stone Book* published in 1976, and the remaining three published across 1977 and 1978), the author offers a set of interlinked stories that, across a single day each, tell the tale of members of Garner's own family at four points in time (in order of narrative, and not of publication – 1864, 1886, 1916, and 1941). In essence, they are, both individually and collectively, prose-poems within which craftsmanship is central to the 'myth' being evoked. In *The Stone Book*, Mary, the daughter of a stonemason desperate to learn to read, is eventually presented with a prayer book carved out of a pebble by her father:

> Mary turned the stone over. Father had split it so that the back showed two fronds of a plant, silk in skeins, silk on the water under the hill ... And Mary sat by the fire and read the stone book that had in it all the stories of the world and the flowers of the flood (Garner, 2006: 35–6).

Then, with blacksmiths and a realisation that such crafts are dying out in the modern era, the quartet's final instalment, *Tom Fobble's Day* (1977 – 'final' in a narrative sense and not with regards the order in which they were published), where William is made a sledge by his grandfather (which, it turns out, is the last thing he was to make before retirement and, then, death): '[T]hough the book ends with exhilaration, as William senses the presence of all his ancestors as he flies down the hill on the sledge' (Carpenter and Prichard, 1995: 498). At night, and with searchlights and anti-aircraft shot slicing through the sky, he slides, again and again, down a snowy slope. There, amongst the many dangers, he undergoes an epiphany of realisation of almost mythical proportions, where craft weaves together the generations:

> He set off. It had not been imagined. He was not alone on a sledge. There was a line, and he could feel it. It was a line through hand and eye, block, forge and loom to the hill. He owned them all: and they owned him (Garner, 2006: 166).

Such an interplay between a mythical past and a convincing contemporality underpins much of Alan Garner's literature. For example, *The Owl Service* (1967) is:

> a perfectly structured piece of work, in which myth and reality exactly fit together and the myth is used to engender catharsis in the lives of three very credible adolescents (Carpenter and Prichard, 1995: 199).

These three central characters are the seductive Alison, her stand-offish stepbrother Roger (both upper middle-class, they belong to an English family that now own the local stately home), and the frustrated 'Valley boy' Gwyn (who serves the English family as one of their domestics), where love, jealousy, anger and a conspicuous class struggle all fuel the tense plot: namely, that an ancient Welsh legend is, once more, violently being played out in the here-and-now. Thus, with *The Owl Service*, '[t]here are three layers of narrative – the adolescents' own story, a similar tragedy in the previous generation, and the Mabinogion myth which lies behind the book and intrudes into it' (Carpenter and Prichard, 1995: 199). Indeed, the Mabinogion myth (more specifically, its 'Fourth Branch', which Garner's *The Owl Service* is, again, a modern-day restaging of) is concerned with the sexually charged triangulated relationship between Lleu Llaw Gyffes (a hero of Welsh mythology), Gronw Pebr (Gronw the Radiant, a warrior-hunter), and Blodeuwedd (a woman in form, but made out of various flora, she is the Lleu's wife, but eventually Gronw's lover). At the end of the tale, Gronw – despite utilising a large circular stone as a shield – is killed by a spear that is thrown by Lleu with such force that it manages to pierce the centre of the stone. As already emphasised, myth, in Alan Garner's work, often manifests itself in the shape of standing stones. So, for the televised adaptation of *The Owl Service* (broadcast late 1969 to early 1970) the Granada production team had a specially commissioned Stone of Gronw – sculpted by a local mason from Aberangell, Edward Rowlands – erected on one of the banks of the Dovey river in time for their three-week's filming in-and-around Dinas Mawddwy, North Wales (for full production details, see McKay, 2008). Circular, and with its characteristic central hole, this recreation of the Stone of Gronw appears as a highly distinctive monolith that features in both the series' chilling title sequences and where Gwyn can be seen, in one episode, on the brow of the distant tree-covered hill (the Bryn), through its carved-out middle.

To place Alan Garner's *The Owl Service* – both the original novel and its TV adaptation – into context, its accomplished bringing together of myth and tragedy amid an ancient landscape (that is, in this instance, a North Wales' landscape dominated by the Stone of Gronw), it manages to both predate and pave the way for a number of other highly respectable small-screen series of the 1970s: In particular, *Children of the Stones*, *Escape into Night*, and *The Stone Tape*, which – collectively – act as a 'back-to-the-soil hippie-era rediscovery of the Myth and Magic of Britain', whereby 'the standing stones and blood-soaked ancient monuments ... recur throughout these stories' (Newman, 2008: 18).

Monoliths and stone circles, dating back 3–4,000 years, were – by the mid-1970s – a fixation of the young and, as such, often were the focus of a whole range of children's texts. The *Puffin Annual 2* (1975), with a three-page article by Judy Allen entitled 'Dragon Paths' (as all in the article derived from beliefs that originated in ancient China), explores the energy to be found amid concentric circles of standing stones; an energy that is as a result of converging ley lines running through such ancient sites (with ley lines themselves referencing the work of Alfred Watkins of the Old Straight Track Society, running in tandem with roads and paths of old). The article encourages its young readers, armed with an OS map, transparent ruler, and pencil, to engage in both mapwork and, this time with map and compass to hand, fieldwork – the latter involving the readers of this *Puffin Annual* actually walking the paths that seemingly follows such leys. This energy that is said to exist when ley lines, monoliths, and stone circles geographically align themselves is explored in considerable depth in *Children of the Stones*.

Children of the Stones – a seven-part serial broadcast across January and February 1977 – revolves around the work of Professor Adam Brake, an astrophysicist, who is conducting a university-sponsored study of the standing stones to be found within the boundary of the quaint (but quite unsettling) rural village of Milbury. There with Matthew, his teenage son, both – very early on in the series – are perturbed by the uniformly false, happy demeanour that the majority of Milbury's inhabitants radiate. With a plot that addresses such unnerving themes as the outsiders' experience of alienation when entering closed rural communities and an adherence to ancient customs that date back to pagan times, *Children of the Stones*, as a result, 'is every bit as complicated, unnerving, scientifically detailed and at times just plain frightening as it might sound' (Worthington, 2011: 11).

Children of the Stones frightens from the opening moments of its first episode – where a monolith (which, expectantly standing in the middle of the road, the Brake's nearly collide with) suddenly takes the form of their eventual female housekeeper – and, even, the opening titles of each and every one of its seven episodes resound to wailing, discordant vocals, as Milbury's stones are filmed from odd angles in a distorted manner. Even the series' tie-in paperback is brimming with such chilling tensions – as the following extract (describing a key scene in Episode One) demonstrates:

> 'I like to do my own research. And I like playing with expensive sonic equipment. Now … you said you wanted me to touch one of these things?'
>
> 'Yes'. She stepped back, as if expecting an explosion.
>
> 'Just … touch it?'
>
> 'That's right'.

He shrugged, stretched out his hand and touched the rock ... completely unprepared for the sudden, excruciating pain that shot up his arm, welding his hand to the stone. He shut his eyes and gritted his teeth, trying to break the contact, but it was no use. The pain seemed to pass through his whole body, transfixing him to the spot. He couldn't move, he couldn't think, he couldn't see ...

Yes, he *could* see. He could see Matthew's picture, and it was as if the ring of shadowy figures had been shocked into life by this current. They were raising their arms in protection against the bright pillar of light in the centre, and turning to flee into the surrounding darkness.

He felt himself falling down and down into the same darkness ... whirling round and round in a whirlpool of night. Then, at last, no pain. No sensation of any kind. Nothing (Burnham and Ray, 1977a: 45).

Thus, with *Children of the Stones* – filmed during the drought-inducing summer of 1976 in Avebury (a village in Wiltshire where an actual Neolithic stone circle stands) – all manner of psychic and paranormal activities, and their relationship with Milbury's characteristic geological topography, are explored and, often, rationalised away by father-and-son's scientific explanations. Discussions to do with the invisible linkages between stone circles and ley lines are mused over, along with a speculation that time itself within Milbury operates along the principal of a cyclical, ever-repeating pattern (that is, Milbury is not only encircled by its standing stones, but it is additionally surrounded by a ring of time that imprisons those within). Following the series' climax where – as already pre-historically depicted in an old oil painting kept by Matthew Brake – all of the villagers are transformed into monoliths by an extra-terrestrial beam of light – normality is seemingly returned to. Adam and Matthew Brake, driving out of Milbury, they (and the viewers) 'realise that in fact time has turned the circle and the whole nightmare is about to begin again' (McGown and Docherty, 2003: 103).

Screened a few years earlier in 1972 by ATV, *Escape Into Night* introduced a young girl, Marianne, who possesses an ultra-vivid imagination that places both herself and a boy called Mark (who is ill, and confined to bed as a result) into mortal danger. Having drawn a house encircled by standing stones, she dreams herself inside it along with Mark. The latter is eventually imprisoned in the house as a result of further – this time, temper-derived – scribbles. Finally, having drawn a single eye on each monolith, they come to life incarcerating Mark further. Ultimately, as it is eventually revealed that he actually exists, Mark is both freed and made well again, by Marianne rescuing him from the house of her dreams. But, it is the one-eyed circle of monoliths, as they slowly approach the house en masse, that provides *Escape Into Night* with its palpable horror, as '[t]he creepy stones and their harsh metallic voices made this a nightmarish serial in all senses of the word', where '[t]he subtext to the psychodrama concerned the capacity that all of us have for evil thoughts' (McGown and Docherty, 2003: 68). Meanwhile, the same year – but this time aimed at an adult audience (as it was broadcast by the BBC on Christmas Night) – *The Stone Tape* introduced a misogynistic male researcher who, set to work in an old empty residence, Taskerlands House, develops a radically new means of recording sound. This ability to record the building's multiple ghostly presences through the structure's stone composition results in the male researcher's fiercely anti-female attitudes to psychic extremes – when, for example, '[t]he first and most 'recent' ghost – a Victorian chambermaid – is cheerfully 'wiped' by the researcher in an echo of his callous treatment of the flesh-and-blood women in his life' (Rigby, 2002: 256).

These latter two televised examples, in particular, not only present (in quite a terrifying manner) the supposed inherent psychic powers to be found in stone – but both, in their own distinct ways, engage in the notion of the house as something paranormal in itself: That is, again, in the case of *Escape Into Night*, a house that only exists in the dreams of a child; and, with *The Stone Tape*, the house is, quite literally, the medium. Thus, taking into account these two televisual texts alone, Ivy Cottage – to Peter, as a young boy – would have, as a result, taken on a far more spiritual dimension. Or, rather, the very stones out of which it was built, back in the late 1800s, would have.

Cemeteries

The horror fiction writer James Herbert, in *James Herbert's Dark Places – Locations and Legends* (1993), discusses a variety of geographical spaces which have provided inspiration for his work. Rather surprisingly, they are often not the obvious haunted houses and the like at night, but everyday areas in broad daylight:

> I like a graveyard on a sunny day. I like the drone of a bee, the trill of a bird, perhaps even the distant sounds of children at play, as I wander down thin paths cut through burial mounds. I remember standing among gravestones once and hearing the thwack of leather on willow as a cricket match progressed in the filed next door to the cemetery. I enjoy these proclamations of life intruding upon the deadness of the graveyard.

> No need for dark brooding skies; sunlight on a sepulchre provides mood enough. No need for rain lashing lichen-diseased tombstones when withered and brittle flowers laid beneath a stone-curved legend tender their own grim ambience. Forget the howling wind, the far-off cry of a frightened animal, the heavy footsteps of some unseen person: just give me a graveyard on a bright summer's day and leave the rest to my own evocations. Let me conjure a figure, perhaps dressed in black or in a shroud, standing there in the middle-distance. Quiet and still. Watching … (Herbert, 1993: 10).

Reinforcing much of what Herbert expresses in the evocative extract above, Ken Worpole makes explicit, in *Last Landscapes – The Architecture of the Cemetery of the West* (2003), that cemeteries, as 'landscapes of the dead', not only 'exert a specific and compulsive hold on the human imagination', as 'they mix feelings of both beauty and anxiety – or even dread – they can rightly claim to be called Sublime' (Worpole, 2003: 21). Yet, such 'landscapes of the dead' – as with Herbert's fond memory of the gentle sound of a cricket match impinging ever-so-slightly upon the 'deadness of the graveyard' – are, at the same time, also 'landscapes of the living', whereby '[i]t is this coterminousness of life and death that gives the burial site its salience and emotional power' (Worpole, 2003: 21). As a result, these 'formal burial sites remain among the most compelling sites of human topography' (Worpole, 2003: 23) that is, a historic topography with its characteristic aesthetic which, being open to the elements, is a landscape of the dead-come-living that, by default, has been, and continues to be, 'one softened by weathering and time' (Worpole, 2003: 77). Moreover, for Sarah Rutherford in *The Victorian Cemetery* (2008), these weathered burial sites are rich places for all manner of human life and wildlife, as 'they provide a local amenity, community focus, social uses for family and other history, wildlife habitats and horticultural collections' (Rutherford, 2008: 60). Thus, especially within both its urban and suburban contexts, the pastoral condition of a cemetery 'is today more often viewed as a sanctuary and secret garden, free of the horrors of recent death and mourning' (Worpole, 2003: 72).

Whilst cemeteries manage to exude such a powerful effect upon the adult imagination, to children this is often a heightened imaginative experience, whereby 'this walled world (a world literally turned upside down) is often a source of unease and superstition' (Worpole, 2003: 22). For both adults and children alike – and as a result of a cognitive state of mind that means that, as humans, we are conscious of the fact that we exist alongside those that have died – 'the cultural marginalization of the cemetery is disquieting' (Worpole, 2003: 73). With St. John's, the Parish Church of Skewen – and its associated cemetery – just across the road from Ivy Cottage (the cemetery bordered the playing field of his primary school, Mynachlog Nedd), such a landscape of the dead was very much part of Peter's day-to-day existence. Quite simply, as Peter and his family lived in such close proximity to the dead, St. John's cemetery – instead of being 'disquieting' – was a comforting geographical aspect of their immediate neighbourhood.

As I walk into the cemetery with Daddy, the grey stone and the green foliage merge with each other in my eyes. Our footsteps crunch loudly as we walk along the gravel path. Dead flowers are everywhere. Never a place we enter into to wander around, or to stay, it is always our route to somewhere else. It is often the start (as it is today) – of our shared walks to the Graig (via Hill Road), to Neath Abbey (via the 'back route'), or even Longford and beyond. This is always the way home as well. Walking further along the path, we are still amid the flat, lower levels of the cemetery. Then, the path gradually gets steeper and steeper as we pass the church and the vicarage behind. Eventually climbing the steep stone steps, we leave the cemetery through the walled rear gate. As we do so, I turn and, looking through the arched opening in the wall, I gaze at the expansive view before and below me: Now able to see not only the entire cemetery but Ivy Cottage nestled amid lower Skewen, it is like looking down on home from Heaven itself.

If we consider the accompanying photograph of the cemetery (Figure 5.2, taken from the elevated perspective described towards the end of Peter's memory, but several decades later), we can now appreciate such a topography as what Ken Worpole terms pivotal landscapes: That is, 'places where life and death, past and future, the material world and the spiritual world are held in balance' (Worpole, 2003: 99). That spirituality of such pivotal landscapes, to Worpole, is not just one of physicality (headstones, the earth itself, and so on), but one which reverberates with near-silent communication between the living and the dead (such as the act of graveside prayer). Taking this notion of cemeteries as topographies of clairaudience between the living and the dead, it can now be appreciated that they 'act as amphitheatres, or echo chambers, in which the conversation of men and women is continued, generation after generation' (Worpole, 2003: 161). Thus, this notion of inter-generational conversations taking place amid such pivotal landscapes, is in line with Doris Francis et al.'s assertions, in *The Secret Cemetery*

Figure 5.2   St John's cemetery, 2005, looking down towards lower Skewen and Ivy Cottage

Source: Author's own collection.

(2005), that 'old cemeteries also become sites of personal consciousness and repositories of group identity and collective memory' (Francis et al., 2005: 201).

Neath Abbey

Burton and Stöber (2011), in their reappraisal of medieval monasteries in Wales note that, especially if the remains of such leviathan architectural structures are a considerable distance away from one's home, 'we tend to conjure up images of seclusion, of monks or nuns in silence and prayer, cut off from the outside world and deeply immersed in their own spiritual lives' (Burton and Stöber, 2011: 42). However, the authors insist, at the time when monasteries were thriving places of both work and worship – approximately 800 years beforehand – we would acknowledge that, far from being isolated from, and blinkered towards, the world outside their walls, they 'were vibrant institutions that were really very much part of medieval society' (Burton and Stöber, 2011: 43). Often providing forms of education, those that lived within the walls of the monasteries farmed the land beyond, and maintained the roads to and from them. More widely, the inhabitants of the monasteries were actively engaged in local and national politics (as part of an international religious network that geographically spanned western Christendom), and they also introduced the communities within which they were immersed to exotic produce (spices and wines and the like). In Wales especially, these monasteries and nunneries, during medieval times, 'were at the heart of the religious life of the country' (Burton and Stöber, 2011: 44), to the extent that 'the prayers of monks, canons and nuns were therefore seen as central to the well ordering of the broader community' (Burton and Stöber, 2011: 44).

With regards to the remains of the Cistercian monastery that is in close proximity to Ivy Cottage at Neath Abbey (hence the related naming of the wider locale), Stephen Absalom and Robert King, in *Around Neath* (2005), note that the site 'was the most hallowed place in the Neath area' (2005: 93), and, as a result, many religious gatherings – since its dissolving – have been conducted at its site, with Corpus Christi processions often ending there, along with multi-denominational festivals also held on its grounds. With a foundation charter being issued by Sir Richard de Granville in 1129, monks of Saxigny, in Normandy, thereafter were awarded 'about ten square miles of rough land between the rivers Neath and Tawe, the Clydach and the Pwllcynon (Crymlyn) Brook' (Eaton, 1987: 35). With the actual Savigniac abbey, the Church of St. Mary, being established a year later, it eventually became Cistercian in 1147, it was then dissolved in 1539 (see New, 1985: 274). With regards its eventual, albeit gradual, ruination, in Robert King's *Haunted Neath* (2009) it is explained that, under orders of Henry VIII, the Vicar General, Thomas Cromwell, 'removed the monks, stripped the roof and allowed the weather in. Nature did the rest' (2009: 29). However, much was rebuilt and reassembled during the Elizabethan period, with the abbot's house being eventually transformed into the mansion of Sir John Herbert, whereby stones from the abbey 'went into this and neighbouring houses and into St Thomas's church in the town' (New, 1985: 274). Many of the historic stones – originally, of course, laid by the builders of the abbey – 'can now be seen to adorn some buildings and walls in the village' (Bailey and Gough, 1998: 21). Thus, it is the weathered remains of Neath Abbey that are, collectively, its impressive legacy, as there exist 'many spectacular masses of fallen masonry, some of them complete with parts of vault ribs and window arches' (New, 1985: 276). Considering the conditions under which this monumental institution was dissolved, it is purported that, with regards Neath Abbey's dispossessed Cistercian Order monks, '[t]heir ghosts continue to frequent the still and now jagged walls to this present day' (King, 2009: 29).

King (2009) is insistent that it is not just the collective spirits of the monks that are tangible amid the ruins of Neath Abbey, but specifically those of both a king and his killer. For, in 1326 Edward II was in hiding there from his enemies (including his wife and her lover), as – during that period – such monasteries stood outside of the law of the land, and, as a result, anyone seeking refuge within their walls could not be seized and prosecuted. For ten days the king remained in the abbey until he eventually attempted an escape. However, one of the monks communicated the king's planned escape route to his pursuers, whereby he was eventually seized and imprisoned at Berkeley Castle where he was finally executed. In turn, the conspirator monk was found out, and it is suspected that he was killed for his disloyal act, and eventually buried in un-consecrated ground. Thus, the monk's troubled spirit is said to still roam the grounds of the abbey:

> Many people claim to have seen a figure dressed in a habit of the Cistercian Order. He always has a sad, if not desperate, expression on his face. Is he wandering for eternity seeking forgiveness? (King, 2009: 31).

Far more explicitly, Richard Holland, in *Haunted Wales – A Survey of Welsh Ghostlore* (2008), claims that the ghost of the king occasionally visits the abbey in search of the monk that betrayed him. Quoting from an older text – Martin Phillips' *The Folklore of the Afan and Margam District* (1933) – Holland notes that '[l]egend has it that "immediately the betrayer perceives his anointed king stalking through the ruins, he disappears, uttering the most blood-curdling shrieks"' (Phillips, 1933, cited in Holland, 2008: 96). Even more chilling is this account by Peter Underwood in *Haunted Wales* (2010):

> The shadowy figure of the king has been observed, it is said, stalking through the ruins on moonlit nights, followed by the dark figure of a monk, and after both figures have disappeared from view, a blood-curdling shriek closes the ghostly episode (2010: 92).

Finally, then, with this photograph in mind, where a parka-clad Peter stands at the railings that surround the grounds of the Abbey (Figure 5.3), it is worth us pondering how such a historic site – that is, a historic site steeped in such spectral

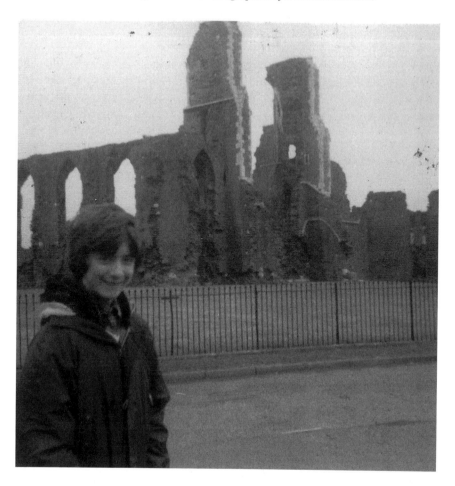

Figure 5.3   Peter, in his parka, in front of Neath Abbey
Source: Author's own collection.

history – is obviously in harmony with its surroundings and those that live in its immediate vicinity despite its supposed haunting. In fact, perhaps it is because of the localness and historic richness of such spirits that those in the neighbourhood have such an affinity with the stones of Neath Abbey.

Railways

Flockton Flyer (Southern Television, 1977–1978) was a children's television series which portrayed the exploits of three siblings who live on a preservation society steam railway: Jimmy Carter (played by Peter Duncan), Jan Carter (Gwyneth

Strong), and Jessica Carter (Annabelle Lanyon – replaced, in Series 2, by Catrin Strong). Billed as an adventure series, '[i]t would be too easy to describe this series glibly as a present-day *Railway Children*' (McGown and Docherty, 2003: 106). For, any adventure is tamed somewhat by the centrality that it gives to the safe, cosy Carter family who act as caretakers of Somerset's Flockton and Lane End branch line (and, specifically, the 'Flockton Flyer' of the title – GWR engine '6412'). Indeed, '[t]he series' real failing was that it was never life-or-death stuff' (McGown and Docherty, 2003: 106). As, even when there was a hint of on-screen danger, a measure of calming rurality gave it all a veneer of middle-class cosseting. Thus, a major accident in one episode is merely a lorry carrying hay which sheds its load at a level crossing, whilst in another episode, which incorporates a mail-train robbery within its plot, the armed culprits turn out to be bungling buffoons. However, despite most episodes leaning towards slapstick comedy amid an idyllic countryside, there are occasional moments – often when rough, urban youths impinge upon such countryside preservation – when the more gritty aspects of 1970s life in Britain are touched upon (and, as a result, provide the series with its most memorable scenes). Even these far-and-few between subversive moments are encountered when watching the *Flockton Flyer*, middle-class values are foisted upon the wayward working-class youths, and, as a result, peace and quiet returns once more to Middle England. For example, '[w]hen a yob vandalises the trains one night the tearaway is taken in and rehabilitated by becoming a useful part in the restoration team' (McGown and Docherty, 2003: 106). Thus, despite this 'yob' (another early performance by Phil Daniels) being made 'safe' and 'cosy' (just like both the Carters and the *Flockton Flyer*), 'it's a shame this more abrasive character couldn't have become a regular part of the cast' (McGown and Docherty, 2003: 106).

With the above in mind, then, it should come as no surprise that the real stars of the *Flockton Flyer* were the trains and the scenery through which they gently puffed. As Series 1 was filmed on location on the West Somerset Railway (which, in reality, runs from Minehead to Taunton), with Series 2 expanding geographically to take in the coast as the Carters relocated downline to Crowcombe Station. Furthermore, as the series' production took place during the fine summers of 1976 and 1978, *Flockton Flyer* has come to encapsulate a particular strand of 1970s children's television that perpetuates the nostalgic notion that, to have experienced childhood during such 'endless summers', was to have been miraculously untouched by the hardships of the time (such as economic downturn and societal decline).

Roy Brown's *The Viaduct* (1967a) is a tale of Victorian railway entrepreneurship and long-lost family riches, and, as such, provides a vibrant account of sidings, rolling stock, and a monumental viaduct, amid the sprawling backstreets of Deptford, south-east London. Against such a gritty backdrop, the relationship between George Benson and his grandson Phil is explored, as they share tales of their ancestor, Ebenezer, a 'genius engineer'. With the Abelard-Schuman first UK publication, the book's orange, wrap-around jacket illustration by James

Hunt presents the viaduct in question, amongst the scrap and barbed wire of Deptford, as an imposing stone and brick structure which spans both front and back covers. Meanwhile, the Macmillan Company's American version with its illustration by Roger Hane (Brown, 1967b), the viaduct – along with the Ebenezer Benson-designed steamtrain, 'Stormrider', terraced housing, and Bensons past and present – emanates as funnel smoke merging with a daydream cloud from a half-drawn boy's head. Yet, inside both editions, the viaduct is described quite graphically as an immense structure of the utmost solidity:

> Grandad paused beneath an arch to get his pipe going. A rare Sunday train thundered over their heads. Then they strolled on, the chill wind whispering in the archways ... Most of the arches were closed in, used as storerooms and workshops. The frontages towered like the entrances to cathedrals. Some were of corrugated iron, others of timber or bricks. Most had man-height inset doors, heavily padlocked or secured with lengths of rusty chain ... At the far end of the path the viaduct, its brick feet striding into the borough of Bermondsey, gathered other branches to itself and became wide and thick and complex (Brown, 1977a: 25–35).

The BBC television three-episode adaptation of *The Viaduct* (1972), chose to adopt the title of the book's last chapter as the title of the series' final instalment, 'Child of Brass and Iron'; and, in doing so, makes a direct correlation between childhood – and children themselves – and the metallic elements to be found all around them. *The Viaduct* – both original novel and the 1970s adaptation for television – bring together the solid elements of railway infrastructure: timber and bricks, brass and iron.

One architectural feature which dominates the geographical area of Skewen within which Ivy Cottage is situated, is the railway viaduct that carries the Swansea to London Paddington line atop of it. In Stephen Absalom and Robert King's *Around Neath* (2005) there is a black-and-white photograph of the viaduct, dated 'c.1970' (2005: 52), in which, daubed upon its masonry, high above its cavernous arches that span 'Mooretown Hill', is a fine example of nationalist-inspired graffiti. In white paint, and in oversized block capitals, is the defiant exclamation: 'LLEWELYN – THE TRUE PRINCE OF WALES'. Dating from just after the Investiture of the Prince of Wales, at Caernafon Castle in 1969, not only can it be read from a great distance away, but it is also Skewen's reminder that, during the 1970s, militancy gripped Wales. For, the 'LLEWELYN' in question here was one of the thirteenth century princes of Gwynedd that ruled over much of Wales, Llewelyn ap Gruffudd, who has been declared by some of the more overtly nationalistic Welsh as 'Llewelyn Ein Llyw Olaf' – that is, 'Llewelyn, Our Last Leader', or, even more truncated (and more emotive) 'Llyewelyn the Last'. Born c. 1223, he fought two wars against English oppression. The first in 1277, which Llewelyn lost, brought about the dissolving of a principality that had been established only ten years earlier. However, he was allowed to retain his title, the

Prince of Wales, and entered into another war with England, that of 1282–83, in which he was killed – a war 'which completed the English conquest of Wales' (Pryce, 2011: 33). Slain on 11 December 1282, Llewelyn ap Gruffudd was the last 'true' prince of an independent Wales before its conquest by the English Plantagenet dynasty.

Thus, the Investiture of 1969 (that is, of an English son, as a new Prince of Wales), took place at a time when, for some elements of the Welsh population, there was a need to disseminate such stirring sentiments and to revisit the history of Wales. Of course, this was all part of a slow-building nationalist move, which – following the Welsh Language Act of 1967 – eventually not only gave the Welsh language legal and political equity, but – with regards both geography and culture – bilingual signs were becoming the norm, and, 1977, the BBC's Welsh-language Radio Cymru launched. Rugby Union played its part, with the Welsh national team – across the entire late-1960s and 1970s – providing Wales with a distinct cultural focus with such masculine sporting heroes as Phil Bennett, Gareth Edwards, and Barry John (to name just a few). Indeed, with Cardiff Arms Park providing the distinctive on-screen backdrop to the exploits of such 'heroes', it was the stadium's deafening rendition of Wales' national anthem, 'Hen Wlad fy Nhadau', ahead of each and every game that Wales played, which encapsulated the Welsh patriotic mood of the 1970s. Winning three Grand Slams, two Triple Crowns, and eight Five Nations between 1969 and 1979, Wales playing at the Arms Park, not only 'became the supreme ritual of Welsh patriotism', but it also provided an opportunity for a select few of the televised spectators to don 'T-shirts proclaiming their support for the tiny Free Wales Army' (Sandbrook, 2012: 511).

Cayo Evans, one of the founding members of the militant Free Wales Army, remembers that, prior to the organisation having to resort to outright violence in order to bring about an awareness of their cause, activities such as politically driven graffiti were the main means by which their message was originally communicated within Wales. Evans recalls that his organisations' initial campaign of propaganda involved 'plastering the slogans and emblem of the FWA all across mid and West Wales', hoping to create 'the impression in people's minds that there was a wide-spread secret army already in existence, instead of the comparative handful that we actually were' (Evans, cited in Clews, 2004: 51). The nationalistic exclamation that adorns the stones of Skewen railway viaduct is a lasting reminder of the earlier, more mannered militancy of Cayo Evans and his Free Wales Army. Yet, a change was underway, as limited acts of graffiti were being replaced by more widespread protests and other forms of physical demonstration. Thus, '[t]o give my small group a rest from the paintbrush I took them to demonstrations organised by the Welsh Language Society and others' (Evans, cited in Clews, 2004: 51).

Whilst many felt that – come the late 1970s – 'Welsh cultural identity genuinely seemed more vibrant and self-confident than at any point in living memory' (Sandbrook, 2012: 512), for others, especially with regards their on-going concerns over the survival of the Welsh language, a high-profile militancy was being entered into 'driven by a perception that, if nothing was done immediately, it would be too late to reverse the trend' (Day, 2002: 218). As this militancy, certainly at first, was language-centered, it was spearheaded by the Welsh Language Society (Cymdeithas yr Iaith Gymraeg), where activists carried out a campaign of both civil disobedience and non-violent direct action in the form of protests, marches, the occupation of public buildings and the haranguing of staff that worked there (post offices, universities, etc.), and acts of symbolic vandalism of aspects of the media, such as television transmitters. But, due to a sense that such tactics were being viewed as slight (and, thus, being ignored) by government, police and the security services, activists were becoming even more agitated and antagonised. As a result, such relative pacifism soon turned to outright violence, whereby 'small numbers of extremists were prepared to resort to more drastic action, such as parading in quasi-military uniforms (the Free Wales Army) and blowing up pipelines carrying 'Welsh water' to English cities' (Day, 2002: 219). Thus, come the late 1970s, the on-going 'battle' was no longer about language alone, but driven by ethnic hatred and an insistency that Welsh land and buildings should no longer remain in the hands of their English owners. Therefore, what resulted was a series of attacks against so-called second-homes (that is, property in Wales, that were only occupied a few weeks a year during the summer months), in the form of quite a wide-spread arson campaign in mostly rural areas of West, North and Mid-Wales. With more than a hundred holiday cottages burnt down by a quasi-spectral organisation that referred to themselves as the Sons of Glyndŵr (Meibion Glyndŵr), their criminal activities even 'extended to attempts to fire-bomb English-owned businesses in Wales and estate agents in Liverpool and Chester who were selling Welsh properties' (Day, 2002: 221).

Wales and its activists were now being perceived of – especially within the corridors of Whitehall – as an increasingly troubling aspect of Cold War internal tensions, as it seems that Wales, from the early 1970s onwards, was under close surveillance. For, as Peter Hennessy uncovers in *The Secret State – Preparing for the Worst, 1945–2010* (2010), the Joint Intelligence Committee, in 1971, had MI5 compile a dossier of all militant individuals and groups (both of the right and of the left) that were then deemed active within the United Kingdom. Within an annex to the JIC document entitled 'Subversive Organisations in the United Kingdom', that, in itself, is 'a rare and fascinating snapshot of what MI5 believed it was facing in the early 1970s' (Hennessey, 2010: 127), details of yet another Welsh militant grouping – the National Patriotic Front (NPF) are provided. Under the subheading 'Other Remarks', it is noted that the NPF was formed when a number of ultra-militant members of the Free Wales Army 'expressed dissatisfaction with that organisation and caused a split amongst its supporters' (cited in Hennessey, 2010: 146). With its headquarters in Cwmbran, Gwent, and with membership of around 30, it was asserted that '[t]he aims of the NPF are to provide Welsh Nationalists with an opportunity to protect Wales against anglicisation and achieve independence' (cited in Hennessey, 2010: 145). Even though non-aggressive acts were still the order of the day with regards militancy in Wales during 1971, the report prophetically warned – with reference to the NPF's activity patterns – that their non-violence was a front, as '[b]ehind this there would be a trained body of saboteurs recruited from those members with experience in the use of explosives' (cited in Hennessey, 2010: 146).

With such Welsh militancy in mind, we now turn to a far gentler rendering of both the Welsh landscape and Welsh culture to be found on television screens during the 1970s – *Ivor the Engine*. Produced by the (extremely) independent and (ever-so-slightly) odd-ball production company Smallfilms (garden-shed based writer-come-producer Oliver Postgate, with Vernon Elliot providing the music), *Ivor the Engine* was originally broadcast in black and white across 1960–1968. Remade, and broadcast in colour, it is its screening by the BBC during the mid-1970s (1975–1977 to be exact) that provided this railway-themed animated series for children its enduring nostalgia imbued appeal. Concerned with 'The Merioneth and Llantisilly Rail Traction Company', and its line than runs, over the viaduct, through Llaniog (and its station), Tan-y-Gwlch, Grumbly Town, Llanmad, and Tewyn Beach, it offers the interwoven tale of Dia Station (who looks after Llaniog Station), Jones the Steam and Owen the Signal (his subordinates), and Jones the Coal and Hughes the Gasworks (local blue-collar workers). Indeed, Ivor the Engine (a steam locomotive) communicates with all through high-pitched, steamed-produced whistles, and is even a member of Grumbly Town's Grumbly and District Choral Society (the master of the choir being one Evans the Song).

With the opening narration of Episode 1 stating that 'Not so long ago, in the top, left-hand corner of Wales, there was a railway', and with these Wenglish-named characters populating such a setting, it is no surprise that, within *Ivor the Engine*, '[r]ailway antics ensued, in Welsh accents, through the barely disguised Ffestiniog valley and the dark wilds of Snowdonia' (Lewis, 2006: 157). Locating *Ivor the Engine* in this particular, and peculiar, geographical area of the United Kingdom was the result of a rational decision based upon belief in the extraordinary. For, as Oliver Postgate enthused:

> Wales was the place. In Wales the railways don't run straight across flat ground at high speeds. They wander up and down the valleys and along the tops of the hills, and in my mind Wales was already a magic place, a place of glorious eccentricities and unlikely logic. I knew this because I was intoxicated by the writings of Dylan Thomas and had been carrying a copy of *Under Milk Wood* in my pocket for years (Postgate, 2000: 210).

Set in such a wild and magical Welsh mountainous landscape that bordered the sea, *Ivor the Engine* possessed a certain element of fantasy based upon traditional Welsh myths, folklore, and customs. In Episode 3, Ivor and Jones notice that Smoke Hill (a previously inactive volcano), now has smoke belching from its summit and, upon investigation, recover an oversized egg from the top of the lava to be found inside. This egg – described as 'round as a rugby football, and red hot' – is placed inside Ivor's fire box, whereupon from it hatches a young, and mischievous, Idris the Dragon. Idris, upon asking the Choral Society 'Do you know 'Land of my Fathers'?', is introduced thus: 'There, looking out of Ivor's funnel, was a dragon. Not one of your lumping-great, fairy-tale dragons. But a small, trim, heraldic Welsh dragon, glowing red-hot and smiling'.

Red, and rather sprite-like, it is worth us referring to Robin Gwyndaf's *Welsh Folk Tales* (*Chwedlau Gwerin Cymru*), and its outlining of the origin and meaning of the Red Dragon in Welsh folk culture. Apparently first appearing as a crest that adorned King Arthur, the mythical dragon was employed by Welsh poets of the Middle Ages as a symbolic acknowledgment of their leaders' bravery. As such, between 1485 and 1603, it became a central motif amid the arms of the Tudors. Then, after a period of being relatively ignored, in 1807 it returned – in its recognisably majestic form as the Red Dragon – when it formed the royal badge of Wales. However, 'it was not until 1959, on the suggestion of the Gorsedd of the Bards, that Queen Elizabeth officially recognised it' (Gwyndaf, 1999: 45).

Significantly, (and bearing in mind the emphasis that Sandbrook places upon rugby in the establishment of Welsh identity during the 1970s in particular), Idris – a mythical creature – is described in *Ivor the Engine* as, upon hatching, 'heraldic', but, beforehand (whilst still in its egg), as 'round as a rugby football'. Idris, then, is a truly Welsh – that is, Wenglish – dragon'; at once, both ancient and modern (well, that is, typically 1970s 'modern').

Additionally, though, it has to be remembered that part-and-parcel of folk-tale humour is a reliance (expectation even) upon stereotypes, and those stereotypes being both locale-based and character-specific. Thus, imbued with such humour, folk-tales' telling of a nation's history, geography, traditions, and so on, not only provide a highly popular form of entertaining escapism, it reminds us that, to the Welsh of old in particular, 'the link between the past and the present was a very real one', whereby '[f]olk memory made people conscious of a long and vivid history' (Gwyndaf, 1999: 25). Thus, Peter, as a young boy in the mid-1970s, was reminded – with *Ivor the Engine* – of Wales' fantasy-enriched history. With steam already a thing of the past, but with the Swansea-to-Paddington line running parallel to the front of Ivy Cottage (and the house itself part of the equally parallel St. John's Terrace), *Ivor the Engine* was a version of Wales' recent history, where the nation's traditions and tales seemed to seep out of its age-old, magical landscape like spring water out of rocks. Yes, *Ivor the Engine* played upon national stereotype, but its characters – both the everyday ones and the far more fantastic ones – seemed to add a folk-tale vitality and dynamism to what would be, otherwise, Smallfilms' rather mundane depiction of a North Wales' railway.

Conclusion

On a banal, everyday level, a child's engagement – that is, contact, when at play – with stones is often one resulting in minor injuries of grazes and scabby knees. Ivy Cottage's garden was full of stone: bits of coal and slate that were constantly being dug up, and paths made out of bricks and flagstones. Yet, with this chapter, Peter finally moves beyond the house, its garden, and the surrounding streets outside – Ivy Cottage's immediate neighbourhood. For, with this chapter, we have examined Peter and his family's wider existence within, and experience of, suburbia during the 1970s. In doing so, we have considered the social institutions of suburbia – that is, those built out of stone, concrete, and other solid materials – that surrounded Peter and his family. Social institutions that they – as both individuals and as a family unit – entered into in order to educate themselves, intoxicate themselves, and so on.

Published by the Reader's Digest, one book that Peter's mother bought for him in 1979 was the weighty, over-sized, and lengthily titled, *The Past All Around Us – An Illustrated Guide to the Ruins, Relics, Monuments, Castles, Cathedrals, Historic Buildings and Industrial Landmarks of Britain*. Bound in Lincoln-green baize, and with gilt lettering and spine, it – to Peter as a 13-year-old boy – was a highly engaging tome that, with its plentiful photographs, illustrations, and maps, very much brought both history and geography to life. For Peter, turning each and every page was an epiphany, with the realisation that each and every stone out of which Ivy Cottage was built – and all of the other pieces of suburban solidity – were pieces of history in themselves.

Crucially, then, such stones were indeed part-and-parcel of the past all around him: The immensity of the stonework that made up Skewen viaduct and the impressive remains of Neath Abbey; the bricks and mortar out of which the public houses and the schools were built; even the prefabricated materials out of which Skewen Library and Rhydhir were hastily constructed. These were, then, stones as institutions and institutions as stone. This was, to Peter, the very solidity of Skewen's suburban permanence. Yet, as well as this macro-suburbia, it was to be the infinite number of microcosmic pieces of coal and slate that existed amid the earth of Ivy Cottage's gardens that, quite fundamentally, his childhood home seemed to comprise of.

Chapter 6

Epilogue – The Hauntology of Childhood

Lovely weather ... On this day we had the news that the fighting has ceased in the Falklands. We have been terribly worried. Lives wasted for nothing (Millie's diary, Monday, 14 June 1982).

If Peter continues to work at this standard then he should obtain some good results in the summer (Peter's school report, Dwr-Y-Felin Comprehensive, form 5A4, Christmas, 1981).

Decades are not convenient. They do not begin, culturally speaking, on the 1 January or end on 31 December. They don't even confine themselves to their respective decades. The Sixties may have swung on both Carnaby Street and the King's Road at some point during those ten years, but, in the South Wales' Valleys, they, in all probability, happened around 1973 or so. With this fluidity of history in mind, the cultural geographies of a 1970s childhood home are equally viscous. As *Remembering the Cultural Geographies of a Childhood Home*, may have opened – well, its first chapter proper, with Peter's memory of entering the overgrown garden of Ivy Cottage – circa September 1970, it now ends, not on New Year's Eve 1970, but amid the coming together of the personal and the global of 1982.

Asking the question, 'When Does Childhood End?', across its concluding chapter, Anthony Burton's *Children's Pleasure* (1996) – whilst admitting that it is a subjective query, dependent upon an individual child's age, upbringing, experiences, etc. – ultimately acknowledges that, in a way, 'we never leave our childhood behind', as, since Freud's early examinations of the human psyche, 'it has been accepted that the experiences of childhood, particularly those beyond the reach of conscious memory, cast a long shadow over adult life' (Burton, 1996: 179). Thus, with *Remembering the Cultural Geographies of a Childhood Home*, it is quite obvious that Peter's childhood does, indeed, 'cast a long shadow over adult life'. This 'shadow' can be understood in terms of the hauntology of childhood. Hauntology, a theory of ghosts founded upon Jacques Derrida's deconstruction methodology (see Lipman, 2014: 5), begs for a sensitivity to both the 'presence of absence' and the 'absence of presence' in our experience of the everyday. Our past self – our childhood – is gone forever. However, our memories of our past self – our memories of childhood – are forever with us.

It is quite an easy task to pinpoint the end of Peter's childhood. His father was to die suddenly, at the age of 56, in August of 1982. Peter left secondary education that same year. Furthermore, it was when the brief, but brutal, Falklands War was fought. Significantly, amongst all of the historical revisitings of the 1970s that have emerged over the past ten years or so, it is, in this respect, that Alwyn W. Turner's *Crisis? What Crisis? Britain in the 1970s* (2008) is at its most insightful. As, with a final chapter entitled 'Outro: FALKLANDS: 'Dignity is valuable ...' (2008: 273–8), the author – quite adamantly – ends the 1970s with that conflict that occurred between April and June, 1982:

> The unexpectedly huge popular support for the action was baffling and bewildering to many socialists who simply hadn't understood the psychological depression into which the country had sunk, nor that, for most people, this was an undesirable condition ... [B]ut by the time that victory became a real possibility, the war in the South Atlantic was considered close enough in terms of morality and outcome to warrant comparison to the finest hour, at least in the eyes of a country grown weary of failure (Turner, 2008: 277).

We're standing outside of our class, just ahead of our 9am registration. Boys in wintery blazers. Girls in summery, gingham-check pinafore dresses. The latter are, huddled together, weeping. They are distraught. They cry, 'Those boys, those poor, poor boys'. The night before, HMS Sheffield has been sunk. I look at the girls, confused, and with great incomprehension. I've just made, a few days ago, a 3-D, papier-mâché map of the Falkland Isles. I've even painted it in true-to-life browns and greens. It is where, after all, the 'Falklands' is being fought, day-by-day, night-after-night. But, when I proudly showed it to Mammy, she – as soon as she realised what it was – scowled at me.

Michael Paris, in *Warrior Nation – Images of War in British Popular Culture, 1850–2000* (2000) critiques Britain as a nation seemingly dependent upon conflict in order to achieve its sense of identity. Paris also pays particular attention to the ways in which children – or, rather, boys – help perpetuate the heroism associated with fighting through play, their choice of reading, the films that they watch, and so on. Thus, come the Falklands War, Paris was concerned with the ways in which boys – perhaps like Peter, aged 16 at the time – interpreted the war as yet another heroic, militaristic exploit. John Branfield's *Falklands Summer* (1987) is explored in order to ascertain the level to which the novel's protagonist – 16-year-old Matthew – is increasingly excited as the conflict's momentum builds:

> Matthew is already a devotee of the pleasure culture of war and is fascinated by World War Two. During the Falklands war he becomes obsessed with this latest conflict, re-enacting its events with his friends and desperately longing to be 'one of the heroes sailing to the South Atlantic'. He rejoices when the *Belgrano* is sunk and when the Argies surrender, but regrets that there will be no more war reports (Paris, 2000: 249).

Meanwhile, both the public and the military were incredulous with regards the astonishing rate by which British ships, during the Falklands War, seemed to be either sunk or crippled. To Peter, this came as no surprise, as he had read and re-read Shelford Bidwell's edited text *World War 3 – A Military Projection Founded on Today's Facts* (1978), and its chapter 'The Land War' (1978: 139–53) that prophesised that a Warsaw Pact invasion of a NATO-defended West Germany would last no more than a mere three days. As, indeed, here is the state of play come 'D+3' (that is, the third day of the conventional war):

> Had it been World War 2, now was the moment for the classic counterattack, for forming reserves for a counteroffensive, accompanied by orders of the day demanding sacrifices and heroism: 'with our backs to the wall'. But there was no wall behind the NATO back. There were no mighty reserve armies: there was not even a reserve stock of munitions. It would not be long before the last missiles were shot away. There was nothing left to stabilize a line (Bidwell, 1978: 152).

Thus, for Peter, coming out of childhood was not only to be a moment of gender-derived confusion, but it was to happen at a time in which the Cold War – and actual conflict (in its present-day form of enactment) – equated ultra-brief wars of rapid attrition of hardware. Gone, then, were the multiple-year struggles of World War One and World War Two as played out by Peter in the gardens and wastelands of Ivy Cottage, and on the carpets of its parlours and living room. Here, in 1982, was the brutal reality of contemporary, short, sharp warfare that kills – to infamously quote *The Sun* – 'Our Boys'. Thus, shortly after the 1970s had ended, boys – on both sides – were being killed. And girls as-mothers-to-be – again, on both sides – cried as a result. A 1970s childhood had, well-and-truly, ended. The seemingly endless summers of the 1970s were no more. Thus, the horizons of Peter's cultural geographies, had, come the end of 1982, moved on forever. From Ivy Cottage's front door, beyond Skewen's suburbia, and out into the South Atlantic, they now stretched from South Wales – at the periphery of NATO's western approaches – eastwards, to the very grass that grew at the foot of the Iron Curtain.

Bibliography

4 Idle Hands (1976) Dir. Jonathan Wright-Miller, Associated Television Limited.

Absalom, Stephen and Robert King (2005, first published 1998) *Around Neath*, Tempus Publishing Limited, Stroud.

Ackroyd, Peter (2010) *The English Ghost – Spectres Through Time*, Chatto and Windus, London.

Adams, Kate, Brendan Hyde and Richard Woolley (2008) *The Spiritual Dimension of Childhood*, Jessica Kingsley Publishers, London.

Aitken, Stuart C. (2001) *Geographies of Young People – The Morally Contested Spaces of Identity*, Routledge, London.

Allen, Judy (1975) 'Dragon Paths' in *Puffin Annual 2*, Penguin Books Ltd., Harmondsworth, 39–41.

Allen, Richard (1970) *Skinhead*, New English Library, London.

Amies, Hardy (2007, first published 1964*) ABC of Men's Fashion*, V&A Publications, London.

Anderson, Anne, Robert Meyrick, and Peter Nahum (2008) *Ancient Landscapes, Pastoral Visions – Samuel Palmer to the Ruralists*, Antique Collectors' Club Ltd., Woodbridge.

Andrews, Virginia (1979) *Flowers in the Attic*, Simon & Schuster, New York.

Anon. (1974) *Images of Youth – Growing up in Birmingham in the 1970's*, City of Birmingham Education Committee, Birmingham.

Anon. (1979) *The Past All Around Us – An Illustrated Guide to the Ruins, Relics, Monuments, Castles, Cathedrals, Historic Buildings and Industrial Landmarks of Britain*, The Reader's Digest Association Limited, London.

Anon. (2006) *My House History – The Historical Researcher's Map Portfolio*, Map Marketing Limited, Hatherleigh.

Anon. (2006) sleeve notes to the CD *Working Man's Soul – Rare Funk, Rock, Soul & Jazz from the UK Cabaret Scene*, Licorice Soul, Sandy.

Anon. (8 February 2011) 'Manics star joins libraries fight' on *BBC News South-east Wales*. Available at: http://news.bbc.co.uk/go/pr/fr/-/local/southeastwales/hi/people_and_places/music/newsid_9390000/9390934.stm

Anon. (n.d.) 'BBC, Comedy, *Butterflies*'. Available at http://www.bbc.co.uk/comedy/butterflies/

Anon. (n.d.) 'Television Heaven, *Butterflies*'. Available at: http://www.television heaven.co.uk/butter.htm

Anon. 'Pan Horror 12' posted 9 June 2008. Available at: http://vaultofevil.proboards.com/index.cgi?board=panspeople&action=display&thread=1267 [accessed 11 March 2011].

Arnold, Graham (2003) *The Ruralists – A Celebration*, Ruralist Fine Art Ltd., London.

Arthur, Ruth M. (1975) *On the Wasteland*, Victor Gollancz Ltd., London.

Ashley, Robert (1978, first published 1971) 'Pieces of Mary', in Herbert van Thal (ed.) *The Twelfth Pan Book of Horror Stories*, Pan Books Ltd., London, 130–32.

Bachelard, Gaston (1971, first published 1960) *The Poetics of Reverie – Childhood, Language, and the Cosmos*, Beacon Press, Boston.

Badmin, S.R. (n.d.) *Trees in Britain*, Penguin Books Limited, West Drayton.

Bagpuss (1974) Dirs. Peter Firmin and Oliver Postgate, BBC.

Bailey, John and Emyr Gough (1998) *Skewen and District – A History*, Gwasg Morgannwg, Neath.

Barker, Martin (1989) *Comics – Ideology, Power & the Critics*, Manchester University Press, Manchester.

Barker, Martin (1990) *Action – The Story of a Violent Comic*, Titan Books Ltd., London.

Barker, Paul (2009) *The Freedoms of Suburbia*, Frances Lincoln Limited, London.

Battle-Action (1977–1983) I.P.C. Magazines Limited, London.

Bayley, Stephen (17 June 2001) 'The Writing on the Walls' in *The Independent on Sunday*, 24–8.

Beasts (1976) 'Special Offer', Dir. Nigel Kneale, Associated Television Limited.

Beckett, Andy (2009) *When the Lights Went Out – Britain in the Seventies*, Faber and Faber Ltd., London.

Bender, Mike and Doug Chernack (2010) *Awkward Family Photos*, Hodder & Stoughton Ltd., London.

Benjamin, Walter (2006) *Berlin Childhood around 1900*, Harvard University Press, London.

Bensley, Lin (2009, first published 2008) *The Village Shop*, Shire Publications Ltd., Oxford.

Beresford, Elisabeth (1976, first published 1973) *The Wombles at Work*, Ernest Benn Limited, London.

Bidwell, Shelford (ed.) (1978) *World War 3 – A Military Projection Founded On Today's Facts*, Book Club Associates, London.

Black, Alistair (2000) *The Public Library in Britain, 1914–2000*, The British Library, London.

Blishen, Edward (ed.) (1969) *The School That I'd Like*, Penguin Books Ltd., Harmondsworth.

Blue Peter (1958–present) Created by John Hunter Blair, BBC.

Bowood, Richard (1963) *The Story of Houses and Homes*, A Ladybird 'Achievements' Book, Wills & Hepworth Ltd., Loughborough.

Bradbury, Malcolm (ed.) (1988) *The Penguin Book of Modern British Short Stories*, Penguin Books Ltd., London.

Bradbury, Ray (1975, first published 1957) *Dandelion Wine*, Corgi Books, London.

Branfield, John (1987) *Falklands Summer*, Orion Publishing Co., London.

Brian Vesey-Fitzgerald (1960) *Garden Flowers*, Ladybird Books Ltd., Loughborough.

Bronco Bullfrog (1969) Dir., Barney Platts-Mills.

Brookes, John (1985) *The Small Garden*, New Orchard Editions Ltd., New Orchard.

Brown, Roy (1967a) *The Viaduct*, Abelard-Schuman Limited, London.

Brown, Roy (1967b) *The Viaduct*, The Macmillan Company, New York.

Brown, Roy (1968) *The Day of the Pigeons*, Abelard-Schuman Limited, London.

Browne, Anthony (2000) *My Dad*, Doubleday, London.

Browne, Anthony (2010, first published 1976) *Through the Magic Mirror*, Walker Books Ltd., London.

Browne, Anthony (2011) *Playing the Shape Game*, Doubleday, London.

Bryson, Bill (2010) *At Home – A Short History of Private Life*, Doubleday, London.

Bullet (1976–1978) D. C. Thomson, Dundee.

Burke, Catherine (2005) 'The edible landscape of school' in Mark Dudek (ed.) *Children's Spaces*, Architectural Press, Oxford, 245–77.

Burnham, Jeremy and Trevor Ray (1977a) *Children of the Stones*, Carousel Books, Ealing.

Burnham, Jeremy and Trevor Ray (1977b) *Raven*, Carousel Books, Ealing.

Burton, Anthony (1996) *Children's Pleasures – Books, Toys and Games from the Bethnal Green Museum of Childhood*, V&A Publications, London.

Burton, Janet and Karen Stöber (2011) 'What Lay Behind those Monastery Walls?', in H.V. Bowen (ed.) (2001) *A New History of Wales – Myths and Realities in Welsh History*, Gomer Press, Llandysul, 42–8.

Busch, Akiko (1999) *Geography of Home – Writings On Where We Live*, Princeton Architectural Press, New York.

Butler, Charles (2006) *Four British Fantasists – Place and Culture in the Children's Fantasies of Penelope Lively, Alan Garner, Diana Wynne Jones, and Susan Cooper*, Scarecrow Press Inc., Lanham.

Butterflies (1978–1983) Created by Carla Lane, BBC.

Cabell, Craig (2003) *James Herbert – Devil in the Dark*, Metro Publishing Ltd., London.

Calcutt, Andrew (2000) *Brit Cult – An A–Z of British Pop Culture*, Prion Books Limited, London.

Callaghan, Richard (2010) *Assigned! The Unofficial and Unauthorised Guide to Sapphire & Steel*, Telos Publishing Ltd., Prestatyn.

Carpenter, Humphrey and Mari Prichard (1995, first published 1984) *The Oxford Companion to Children's Literature*, Oxford University Press, Oxford.

Chapman, James (2011) *British Comics – A Cultural History*, Reaktion Books Ltd., London.

Children of the Stones (1977) Dir. Peter Graham Scott, HTV West.

Clapson, Mark (2003) *Suburban Century – Social Change and Urban Growth in England and the USA*, Berg, Oxford.

Clarke, Brian M. (2008) 'Let's Look at … *Spellbound*' in *Crikey! – The Great British Comics Magazine!*, Issue 4, 36–9.

Clews, Roy (2004, first published 1980) *To Dream of Freedom – The Story of MAC and the Free Wales Army*, Y Llofa Cyf., Talybont.

Clifton House Mystery, The (1978) Created by Leonard White, HTV West.

Clutterbuck, Richard (1978) *Britain in Agony – The Growth of Political Violence*, Faber and Faber Limited, London.

Cohen, Stanley (1973) 'Campaigning against vandalism' in Colin Ward (ed.) *Vandalism*, The Architectural Press, London, 215–57.

Collins, Andrew (2003) *Where Did It All Go Right? Growing Up Normal in the 70s*, Ebury Press, London.

Conran, Terence (1978) *The Bed and the Bath Book*, Mitchell Beazley Publishers Limited, London.

Conran, Terence (1999, first published 1985) *Terence Conran's New House Book – The Complete Guide to Home Design*, Conran Octopus Ltd., London.

Coote, Trevor (2011) *Lemon Socks*, self-published.

Corrigan, Paul (1979) *Schooling the Smash Street Kids*, The MacMillan Press Limited, London.

Cross, Roy and Arthur Ward (2002) *Celebration of Flight – The Aviation Art of Roy Cross*, Airlife Publishing Ltd., Shrewsbury.

Crunch, The (1979–1980) D.C. Thomson, Dundee.

Crystal Tipps and Alistair (1972) Produced by Michael Grafton-Robinson, BBC.

Cunningham, Hugh (2006) *The Invention of Childhood*, BBC Books, London.

Curry, John (ed.) (2009) *Donald Featherstone's War Games – Battles and Manoeuvres with Model Soldiers*, Lulu.com.

Curry, John (ed.) (2008) *Donald Featherstone's Skirmish Wargaming*, Lulu.com.

Dave Allen at Large (1971–1979) Dir. Peter Whitmore, BBC.

Davies, Owen (2007) *The Haunted – A Social History of Ghosts*, Palgrave MacMillan, Basingstoke.

Davis, Michael (2008) *Street Gang – The Complete History of Sesame Street*, Viking Penguin, New York.

Day, Christopher (2007) *Environment and Children – Passive Lessons from the Everyday Environment*, Architectural Press, Oxford.

Day, Graham (2002) *Making Sense of Wales – A Sociological Perspective*, University of Wales Press, Cardiff.

Deakin, Roger (2007) *Wildwood – A Journey Through Trees*, Hamish Hamilton, London.

Dickens, Monica and Rosemary Sutcliff (eds) (1978) *Is Anyone There?*, Penguin Books Ltd., Harmondsworth.

Dillon, Brian (2005) *In the Dark Room – A Journey in Memory*, Penguin Ireland, Dublin.

Doctor Who (1970) 'Spearhead from Space', Dir. Derek Martinus, BBC.

Dunne, Anthony (2005) *Hertzian Tales – Electronic Products, Aesthetic Experience, and Critical Design*, Massachusetts Institute of Technology Press, London.

Dunne, Anthony and Fiona Raby (2001) *Design Noir – The Secret Life of Electronic Objects*, Birkhäuser, Basel.

Dyer, Geoff (2005) *The Ongoing Moment*, Little. Brown, London.

Eaton, George (1987) *A History of Neath from Earliest Times*, Christopher Davies (Publishers) Ltd., Swansea.

Elms, Robert (2005) *The Way We Wore – A Life In Threads*, Picador, London.

Escape Into Night (1972) Dir. Richard Bramall, ATV.

Esmonde, John and Bob Larbey (1977, first published 1976) *The Good Life*, Penguin Books Ltd., Harmondsworth.

Evans, Bill and Andrew Lawson (1986, first published 1981) *A Nation of Shopkeepers*, Plexus Publishing Limited, London.

Faces, The (1973) *Ooh La La*, LP, Warner Bros.

Farley, Paul and Michael Symmons Roberts (2011) *Edgelands – Journeys Into England's True Wilderness*, Jonathan Cape, London.

Finucane, R.C. (1996) *Ghosts – Appearances of the Dead & Cultural Transformation*, Prometheus Books, New York.

Flanagan, Matthew (2008) 'The Poetic of Childhood – Form and Structure in the Trilogy' in

'Bill Douglas Trilogy' (booklet that accompanied the BFI 2008 DVD release of *Bill Douglas Trilogy – My Childhood, My Ain Folk, and My Way Home*), 10–11.

Flockton Flyer (1977–1978) Prod./Dir. Colin Nutley, Southern.

Fowler, Christopher (2009) *Paperboy – A Memoir*, Doubleday, London.

Francis, Doris, Leonie Kellaher, and Georgina Neophytou (2005) *The Secret Cemetery*, Berg, Oxford.

From Beyond the Grave (1973), Dir. Kevin Conner, Amicus.

Gainsborough, Thomas (1748–1749) *Mr and Mrs Andrews*, oil on canvas.

Garde-Hansen, Joanne (2011) *Media and Memory*, Edinburgh University Press, Edinburgh.

Gardener's World (1968–present) BBC.

Garner, Alan (1967) *The Old Man of Mow*, Collins, London.

Garner, Alan (1967) *The Owl Service*, Collins, London.

Garner, Alan (2006, first published 1983) *The Stone Book Quartet*, Harper Perennial, London.

Garnett, Mark (2007) *From Anger to Apathy – The British Experience since 1975*, Jonathan Cape, London.

George, David Graham (n.d.) *A Skewen Boy Looks Back*, Glamorgan Press, Neath Abbey.

Ghosts of Motley Hall (1976) Dir. Quentin Lawrence, ITV.

Gikow, Louise A. (2009) *123 Sesame Street – 40 Years of Life on the Street*, Black Dog & Leventhal Publishers, Inc., New York.

Gill, Tim (2007) *No Fear – Growing Up in a Risk Averse Society*, Calouste Gulbenkian Foundation, London.

Goffman, Erving (1961) *Asylums*, Anchor Books, New York.

Goodenough, Elizabeth (2003) 'Introduction' in Elizabeth Goodenough (ed.) *Secret Spaces of Childhood*, University of Michigan Press, Michigan, 1–16.

Gordon, Avery F. (2008, first published 1997) *Ghostly Matters – Haunting and the Sociological Imagination*, University of Minnesota Press, Minneapolis.

Grange Hill (1978–2008) Created by Phil Redmond, BBC.

Greenhalgh, Liz and Ken Worpole with Charles Landry (1995) *Libraries in a World of Cultural Change*, UCL Press Limited, London.

Greenland, Colin (1983) *The Entropy Exhibition – Michael Moorcock and the British 'New Wave' in Science Fiction*, Routledge & Kegan Paul Plc., London.

Gwyndaf, Robin (1999, first published 1989) *Welsh Folk Tales*, National Museum of Wales, Cardiff.

Hall, Stuart, Chas Critcher, Tony Jefferson, John Clarke, and Brian Roberts (1978, reprinted 1979) *Policing the Crisis – Mugging, the State, and Law and Order*, The MacMillan Press Ltd., London.

Harwood, Elain (2010) *England's Schools – History, Architecture, and Adaptation*, English Heritage, Swindon.

Haslam, Dave (2005) *Not Abba – The Real Story of the 1970s*, Fourth Estate, London.

Hauser, Kitty (2007) *Shadow Sites – Photography, Archaeology, and the British Landscape 1927–1955*, Oxford University Press, Oxford.

Havenhand, I. & J. (1965) *The Miner – 'People at Work'*, A Ladybird 'Easy-Reading' Book, Wills & Hepworth Ltd., Loughborough.

Hawkins, John and Susan Meredith (1982) 'Audio and Radio', in Lisa Watts (ed.) *The Usborne World of Electronics – A Colourful Introduction to Computers, TV, Video, Audio and Radio*, Usborne Publishing Ltd., London, 65–95.

Hennessy, Peter (2010, first published 2002) *The Secret State – Preparing for the Worst, 1945–2010*, Penguin Books Ltd., London.

Herbert, James (1977) *Fluke*, New English Library, Sevenoaks.

Herbert, James (1979) *Lair*, New English Library, London.

Herbert, James (1980) *The Dark*, New English Library, London.

Herbert, James (1986) *The Magic Cottage*, Book Club Associates, London.

Herbert, James (1993) *James Herbert's Dark Places – Locations and Legends*, BCA, London.

Herbert James (2001) *Once ...,* MacMillan, London.

Hewitt, Paolo (2002) *The Looked After Kid – Memoirs From A Children's Home*, Mainstream Publishing Company (Edinburgh) Ltd., Edinburgh.

Hide and Seek (1972) Dir. David Eady, The Children's Film and Television Foundation.

Hirsch, Marianne (1997, reprinted 2002) *Family Frames – Photography, Narrative and Postmemory*, Harvard University Press, Cambridge.

Hoggart, Richard (2010, first published 1957) *The Uses of Literacy – Aspects of Working-Class Life*, Penguin Books Ltd., London.

Holland, Richard (2008) *Haunted Wales – A Survey of Welsh Ghostlore*, Ashbourne Hall, Ashbourne.

Howe, David J. and Stephen James Walker (1996) *Doctor Who, The Handbook – The Third Doctor, The Jon Pertwee Years: 1970–1974*, Doctor Who Books, London.

Humphreys, Richard (1990, first published 1989) *The British Landscape*, The Hamlyn Publishing Group Limited, London.

Hunt, Leon (1998) *British Low Culture – From Safari Suits to Sexploitation*, Routledge, London.

Hutber, Patrick (1976, reprinted 1977) *The Decline and Fall of the Middle Class – And How it Can Fight Back*, Penguin Books Ltd., Harmondsworth.

Hutber, Patrick (1978) *What's Wrong With Britain?*, Sphere Books Ltd., London.

Hutchings, Peter (2002) 'The Amicus house of horror', in Steve Chibnall and Julian Petley (eds) *British Horror Cinema*, Routledge, London, 131–44.

Hyde, Brendan (2008) *Children and Spirituality – Searching for Meaning and Connectedness*, Jessica Kingsley Publishers, London.

Ingram, Tony (2008) 'Supercats and Orphan Brats – DCT's Spellbinding Girls' Comic', in *Crikey! – The Great British Comics Magazine!*, Issue 6, 4–7.

Inshaw, David (1972–1973) *The Badminton Game*, oil on canvas.

Jackson, Peter (1989) *Maps of Meaning – An Introduction to Cultural Geography*, Unwin Hyman Ltd., London.

Johannessen, Neil (2010, first published 1994) *Telephone Boxes*, Shire Publications Ltd., Oxford.

Johnston, Keith M. (2010) '"Underground, overground": Remembering the Wombles', in Laurel Forster and Sue Harper (eds) *British Culture and Society in the 1970s – The Lost Decade*, Cambridge Scholars Publishing, Newcastle upon Tyne, 154–63.

Jones, Ken and Hannah Davies (2002) 'Keeping It Real: *Grange Hill* and the Representation of "the Child's World" in Children's Television Drama', in David Buckingham (ed.) *Small Screens – Television for Children*, Leicester University Press, London, 141–58.

Jones, Owain (2005) 'An Ecology of Emotion, Memory, Self and Landscape', in Joyce Davidson, Liz Bondi and Mick Smith (eds) *Emotional Geographies*, Ashgate Publishing Limited, Aldershot, 205–18.

Jones, Owain and Paul Cloke (2002) *Tree Cultures – The Place of Trees and Trees in Their Place*, Berg, Oxford.

Jones, Stephen (ed.) (1992) *James Herbert – By Horror Haunted*, New English Library, Sevenoaks.

Kibble-White, Graham (2005a) *TV Cream – The Ultimate Guide to 70s and 80s Pop Culture*, Virgin Books, London.

Kibble-White, Graham (2005b) *The Ultimate Book of British Comics – 70 Years of Mischief, Mayhem and Cow Pies*, Allison & Busby Limited, London.

King, Clive (1976, first published 1963) *Stig of the Dump*, Puffin Books, Harmondsworth.

King, Robert (2009) *Haunted Neath*, The History Press, Stroud.

King, Robert and Brian King (1999, reprinted 2005) *Around Neath – The Second Selection*, Tempus Publishing Limited, Stroud.

Knobler, Peter and Greg Mitchell (1995) 'Introduction', in Peter Knobler and Greg Mitchell (eds) *Very Seventies – A Cultural History of the 1970s, from the Pages of* Crawdaddy, Fireside, New York, 13–19.

Kuhn, Annette (2008) *Ratcatcher*, Palgrave Macmillan, Houndmills.

Laermans, Rudi and Carine Meulders (2006, first published 1999) 'The domestication of laundering', in Irene Cieraad (ed.) *At Home – An Anthropology of Domestic Space*, Syracuse University Press, New York, 118–29.

Lea, John and Jock Young (1984) *What is to be Done About Law and Order?*, Penguin Books Ltd., Harmondsworth.

Leather, Alan and Antony Matthews (1973) 'What the architect can do: A series of design guides' in Colin Ward (ed.) *Vandalism*, The Architectural Press, London, 117–72.

Lee, Laurie (2002, first published 1959) *Cider With Rosie*, Vintage, London.

Leggott, James (2010) 'Dead ends and private roads: The 1970s films of Barney Platts-Mills', in Paul Newland (ed.) *Don't Look Now – British Cinema in the 1970s*, Intellect, Bristol, 229–39.

Leonard, Kevin (24 March 2011) 'BT says quarter of phone boxes in Wales rarely used' on *BBC News Wales* online. Available at: http://www.bbc.co.uk/news/uk-wales-12784596 [accessed 27 March 2011].

Lewis, C.S. (1950) *The Lion, the Witch, and the Wardrobe*, Geoffrey Bles, London.

Lewis, Richard (2005) *The Bumper Book of Fads and Crazes*, Atlantic Books, London.

Lewis, Richard (2006, first published 2002) *The Encyclopaedia of Cult Children's TV*, Allison & Busby Limited, London.

Lewis, Robert (2008) *Wenglish – The Dialect of the South Wales Valleys*, Y Lolfa Cyf., Talybont.

Lewisohn, Mark (n.d.) 'Butterflies'. Available at: http://www.carlalane.com/butterflies.php

Lipman, Caron (2014) *Co-habiting with Ghosts – Knowledge, Experience, Belief and the Domestic Uncanny*, Ashgate, Farnham.

Lockey, B. (1968, first published 1938) *The Interpretation of Ordnance Survey Maps and Geographical Pictures*, George Philip and Son Limited, London.

Londei, John (2007) *Shutting Up Shop – The Decline of the Traditional Small Shop*, Dewi Lewis Publishing, Stockport.

Louv, Richard (2009, first published 2005) *Last Child in the Woods – Saving Our Children from Nature-Deficit Disorder*, Atlantic Books, London.

Lovell, Andrew (2008) *Tiswas and Tanktops – The Pocket Diary of a 1970s Boy*, RUL, Rugeley.

Lucie-Smith, Edward (1980) *Art in the Seventies*, Phaidon Press Limited, Oxford.

Lurie, Alison (1981) *The Language of Clothes*, William Heinemann Ltd., London.

Lyall, Gavin (1976) *Operation Warboard – Wargaming World War II Battles in 20–25mm Scale*, A&C Black Limited, London.

Mabey, Richard (1974, first published 1973) *The Unofficial Countryside*, Readers Union, Glasgow.

MacBeth, George (1977) 'Birth', in Giles Gorden (ed.) *A Book of Contemporary Nightmares*, Michael Joseph Ltd., London, 115–27.

Magic (1978) Dir. Richard Attenborough.

Magic Ball, The (1971) Dir. Brian Cosgrove, Granada Television.

Mains, Johnny (2010) 'A Brief History of the Horrors' in Herbert van Thal (2010, first published 1959) *The Pan Book of Horror Stories*, Pan Books, London, ix–xv.

Manning, Matthew (1974) *The Link – The Extraordinary Gifts of a Teenage Psychic*, Colin Smythe Ltd., Gerrards Cross.

Manning, Matthew (1978) *The Strangers – My Conversations with a Ghost*, W.H. Allen and Co. Ltd., London.

Marson, Richard (2008) *Blue Peter – 50th Anniversary*, Hamlyn, London.

Martin, Christopher (ed.) (1991) *The Ruralists*, Academy Group Ltd., London.

Mary, Mungo and Midge (1969) Prod. John Ryan, BBC.

Matheson, Richard (1979, first published 1978) *What Dreams May Come – A Novel of Life After Death*, Michael Joseph Ltd., London.

Maxwell-Stuart, P.G. (2006) *Ghosts – A History of Phantoms, Ghouls & Other Spirits of the Dead*, Tempus Publishing Limited, Stroud.

McCallum, Simon (2010) Notes to 'Fire Prevention – *Fire Routine*, 1979' in the booklet that accompanies the BFI's 2010 DVD release *Stop! Look! Listen! – The COI Collection, Volume Four*, 32.

McCann, Graham (ed.) (2005) *The Essential Dave Allen*, Hodder and Stoughton Ltd., London.

McGahan, Katy (2010) 'Warning! This film might be dangerous' in the booklet that accompanies the BFI's 2010 DVD release *Stop! Look! Listen! – The COI Collection, Volume Four*, 1–3.

McGown, Alistair D. and Mark J. Docherty (2003) *The Hill and Beyond – Children's Television Drama – An Encyclopedia*, British Film Institute, London.

McKay, Stephen (2008) 'The Owl Service – The Legend Unravelled' in 'Programme Notes' (booklet that accompanied the Network 2008 DVD release of *The Owl Service*), 2–14.

Melly, Jim (2003) *'Last Orders, Please' – Rod Stewart, The Faces, and the Britain We Forgot*, Ebury Press, London.

Meneley, Anne and Donna J. Young (2005) *Auto-Ethnographies – The Anthropology of Academic Practices*, Broadview Press, Plymouth.

Misty (1978–1980) I.P.C. Magazines Ltd., London.

Montgomery, Heather (2009) *An Introduction to Childhood – Anthropological Perspectives on Children's Lives*, Wiley-Blackwell, Oxford.

Moore, Jerrold Northrop (2007) *The Green Fuse – Pastoral Vision in English Art, 1820–2000*, Antique Collectors' Club Ltd., Woodbridge.

Moore, Jerrold Northrop, Laurie Lee, and Peter Hahum (n.d.) *The Ruralists – A Celebration*, Ruralist Fine Art Ltd., Barley Splatt.

Moore, Robin C. (1986) *Childhood's Domain – Play and Place in Child Development*, Croom Helm Ltd., Beckenham.

Moore, Robin C. (2003) 'Childhood's Domain: Play and Place in Child Development', in Elizabeth Goodenough (ed.) *Secret Spaces of Childhood*, The University of Michigan Press, Michigan, 57–61.

Moore-Gilbert, Bart (1994) 'Introduction: cultural closure or post-avantgardism?' in Bart Moore-Gilbert (ed.) *Cultural Closure? The Arts in the 1970s*, Routledge, London, 1–28.

Moreman, Christopher M. (2010, first published 2008) *Beyond the Threshold – Afterlife Beliefs and Experiences in World Religions*, Rowman & Littlefield Publishers Inc., Lanham.

Morrison, Kathryn A. (2003) *English Shops and Shopping*, Yale University Press, New Haven.

Morrow, Robert W. (2006) *Sesame Street and the Reform of Children's Television*, The Johns Hopkins University Press, Baltimore.

Moynahan, Brian (Sunday, 3 October 1976) 'The Brotherhood of Ruralists', in *The Sunday Times Magazine – The Sunday Times*, 78–84.

Mr Benn (1971–1972) Dir. David McKee, BBC.

Mr Smith's Vegetable Garden (1976) BBC.

Murphy, Dominic (2 April 2011) 'All about my mother', in *Guardian Weekend*, 82–5.

My Ain Folk (1973) Dir. Bill Douglas.

My Childhood (1972) Dir. Bill Douglas.

My Way Home (1978) Dir. Bill Douglas.

Neve, Christopher (4 October 1984) 'One Moment One Summer – David Inshaw: Recent Paintings' in *Country Life*, 954–5.

New, Anthony (1985) *A Guide to the Abbeys of England and Wales*, Constable and Company Ltd., London.

Newkey-Burden, Chas (August, 2000) 'Archer out of *Scum*', in *Loaded – Greatest Ever Englishmen*, Arcturus Publishing Ltd., London, 88–9.

Newman, Kim (2008) '*The Owl Service* – Unexplained Mysteries' in *Alan Garner's* The Owl Service – *Programme Notes*, booklet accompanying the Network DVD, 18–19.

Noah's Castle (1979) Dir. Colin Nutley, Southern Television.

O'Brien, Stephen (1989) *Visions of Another World – The Autobiography of a Medium*, The Aquarian Press, Wellingborough.

Odgers, Caroline (23 April 1981) 'A Move to the Country – The Brotherhood of Ruralists', in *Country Life*, 1112–13.

Offutt, Jason (2010) *What Lurks Beyond – The Paranormal in Your Backyard*, Truman State University Press, Kirksville.

Open All Hours (1976) Dir. Sydney Lotterby, BBC.

Owl Service, The (1969–1970) Dir. Peter Plummer, Granada.

Paris, Michael (2000) *Warrior Nation – Images of War in British Popular Culture, 1850–2000*, Reaktion Books Ltd., London.

Parsons, Tony (1976) *The Kids*, New English Library, London.

Pask, Trevor (2011, first published 2010) *Airfix Kits*, Shire Publications Ltd., Oxford.

Patten, Brian (1972, first published 1969) 'Making a Call', in Monica Dickens and Rosemary Sutcliff (eds) (1978) *Is Anyone There?*, Penguin Books Ltd., Harmondsworth, 9.

Pautz, Peter D. (1987) 'Introduction', in Kathryn Cramer and Peter D. Pautz (eds) *The Architecture of Fear*, Arbor House Publishing Company, New York, xi–xii.

Peacock, Paul (2005) *A Good Life – John Seymour and his Self-sufficiency Legacy*, Farming Books and Videos Ltd., Preston.

Pearce, Philippa (1976, first published 1958) *Tom's Midnight Garden*, Penguin Books Ltd., Harmondsworth.

Pearson, Harry (2007) *Achtung Schweinehund! A Boy's Own Story of Imaginary Combat*, Little, Brown, London.

Pennartz, Paul J.J. (2006, first published 1999) 'Home: The Experience of Atmosphere', in Irene Cieraad (ed.) *At Home – An Anthropology of Domestic Space*, Syracuse University Press, New York, 95–106.

Perry, Mark (1976–1977) *Sniffin' Glue*, self-published fanzine.

Postgate, Oliver (2000) *Seeing Things – An Autobiography*, Sidgwick and Jackson, London.

Powers, Alan (2003) *Children's Book Covers – Great Book Jacket and Cover Design*, Mitchell Beazley, London.

Prosser, Jay (2005) *Light in the Dark Room – Photography and Loss*, University of Minnesota Press, Minneapolis.

Pryce, Huw (2011) 'Llywelyn the Great and Llywelyn the Last – For Themselves or for Wales?', in H.V. Bowen (ed.) *A New History of Wales – Myths and Realities in Welsh History*, Gomer Press, Llandysul, 28–34.

Ratcatcher (1999) Dir. Lynne Ramsay.

Raven (1977) Dir. Michael Hart, ATV.

Raw, Laurence (1997) *The Country and the City*, The British Council, Manchester.

Read, John (broadcast 15 January 1978, BBC2) 'The Lively Arts – "Summer with the Brotherhood"'.

Read, Tess (2001) *Mr Benn's Little Book of Magic*, Arrow Books, London.

Remembering the Secret Garden (2004), a documentary that accompanies the 2004 DVD release of *The Secret Garden* (1975), BBC.

Rentaghost (1975–1984) Created by Bob Block, BBC.

Rigby, Jonathan (2002, first published 2000) *English Gothic – A Century of Horror Cinema*, Reynolds & Hearn Ltd., Richmond.

Robertson, Gary (2010) *Skeem Life – Growing Up in the Seventies*, Black & White Publishing Ltd., Edinburgh.

Robinson, Ian (2010) *The Rupert Companion – A History of Rupert Bear*, Egmont UK Limited, London.

Rose, Jonathan (2010, first published 2001) *The Intellectual Life of the British Working Classes*, Yale University Press, New Haven.

Rosselin, Céline (2006) 'The Ins and Outs of the Hall: A Parisian Example', in Irene Cieraad (ed.) *At Home – An Anthropology of Domestic Space*, Syracuse University Press, New York, 53–9.

Rowe Townsend, John (1975) *Noah's Castle*, Oxford University Press, Oxford.

Rudd, Natalie (2003) *Peter Blake*, Tate Publishing, London.

Rupert Annual, The (1967) Beaverbrook Newspapers Ltd., 1966.

Russell, Patrick (2010) Notes to 'Fire Prevention – *Searching*, 1974' in the booklet that accompanies the BFI's 2010 DVD release *Stop! Look! Listen! – The COI Collection, Volume Four*, 30.

Rutherford, Sarah (2008) *The Victorian Cemetery*, Shire Publications Ltd., Oxford.

Sabol Jr., John G. (2007) *Ghost Culture – Theories, Context, and Scientific Practice*, AuthorHouse, Bloomington.

Sabol Jr., John G. (2009) *Bodies of Substance, Fragments of Memories – An Archaeological Sensitivity to Ghostly Presence*, AuthorHouse, Bloomington.

Sabol Jr., John G. (2012) *Ghost Culture Too – Expanding the Contemporary Reality of Past Interactive Interactions*, Ghost Excavator Books Inc., Brunswick.

Sandbrook, Dominic (2010) *State of Emergency – The Way We Were: Britain, 1970–1974*, Allen Lane, London.

Sandbrook, Dominic (2012) *Seasons in the Sun – The Battle for Britain, 1974–1979*, Penguin Books Ltd., London.

Sapphire and Steel (1979–1982) Created by Peter J. Hammond, ATV.

Schwartz, Susan L. (April, 2000) 'I Dream, Therefore I Am: *What Dreams May Come*' in *Journal of Religion & Film*, Vol. 4, No. 1. Available at: http://www.unomaha.edu/jrf/IDream.htm

Sconce, Jeffrey (2005, first printed 2000) *Haunted Media – Electronic Presence from Telegraphy to Television*, Duke University Press, Durham.

Scott, Jenni (2008) '*Misty, Jinty*, and *Tammy* – Female Identities and Socialisation in the 1970s Wave of British Girls' Comics', in *Crikey! – The Great British Comics Magazine!*, Issue 4, 4–9.

Scott, Nancy (1967) *Understanding Maps*, Wills and Hepworth Ltd., Loughborough.

Scum (1979) Dir. Alan Clarke.

Sesame Street (1969–present) Created by Joan Ganz Cooney, PBS.

Seymour, John (2007) *The Complete Guide to Self-Sufficiency*, Dorling Kindersley Limited, London.

Shadows – The Classic First Series of the BAFTA-Nominated '70s Supernatural Kids' Drama (1975), Network DVD (2010).

Shepherd, Janet and John Shepherd (2012) *1970s Britain*, Shire Publications Ltd., Oxford.

Shurmer-Smith, Pamela (2002) 'Reading Texts' in Pamela Shurmer-Smith (ed.) *Doing Cultural Geography*, Sage Publications Ltd., London, 123–36.

Sibley, David (2005) 'Private/Public' in David Atkinson, Peter Jackson, David Sibley, and Neil Washbourne (eds.) *Cultural Geography – A Critical Dictionary of Key Concepts*, I. B. Tauris & Co. Ltd., London, 155–60.

Simpson, Jacqueline (2010) *Green Men & White Swans – The Folklore of British Pub Names*, Random House Books, London.

Sixth Sense, The (1999) Dir. M. Night Shyamalan.

Slater, Nigel (2007) *Eating for England – The Delights & Eccentricities of the British at Table*, Fourth Estate, London.

Solnit, Rebecca (2002, first published 2001) *Wanderlust – A History of Walking*, Verso, London.

Sounes, Howard (2006) *Seventies – The Sights, Sounds and Ideas of a Brilliant Decade*, Simon & Schuster Ltd., London.

Spellbound (1976–1978) D.C. Thomson, Dundee.

Spencer, Amy (2005) *DIY: The Rise of Lo-Fi Culture*, Marion Boyars Publishers Ltd., London.

Sterry, Paul (2007) *Collins Complete British Trees*, Harper Collins Publishers Ltd., London.

Stranglers, The (1977) *Rattus Norvegicus*, LP, United Artists.

Stone Tape, The (1972) Dir. Peter Sasdy, BBC.

Survivors (1975–1977) Created by Terry Nation, BBC.

Sweetman, Tom (2007a) 'Play *Misty* For Me' in *Crikey! – The Great British Comics Magazine!*, Issue 1, 30–34.

Sweetman, Tom (2007b) 'The Devil in the Shop' in *Crikey! – The Great British Comics Magazine!*, Issue 1, 41–3.

Tait, Derek (2011) *A 1970s Childhood – From Glam Rock to Happy Days*, The History Press, Stroud.

Tanizaki, Junichirō (2001, first published 1977) *In Praise of Shadows*, Vintage, London.

Thrift, Nigel (1994) 'Inhuman Geographies: Landscapes of Speed, Light and Power', in Paul Cloke, Marcus Doel, David Matless, Martin Phillips and Nigel Thrift (eds) *Writing the Rural – Five Cultural Geographies*, Paul Chapman Publishing Ltd., London, 191–248.

Thriller (1973–1976) Created by Brian Clemens, ITV.

Tincknell, Estella (2005) *Mediating the Family – Gender, Culture and Representation*, Hodder Education, London.

Toop, David (2010) *Sinister Resonance – The Mediumship of the Listener*, The Continuum International Publishing Group Ltd., London.

Torrance, Chris (1977) *Citrinas – The Magic Door Book II*, Albion Village Press, London.

Townsend, John Rowe (1987, first published 1965) *Written for Children – An Outline of English-Language Children's Literature*, Penguin Books Ltd., London.

Tuan, Yi-Fu (1998) *Escapism*, The Johns Hopkins University Press, Baltimore.

Turner, Alwyn W. (2008) *Crisis? What Crisis? – Britain in the 1970s*, Aurum Press Ltd., London.

Turner, Robin (7 February 2011) "If you tolerate this … '; Nicky Wire on library closures' on *Guardian.co.uk Music Blog*. Available at: http://www.guardian.co.uk/books/2011/feb/07/nicky-wires-library-closures-manics

Underwood, Peter (2010, first published 1978) *Haunted Wales*, Amberley Publishing, Stroud.

Usherwood, Nicholas (1981) *The Brotherhood of Ruralists*, Lund Humphries Publishers Ltd., London.

Usherwood, Nicholas (August 2004) introduction to 'Moments of Vision (Between Fantasy and Reality – David Inshaw, 29 September–22 October 2004', exhibition catalogue, Agnew's, Old Bond Street, London.

Usherwood, Nicholas (June 1981) 'David Inshaw: Paintings and Photographs', in *London Magazine*, 65–72.

Usherwood, Nicholas (October 1984) 'David Inshaw Drawings' in *Antique Collector*, 88–9.

Viaduct, The (1972) Producer Dorothea Brooking, BBC.

Viner, Brian (2009) *Nice to See It. To See It, Nice – The 1970s in Front of the Telly*, Simon & Schuster UK Ltd., London.

Ward, Arthur (1999) *Airfix – Celebrating 50 Years of the Greatest Plastic Kits in the World*, Harper Collins Publishers, London.

Ward, Arthur (2004) *Classic Kits – Collecting the Greatest Model Kits in the World, from Airfix to Tamiya*, Collins, London.

Ward, Arthur (2009) *The Boys' Book of Airfix – Who Says You Ever Have to Grow Up?*, Ebury Press, London.

Ward, Colin (1970) *Violence – It's Nature, Causes and Remedies*, Penguin Books Ltd., Harmondsworth.

Ward, Colin (1973) 'Notes on the future of vandalism', in Colin Ward (ed.) *Vandalism*, The Architectural Press, London, 276–311.

Ward, Colin (1978) *The Child in the City*, The Architectural Press Ltd., London.

Ward, Colin (ed.) (1976) *British School Buildings – Design and Appraisals, 1964–1974*, The Architectural Press Ltd., London.

Warlord (1974–1986) D.C. Thomson, Dundee.

Warner, Marina (2006) *Phantasmagoria – Spirit Visions, Metaphors, and Media into the Twenty-first Century*, Oxford University Press, Oxford.

Wheeltappers and Shunters Social Club, The (1974–1977) Produced by Johnnie Hamp, Granada.

Wheen, Francis (2009) *Strange Days Indeed – The Golden Age of Paranoia*, Fourth Estate, London.

Whitehead, Phillip (1985) *The Writing on the Wall – Britain in the Seventies*, Michael Joseph Limited, London.

Whiting, Roger (1986) *Crime and Punishment – A Study Across Time*, Stanley Thornes (Publishers) Ltd., Cheltenham.

Williamson, Howard (2004) *The Milltown Boys Revisited*, Berg, Oxford.

Williamson, Howard and Pip Williamson (1981) *Five Years*, National Youth Bureau, Leicester.

Willis, Paul (1977) *Learning to Labour – How Working Class Kids Get Working Class Jobs*, Saxon House, Westmead.

Winter, Jay (1997, first published 1995) *Sites of Memory, Sites of Mourning – The Great War in European Cultural History*, Press Syndicate of the University of Cambridge, Cambridge.

Wolfreys, Julian (2010) 'Ghosts: Of Ourselves or, Drifting with Hardy, Heidegger, James, and Woolf', in María del Pilar Blanco and Esther Peeren (eds) *Popular Ghosts – The Haunted Spaces of Everyday Culture*, The Continuum International Publishing Group Ltd., London, 3–18.

Wombles, The (1973–1977) Ivor Wood, BBC.

World of Sport (1965–1985) ITV.

Worpole, Ken (2003) *Last Landscapes – The Architecture of the Cemetery in the West*, Reaktion Books Ltd., London.

Worthington, Tim (2011) 'Completing the Circle – A Retrospective of HTV's Cult Children's Programming', in 'Completing the Circle' (booklet that accompanied the Network 2011 DVD release of *Children of the Stones*).

Index